THE FIJIAN
COLONIAL
EXPERIENCE

A STUDY OF THE NEOTRADITIONAL ORDER UNDER BRITISH COLONIAL RULE PRIOR TO WORLD WAR II

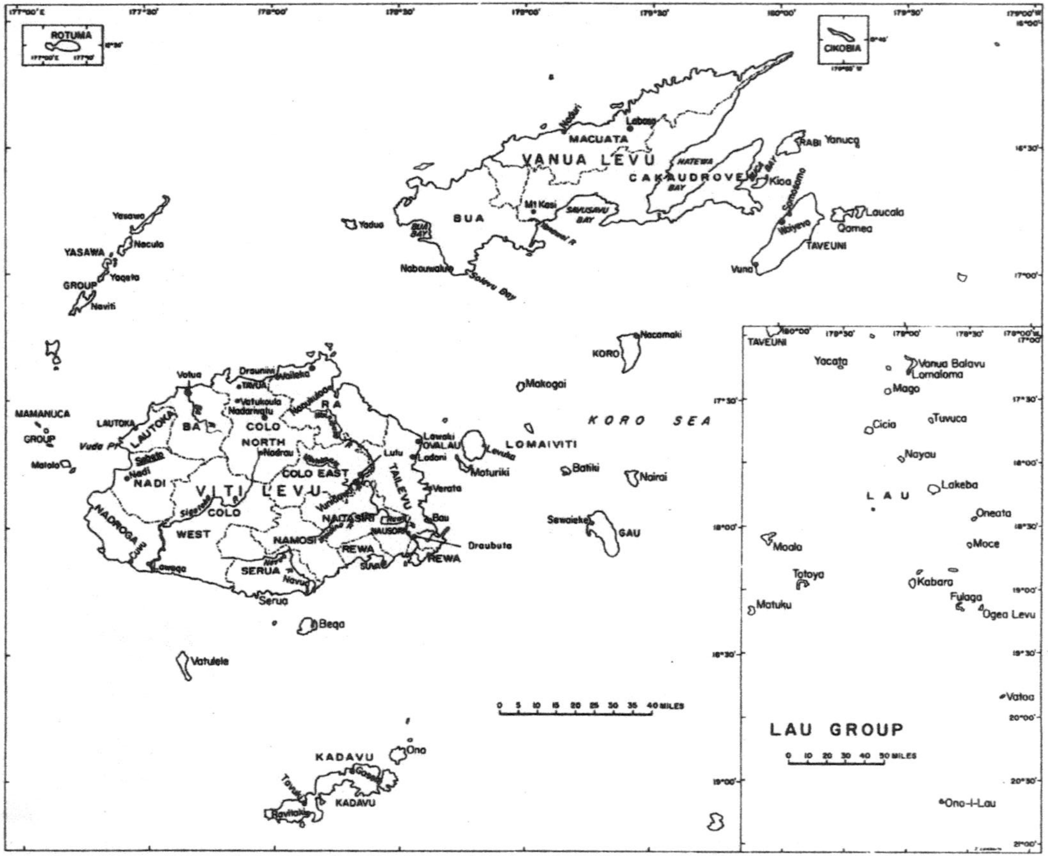

Map 1 Colony of Fiji, 1920-1944

VANUA LEVU

MACUATA

CAKAUDROVE

BUA

TAVEUNI

RABI

KIOA

QAMEA

KORO SEA

KORO

LOMAIVITI

GAU

Nairai

Batiki

Makogai

Moturiki

Wakaya

Ovalau

Levuka

NAITASIRI

REWA

TAILEVU

VITI LEVU

COLO NORTH

COLO EAST

COLO WEST

NADI

LAUTOKA

BA

RA

SERUA

NAMOSI

NADROGA

Beqa

Serua

Vatulele

KADAVU

Ono

YASAWA GROUP

MAMANUCA GROUP

ROTUMA

CICIA

LAU GROUP

LAU

Vanua Balavu
Lomaloma
Mago
Cicia
Nayau
Lakeba
Oneata
Moce
Kabara
Fulaga
Ogea Levu
Ono-i-Lau
Vatoa

Yacata
Vanua Balavu

Moala
Totoya
Matuku

TAVEUNI

0 10 20 30 40 MILES

0 10 20 30 40 50 KILOMETRES

THE FIJIAN COLONIAL EXPERIENCE

A STUDY OF THE NEOTRADITIONAL ORDER UNDER BRITISH COLONIAL RULE PRIOR TO WORLD WAR II

TIMOTHY J. MACNAUGHT

Australian National University

eVIEW

Published by ANU eView
The Australian National University
Acton ACT 2601, Australia
Email: enquiries.eview@anu.edu.au
This title is also available online at eview.anu.edu.au

National Library of Australia Cataloguing-in-Publication entry

Creator:	Macnaught, Timothy J. (Timothy John), 1945- author.
Title:	The Fijian colonial experience : a study of the neotraditional order under British colonial rule prior to World War II / Timothy John Macnaught.
ISBN:	9781921934353 (paperback) 9781921934360 (ebook)
Subjects:	British--Fiji--History. Fiji--History. Fiji--Colonial influence.
Dewey Number:	996.11

Cover design and layout by ANU Press.
Cover photograph source: Mitchell Library, State Library of New South Wales.

First published 1982 by The Australian National University
This edition © 2016 ANU eView

Summary

This book analyses thematically much of the colonial experience of the Fijians earlier this century - their land rights, village and district politics, chiefly leadership, underground movements and various British efforts to 'improve' them.

The major theme is the failure of vague policies fostering individualism and enterprise to interrupt the continuities of a vigorously autonomous social and political world maintaining eight of ten Fijians in a relatively affluent neotraditional order until World War II, despite the deep vein of discontent and material aspirations manifested most clearly in Apolosi R. Nawai's movement, the Viti Company. The epilogue briefly chronicles some of the recent changes in Fijian life which, it is argued, throw into sharper relief the accomplishments of the earlier partnership between Fijian leaders and British officials. Therein lie the historical antecedents of both the economic problems of the Fijian people and their ascendancy in national political life through the first decade of independence.

Contents

Acknowledgements

The Government of Fiji and the generous support of the Research School of Pacific Studies, Australian National University, made possible a total of eighteen months' fieldwork and archival research in Fiji between 1972 and 1974, and this book is a revision of a doctoral dissertation accepted by A.N.U. in 1976. Deryck Scarr, to whose vigilance, insights and friendship I am enormously indebted, was my original adviser, and since then I have profited from his further writings on Fiji and those of Ahmed Ali and Ken Gillion in their parallel explorations of the Fiji Indian experience. John Nation's excellent study of contemporary Fijian politics strengthened me in the conclusion that the Fijian colonial experience had something to say to the present, and alone made it intelligible.

In Fiji the National Archivist, Setariki T. Tuinaceva, gave me extraordinary assistance in providing thousands of files as did dedicated staff: Helen White, Etuate Bakaniceva, Masood Khan, Tomasi Saladuadua, Paula Moceisadrau, Eparama Ulutegu, Samisoni I. Kafoa and Josateki Bakeidau. My friends Pio Manoa and Josefo R. Meke and numerous others taught me much in the field, and in Suva I was frequently the guest of Ratu Tiale W.T. Vuiyasawa and Ratu Penaia Lalabalavu Latianara whose memories and stories greatly spiced or clarified the colonial record. Petero Vakaoqotabua, Felise Daveta, Lepani Siga of Naroi, Sesili Sili, Petero Sikeli, and most especially George Cama, his wife Lako and their kindred from Moala and Matuku gave us a family to join in Suva and nearly every part of the group and as happy times as we have ever had; experiences which convinced us that the Fijians had 'come through' the colonial experience with a distinctive integrity and grace an historian such as myself should respect - and dare to interpret for a wider world.

Gavan Daws and Walter Johnson gave me the encouragement I needed to bring this book to press; Michael and Kitty Dabney typed and Ann Neale edited the final manuscript with extraordinary speed and care, while the maps were drawn by Imants Lamberts. My wife Alice-Anne, our children, parents and families know how much I have been sustained by their love and support.

Finally I am grateful to the University of Hawaii for research leave to complete this work, and to the Australian National University for publishing it in a format which lowers the cost of sharing my thoughts with the people of Fiji.

Guide to pronunciation

Vowel sounds approximate those of Latin or Spanish. Long or stressed vowels, marked for convenience in the glossary following, are not identified by macrons in print. The orthography of Fijian consonants employs several simple conventions that can mislead the foreign speaker.

b is mb as in member
c is th voiced as in then
d is nd like nd in candy
g is ng as in sing but may also occur at the
       beginning of a word
   (as does q)
q is ng voiced as in finger

Glossary of Fijian words

Bai Tabua	'sacred fence of whales' teeth', secret society of Tuka adherents
bose	council
Buli	official title of government district chief
burua	mourning feast and ceremonies
dalo	taro, staple Fijian tuber
draunikau	sorcery
galala	'free' farmer legally exempted from communal obligations; in current usage a man living apart from the village
gauna	time, era
isevu	first fruits offering
itaukei	the (original) owners of the land; often, by extension, the term used by Fijians to refer to themselves as against other races
kai	inhabitant of, man of
kaisī	commoner, low-born (pejorative)
kai vale	chief's household servants
kerekere	the practice of 'requesting' goods of a friend or relative
koro	village
lala	chief's conscription of goods and services
lali	wooden drum
lotu	church
luveniwai	spirit-'children of the water'

magiti	feast
mana	supernatural power
masi	cloth made from bark of the paper mulberry tree
mata	envoy
matanitū	political confederation of vanua; the government
matanivanua	spokesman for the chiefs
mataqali	social unit of second order of inclusiveness; legally a patrilineal descent group and the proprietary unit of most Fijian land
meke	a song integrated with dance movements
noi	dialectal variant of kai
oco	food given in return for work, especially housebuilding
ovisa	officer
papālagi	country of the white man
qali	tribute-paying, or dependent social group
qalivakabau	dependants of Bau in Lomaiviti and elsewhere
Roko Tui	government title of heads of provinces - in some areas also a hereditary title
sōlevu	a large ceremonial exchange of food and goods between two sides
sulu	length of cotton print wrapped round the loins (lava lava)
tabu	taboo

tabua	sperm whale's tooth
Talai	Fijian title for the variously styled officer in charge of the Fijian Administration, since 1944 the Secretary for Fijian Affairs
tama	a muted shout of respect in unison on the first approach of a chief, as e.g. duo! o!
taralalā	dancing European-style with body contact
tikina	government district
Tui	leading chief of a vanua
Tuka	an immortality cult
tūraga	chief (general word)
tūraga ni koro	government chief of the village
vakamisioneri,	an annual Wesleyan collection for support of the church
vakarorogo	'go to', acknowledge allegiance to
vakatūraga	in a chiefly fashion
vakavanua	pertaining to the land, customary, traditional
vakaveiwekani	in the manner of relatives
vakaviti	Fiji-style - often used pejoratively by local Europeans
vanua	land, small polity, local chiefdom of several villages of yavusa
vata	raised sleeping-shelf or platform
Viti Cauravou	Young Fiji Society
vulagi	visitor, outsider

<u>Vuniduvu</u>	high priest of <u>Tuka</u> cult; inspired author of <u>meke</u>
<u>vunivalu</u>	best-known title of dominant chief of Bau; often in other places the executive chief's title, as distinguished from a sacred titleholder
<u>yaqona</u>	kava, liquid from the pounded or masticated root of <u>Piper methysticum</u> strained through water
<u>yavusa</u>	social unit of third order of inclusiveness; legally a group of ranked <u>mataqali</u> with kinship ties fictionalized as descent from a common ancestor

Abbreviations

CO	Colonial Office, London
CP	Fiji Legislative Council Paper
CS	Colonial Secretary, Fiji
CSO	The Colonial Secretary's Office Series, Suva
MM	Methodist Mission Collection in the National Archives of Fiji
NC	The Native Commissioner or Talai later SNA
PMB	Pacific Manuscripts Bureau, Canberra
SNA	The Secretary for Native Affairs; in documentary call numbers refers to the secretariat's series.

Unless otherwise specified, all references in these notes are to documents in the National Archives of Fiji. Despatches to and from the Governors of Fiji cited without the CO series number were read in the bound volumes of originals and carbon copies in the National Archives of Fiji; the others on microfilm from the Public Record Office supplied to the National Library of Australia and libraries associated in the Australian Joint Copying Project. Citations in the text from Fijians' correspondence are either my own translations or, wherever adequate, official translations in the files. Ratu Sukuna, frequently cited in later chapters, wrote in English, or in the case of land records, made his own translations for official consumption.

Introduction

The death on 7 February 1897 of Governor Sir John B. Thurston, champion of the integrity of Fijian community life for a quarter century, closed a remarkable segment in the history of European expansionism in the South Pacific.[1] An exuberant, tumultuous, and sophisticated collection of warring Fijian societies inhabiting some eighty islands in the group had been threatened but not overwhelmed by the relentless pressures of the Australasian frontier on their land and their autonomy, even though they had ceded sovereignty to Queen Victoria on 10 October 1874. According to a cherished Fijian myth, a pleasant reduction of the tortuous politics of those events, Fiji had not been ceded 'in anger to her late Majesty Queen Victoria; it was ceded in loving trust (loloma)' - a chiefly presentation, no less, which had obliged the gratified recipient, now Supreme Chief of Fiji, to redistribute power and privileges to the original donors and to assume part of the responsibility for safeguarding the prosperity and rights of the people.[2] In short the Deed of Cession, far more effectively than the New Zealander Maoris' Treaty of Waitangi, came to be seen by Fijians as a solemn charter for a British - Fijian partnership premised on verbal assurances (the cession itself was unconditional) that colonial rule would respect and maintain the interests of Fijian society as paramount. The needs of some 140,000 Fijians and their expectations of being governed 'righteously and in accordance with native usages and customs' were not to be subordinated to the contrary expectations of some 1500 European settlers and resident adventurers.[3]

The latter had done everything possible to disrupt preceding attempts to elaborate an independent government (on the lines of royal Hawaii or Tonga). Thurston, as chief minister to King Cakobau from mid 1872, had earned their enmity for exposing the ruthless self-interest in their 'patriotic' determination that Fiji would become a British bastion in the South Seas, a proper British colony run in the interests of Englishmen and Empire. The Fijians would be pacified and disarmed, in time an influx of European settlers and their descendants would gain internal self-government (as in New Zealand and the Australian colonies from which most of the settlers had come); it would then be an easy matter to dismantle whatever British protectionist legislation stood in the way of completing the transfer of splendid lands lying waste in the hands of

1

the idle natives to those better equipped by race and destiny to bring them into full production. Poll taxes would ensure that Fijians would learn the dignity of a disciplined day's work on European plantations, and wage rates would be so regulated that Fijians would continue to subsidize the capitalist economy by feeding and housing their dependants from their own labour and resources as before - either that, or choose to withdraw into reserves like the Melanesians of New Caledonia and watch the importation of more willing Pacific Islanders or Asians to work under indenture and reap the rewards of honest labour. (The machinery was already in place: many estates before Cession were worked and defended by New Hebrideans and Solomon Islanders.)

The dreams of 'rampant Anglo-Saxons' had not materialized.[4] The first Governor, Sir Arthur Hamilton Gordon, felt he had a divine mission to make the islands an exception to the dismal history of colonialism. Fiji did not become a white man's country, although enormous concessions were made to maintain the viability of the better established planters and, in the 1880s, to develop a substantial sugar economy on lands already alienated before Cession or leased from the Fijians. Between 1879 and 1919 over 60,000 Indians were brought in under indenture to solve the labour problems of the European sector. Most were encouraged to stay on as free settlers, with remarkably little thought for the demographic repercussions that were to see their descendants outnumber the Fijians themselves by World War II, and embark on a long struggle, never fully realized, to win for themselves the equal place of dignity and power that was their birthright.[5] In the year that Thurston died, however, when this story begins, some 11,000 Indians were isolated under indenture on company estates and only about a thousand time-expired men and their families were beginning to cultivate 1500 acres of land at Rewa and Navua. The success of Indian labour in developing an export economy, crucial for the expanding revenues of an impoverished government (£74,492 in 1897, £138,167 in 1903), was seen as giving the Fijians the time they needed - time to absorb the impact of colonial rule, to arrest the steady decrease in their numbers, and to enjoy the unusual institutions that had given them a powerful voice in colonial policy and wholly unprecedented peace and unity.

For colonial rule had brought to fruition the seeds of national unity sown over three millennia of migrations, trading and kinship connections, shifting political alliances between dominant lineages in war and peace, and common problems with Tongan imperialism. Though a substantial literature has explored many aspects of Fijian history through to the end of the nineteenth century, no systematic ethnohistorical reconstruction has lifted the veil over the era Fijians were taught to dismiss as 'the time of darkness', despite profoundly felt continuities with the past underpinning modern Fijian pride in their way of life.[6] Many of the sources on which this history rests are written by Fijians to other Fijians in the Bauan dialect of the Bible, and are perhaps the best possible sources anywhere in the Pacific for illuminating island dimensions of the colonial experience. Nevertheless the interaction is predicated on a thoroughgoing penetration of 'the traditional' by a powerful neotraditional set of institutions (and often quite arbitrary regulations) vertically integrating Fijian society under the Crown. Select principles operating in traditional societies, notably those that were, like patriarchal authority, more immediately intelligible to European observers, became codified in an altogether new way. This was often at the expense of other principles such as a pervasive dualism inherent, for instance, in the allocation of spiritual and temporal power between complementary chiefly offices, or in the division of roles within many villages between two privileged groups, the original owners (itaukei) and the group which provided a chief to be installed by the itaukei. A traditional chief presiding over the cycle of service and tribute, drawing together the constituent groups of a local society under the aegis of ancestral and other gods, was only superficially the autocratic paterfamilias he seemed to outsiders. In truth he was at one intersection of a flexible web of horizontal and hierarchical 'paths of the land'. The regional varieties of kinship and social organization in old Fiji, the underlay of colonial reconstruction, defy summary analysis and description: suffice to emphasize here that the colonial order devised and imposed new, very much simplified principles of authority and territorial organization which may or may not have meshed with pre-existing sociopolitical realities. The resultant ambiguities, the continuing interplay of local and colonialist priorities, will often emerge in the chapters that follow. But with the poverty of local and regional studies in Fijian history and anthropology, there are

severe limits in a work of this scale to the illumination
of local processes. The only solid framework of reference
for the analysis of Fijian affairs is that which Gordon and
Thurston created, and which Fijians rapidly made their own
and defended tenaciously for a century as the bulwark of
their neotraditional identity, of everything that was still
distinctively Fijian.

Similarly there is no need here to pursue further the
well-documented extravagance of Gordon's claim that the
institutions of the Fijian Administration were 'purely
native, and of spontaneous growth'.[7] Had he argued that the
system operated in a Fijian idiom and style that was very
congenial to the participants, had he defended his and
Thurston's innovations solely on the grounds that they were
better suited than the machinery and laws of Westminster to
meet both the needs of Fijian society and the minimal
demands of colonial rule, his rationale would have better
stood the test of time.[8]

The Governor was solemnly installed as the
representative of the Supreme Chief, and in turn personally
installed leading men as salaried governors or Roko Tui of
fourteen provinces in which, more often than not, they were
entitled to some kind of allegiance or cooperation from the
constituent polities. For most of the provincial
boundaries approximated the spheres of influence of the
chiefly lineages dominant at Cession. High chiefs of
character, and some of none, were virtually assured of
government appointment. In feudal style the Governor
administered an oath of allegiance and presented each new
Roko Tui with a staff of office. (The symbolism of the
latter was suitably ambiguous. While the quaint words of
installation enjoined the Roko to shepherd his people with
fatherly care, in the hands of more than one Roko the staff
was only a little less lethal than a club.)

From its inception the powerful position of Roko Tui
was highly acceptable to the high chiefs. In 1897 there
were thirteen Rokos and four European Governor's
Commissioners. The three provinces finally established for
the interior - Colo North, Colo East and Colo West -
preferred European rule to the elevation of any one of
their broken and disunited social groups, while in
Naitasiri the highest hereditary chief and his family were
out of favour with the people and had reluctantly been
dismissed. Ten of these Rokos could claim to be high
chiefs of their provinces; none of the thirteen was

without status or connection with the provinces they ruled.
Ra for instance was ruled by Ratu Joni Madraiwiwi, one of
the highest chiefs of Bau, which, as the dominant power in
eastern Fiji, had long been able to call on parts of Ra to
provide men for the Bauan armies. The salary of a senior
Roko was on a par with a junior European stipendiary
magistrate's (£350); in addition they received a twentieth
share of all lease monies in their province. In the sugar
provinces this share amounted to £200 or £300 a year.
'Fringe benefits', such as the use of 'prison' labour on
private plantations, were considerable.

The strongest unit of local government was the
district on tikina. The provinces were originally
subdivided into eighty-four tikina, not primarily for
administrative efficiency, but to correspond as closely as
was convenient to less inclusive federations of allied
social groups known as vanua. Usually the installed chiefs
of the vanua were appointed to take charge of the
preparation of taxes and all government work. They were in
this capacity styled Buli and were generally responsible to
the Roko for the state of the villages and for implementing
the resolutions of the various councils and the Native
Regulations described below. Their salary was only
nominal, £3 and £10 a year, because they had the right both
by custom as chief (in most areas) and by regulation as
Buli to levy services (lala) from their people in food
contributions, traditional manufactures and labour to meet
their own personal needs and those of the community. (The
Rokos enjoyed a similar right, and likewise all hereditary
chiefs, subject to the discretion and definition of the
Roko or Buli.) The Buli also received a twentieth share of
the rent monies of his district.

The power of the Buli was reinforced by a system of
courts. Native stipendiary magistrates presided alone on
district courts and sat with the European stipendiary
magistrate on provincial courts, which were the courts of
first instance only for serious charges such as arson or
rape. These courts implemented a stringent code of Native
Regulations which were framed by a board in close
consultation with Fijian leaders. They gave the force of
law to what was defined as reasonable and just if Fijian
hierarchical societies were to survive the superimposition
of colonial rule. A man had to remain in his village,
then, and keep planting (actual quantities were specified),
cooperate with the chiefs in the communal enterprises
(disobedience became a legal offence), bring his grievances

to orderly councils and courts, and play his part in all the ceremonial occasions demanded either by custom or the new order. To European observers the Native Regulations appeared to work only in the interests of particular chiefs; in the absence of democracy the people apparently had no redress against the abuse of power. But it was easy to intrigue against an oppressor and bring district or provincial administration to a standstill until Government House intervened. Nothing could be more misleading, it will be seen, than the idea that Fijian political processes were 'frozen' by the new colonial order.

The weakest link in the system was at village level, where the elected turaga ni koro or village headman had the unenviable task of implementing all the orders of higher officials while answering for the conduct of his relatives and friends in the village. He could in practice do very little without the support of village leaders who were often reluctant to assume a position that gave responsibility without reward. The Buli summoned these turaga ni koro and 'chiefs of the land' (however defined locally) to a monthly district council. They discussed every aspect of village life, not distinguishing between traditional activities and the work of government proper. Then in October or November of each year the Bulis and chiefs of the whole province met in a more formal provincial council and submitted for the Governor's assent resolutions which then had the force of law. Finally, from time to time - but in principle annually - the Governor convened the Council of Chiefs (Bosevakaturaga) where the assembled Rokos and representatives of lesser officials advised the colonial government on many matters referred to them or raised on their own initiative. It provided an infinitely more congenial forum than the incomprehensible offshoot of Westminster existing in the Legislative Council, though later the chiefs were represented there as well.[9] The resolutions of the assembled chiefs could not be disregarded lightly so long as the government was serious in maintaining the paramountcy of Fijian interests. A committee of the Council sent a personalized report of the state of the people to the Sovereign, who replied with suitable expressions of interest in their welfare and pleasure in their abiding loyalty.[10]

The surprising trust Fijians began to develop in British rule was strained but not undermined by the obligation to pay substantial taxes in kind. Thurston, first Auditor-General of the colonial government, designed for Gordon a taxation scheme that made unaccustomed demands on the villages by requiring all able-bodied men to cultivate a marketable crop in a communal tax field under the direction of the chiefs. The scheme was defended as a development of the traditional lala rights of chiefs to command garden planting to meet their own needs and ensure the prosperity of the people. The produce of each district had to realize a cash figure as part of the sum allocated to the province by the Legislative Council. The produce was collected at central points, shipped to Suva or Levuka and sold by tender to the highest bidder. Prices realized were often double the price Fijians would have received in small, direct dealings with the storekeeper-agents of the European commercial houses, more than double if payment was made - as was the practice - in goods marked up at a higher price to Fijians. In good years cash refunds were returned to the producers, too late perhaps to act as a direct incentive to production, but pleasant windfalls which helped them buy imported drapery and foods, build churches and schools, and especially to maintain a fleet of sailing cutters which gave them an independent means of transport probably better than villages in more remote coastal areas have ever had.

Thurston championed the scheme under Gordon and expanded it during his own governorship (1888-97) as a rational management of the colony's natural resources and the only feasible way of making Fijians substantial producers in their own right. Although he experimented with a variety of new commodities such as coffee and cinnamon, bananas and especially coconuts were the only promising export crops until the expansion of the sugar industry. Before Gordon's departure in 1880, Thurston went as Colonial Secretary to Sydney where he persuaded the Colonial Sugar Refining Company (CSR) to establish its first mill at Nausori, and shortly afterwards another was built at Rarawai, Ba. In the first decade of cane production to 1889 Fijians grew 53,870 tons worth £29,599 at the Nausori mill, earning considerable refunds above the provincial tax assessments. The western side of Viti Levu was better suited to cane. In a good year such as 1889 the 5963 people of Ba and Yasawas earned a refund of £2339 from the proceeds of their cane fields. [11]

Despite its financial success and political advantages to Fijians, the immediate physical demands of tax work were a chronic source of the grumbling that seems endemic in any society where initiative comes from above. The scheme

presented major logistical problems and required a level of
managerial or accounting skill that was not easily found
among Fijian leaders. European tax inspectors had to be
employed to supervise the work, and a colony as poor as
Fiji often had to make do with men recruited locally.
Little love was lost between many of these men and Fijian
officials. When Thurston's strong but sympathetic hand was
taken away in 1897, the scheme began to generate a pattern
of non-cooperation that led to its collapse, as will be
seen, within a decade.

The native taxation scheme was particularly resented
by the European settlers: more than anything else it gave
teeth to the government policy of insulating Fijians from
the need to divert their labour resources to the
plantations, and to become wholly dependent on local
merchants. Excluded from any real say in the colony's
affairs, deprived even of elected members in the
Legislative Council until 1904, local Europeans despaired
of Fijians ever being accorded the full personal liberty of
British subjects, the liberty above all else to sell their
lands and become a free-floating pool of labour. Although
the Europeans and the Indians were entirely exempt from
legislation designed to meet the needs of Fijian societies,
they were severely restricted in their dealing with
Fijians. Native Dealings ordinances limited the amount
that could be recovered from a Fijian in the courts.
Labour recruiting was closely regulated. Alienation of
Fijian land, except to the Crown, was halted, and leases
limited to twenty-one years. All pre-Cession claims were
submitted to a Lands Claims Commission. True, the
Commissioners took a generous view of some quite outrageous
pre-Cession transactions by which thousands of prime acres
had been exchanged for muskets, whisky and trade goods, but
less than a third (517) of the 1683 applications were
granted as claimed; 390 were granted ex gratia in whole or
part, and about half the 800,000 acres claimed were
returned to the Fijian owners. [12]

Gordon had wanted the finality of legal tenure to
apply not only to lands alienated before Cession but also
to Fijian lands, the whole of which had been theoretically
transferred to the Crown by the Deed of Cession. He had
come with instructions to make a settlement that did full
justice to the existing rights and future needs of Fijian
communities, and Thurston would have filled him in on the
ample assurances given to the chiefs on that score. The
problems of leaving Fijian lands under customary tenure

were obvious: where rights were vague or conflicting,
where ownership was disputed or uncertain, there could be
no easy way of settling the kind of disputes that in former
times had been resolved by war, no way of knowing which
land was unclaimed and at the disposal of the Crown, and no
efficient way of arranging leases to Europeans and, later,
the Indians.

To make matters worse, Fijian systems of land tenure
were little understood even by the most experienced
observers. In no area of Fijian life was Gordon's
ostensible policy of building on existing institutions more
fraught with difficulty; the very desire to codify and
standardize what in reality were flexible sets of
principles pertaining to decisions about land (and
different from one community to another) was contradictory.
It has been brilliantly shown by Peter France in The
Charter of the Land that Gordon and his advisers were
creating an ill-founded orthodoxy when they insisted that
Fijian land customs had 'the inflexibility and precision of
a legal system' which they then thought they were merely
writing into the laws of the colony.[13]

What Gordon did, it seems, was to elicit the consent
of the Council of Chiefs to the notion that Fijian land was
inalienable and that there had to be an 'authentic'
land-owning unit. The chiefs chose the mataqali, the word
that was in general use to describe the kinship or
household groups with which chiefs had dealings at village
level. (It later came for legal purposes to have
everywhere the meaning it had in Bau, a clan or patrilineal
descent group of second order inclusiveness.) When the
first Native Lands Commission was established in 1880 to
begin the long task of registering land ownership to
mataqali throughout the group, the Commissioners met
resistance and confusion, and the work was abandoned.
Thurston revised Gordon's original legislation in 1892 and
the new Native Lands Commissioner, Basil Thomson, conducted
investigations in Rewa, Ba and Tailevu. He provided the
first detailed evidence of actual tenure practice: in
Rewa, land and sometimes many scattered pieces of land were
held by individuals, bequeathed to male heirs, and leased
to other individuals. Thomson recorded ten conditions
under which land rights could be transferred: so much for
inalienability. In Ba, a province full of recently
dislocated people, the people wanted to revive dormant
rights to ancestral lands that now offered the prospect of
income from rents. In Tailevu, Thomson discovered that

land rights were in most cases recently established and often conflicting, and that no one wanted the _mataqali_ to be the unit of ownership. 'The self-conscious solicitude evinced by European legislators for the preservation of an immemorial system of Fijian land tenure', concludes France, 'was not shared by those Fijians who gave evidence before Thomson's Commission: they sought to provide for the future rather than to preserve the past.'[14]

Under Thomson's successors the Native Lands Commission tried to resolve the chaos by first classifying the people into descent groups and then awarding blocks of land to each _mataqali_. Though the people had pressed for family holdings to be recorded, it was felt that the monumental task of surveying and registering the boundaries of every small parcel of land was beyond the resources of the colony. Like it or not, Fijians had to learn to live with an arbitrary settlement and a cumbersome unit of ownership.

Despite the weakness of its theoretical justification, it will be argued that in the long run there were advantages in compromise and legal clarity. Fijian land rights as established by colonial law, with all the clumsy contradictions analysed by scholars, were to withstand the attacks of those Europeans who recognized from the beginning that the easier alternative - individualized land tenure in fee simple - was the classic solution (as in Hawaii and New Zealand) for the rapid transfer of native land to alien lands. If Gordon's belief that every inch of Fiji had an undisputed communal owner from time immemorial was a misconception, it was, from the Fijian point of view, a singularly fortunate one. The rights of the Crown under the Deed of Cession were never exercised except to acquire land so poor or remote that no community bothered to pursue or invent a claim. (To these Crown lands were later added the lands of registered _mataqali_ that became extinct.) Gordon's manifest unwillingness to pursue the rights of the Crown more aggressively meant that future government-sponsored schemes for European settlement would be limited to offering leases of Fijian lands. Fiji's existing European estates, though very extensive indeed in places such as Taveuni, had little hope of further expansion so long as Gordon's policies were maintained.

Despite problems that will become more apparent in later chapters, it was no mean legacy of power, security and dignity that Gordon and Thurston bequeathed the Fijian people. The irony is that the very success of their

administrative and political arrangements to dispel the
chiefs' disarray and despair at Cession, to keep Fiji
Fijian, was taken for granted by the end of the century.
More often than not Fijians chose to exercise their local
autonomy in ways that did not conform to more conventional
British concepts of progress. And now there were newcomers
in government who yearned to redefine the white man's
burden in Fiji.

Chapter 1

New white men without knowledge

'We are peculiarly situated here as regards natives', complained the Governor in 1907, considerably understating the differences he perceived between the powerful position of the Fijians and the more depressed situation of the aboriginal inhabitants of other British colonies.[1] The Governors who followed Gordon and Thurston viewed the system of Fijian administration bequeathed them with feelings ranging from kindly forbearance to cynical despair. Nearly all of them voiced hopes of reform, insisting that Fijians could not forever opt out of the twentieth century or the colonial version of 'the modern world'. Every address of a Governor to the Council of Chiefs employed quaintly translated clichés of the conventional wisdom the privileged classes of England had always directed to the lower orders at home, and much more confidently to the subject peoples overseas. Many of these Governors lacked personal credibility in their role as Supreme Chief. It could hardly be expected that in three or six years a Governor would achieve the kind of rapport with Fijians Thurston had built up over much of his life. Some of them made no attempt to learn Fijian - they were past the stage of their career where language tests could be considered reasonable. While most seemed to have enjoyed the impressive chiefly rituals that had become a gratifying tradition of the Fiji post, few were sensitive to the reciprocal commitments to which the same ceremonial solemnly bound them in Fijian eyes. With the death of Thurston in 1897, the partnership of the British and the Fijians entered a long period of strain, rather like a lukewarm marriage that had lasted long enough for each partner to value the convenience and fear the consequences of a rupture. With the best of intentions Thurston's successor in Fiji, Sir George T.M. O'Brien, began a process of almost continuous review of Fijian policy and ineffective piecemeal reform intended to bring Fijians gradually into line with more conventional British ideals of individualism and democracy. It is a theme that underscores the history of the British administration for the next fifty years.

O'Brien was a quiet bachelor who preferred the company of his spinster sister and Roman Catholic clerics to Suva's raucous society of planters, lawyers and merchants - nor did he have any inclination to maintain the intimate

12

relations Fijian leaders had previously enjoyed with their supreme chief. A painstaking and practical man, he had the views of the age on the importance of cleanliness, privacy, the one-family household, thrift and enterprise. If he brought to his review of the government's Fijian policy a sense of decency and much patience, he lacked the cross-cultural insight that had distinguished the career of his predecessor. O'Brien took for granted that Thurston's long political battle for the survival of a Fijian polity had been won: it was now urgent that something more be done to ensure the physical survival of the appalling number of children dying in their first year and later.

Between the census of 1891 and that of 1901, annual birth and death tallies monitored a decline in the Fijian population of 11,397 to a new low of 94,397 - despite a birth rate as high as thirty-seven per thousand. One-third of Fijian children failed to reach their first birthday; in the Yasawas and the Colo provinces the proportion was four out of ten. The Colonial Office and the colonial government in Suva were sensitive to these statistics for political as well as humane reasons. The decrease figures were ammunition for the vociferous section of the European community who resented their lack of elected representation in the Legislative Council and the economic self-sufficiency of the Fijians, and sought a solution in federation with New Zealand or even Australia where governments had dealt with 'the native problem' in ways far more conducive to economic progress. In Fiji the federationists tried to drum up support amongst the Fijians themselves, telling them that they were oppressed by the government, unjustly taxed, that obedience to hereditary chiefs was shameful in a British country, and that they should disregard the restrictions imposed on their liberty to leave their districts and find work.[2] They took every opportunity to vilify the Fijian Administration in the sympathetic columns of the Fiji Times and Australasian newspapers: 'coddling administration. . . has resulted in the unfortunate aborigines being relegated off the face of the earth at a most alarming rate. . . when overtaken by sickness he quietly succumbs as a happy release from his troubles'.[3]

The decrease in population had been a worry to the government for over twenty years. The measles epidemic of 1875 had carried off about one-fifth of the pre-Cession population of perhaps 140,000. Subsequent epidemics of whooping cough, dengue fever, dysentery and influenza took

several thousand more lives. After 1891 there was a decade
free of epidemics yet deaths consistently exceeded births.
Norma McArthur has correlated the continuing decline in the
number of births in these years with the arrival at
reproductive age of the seriously depleted cohorts born
just before and just after the 1875 measles.[4] No such
explanation was evident to the anxious government officials
of 1893 when they sent circulars to everyone of note or of
long residence in the colony inviting them to submit
opinions to a commission of inquiry into the decrease.
Basil Thomson, who served on the Commission, later wrote
amusingly that it appeared from the collected replies as if
Fijians were suffering from 'a combination of every known
physical, moral and social disease in its most acute form.
Collectively they were cankered through and through with
monogamy, in-breeding, unchivalry, communism and dirt;
individually by insouciance, foreign disease,
kava-drinking, and excessive smoking.'[5] 'But the most
potent cause of all', pronounced a planter from Serua, 'is
Tobacco and self-abuse amongst men, women, girls and
boys.'[6] If the respondents agreed on one thing, it was
that Fijian mothers were bad mothers - 'a race of blunted
sensibilities', claimed one official: 'I have lived
amongst natives during the past 23 years and have never
seen any particular affection shown to a child by its
mother.'[7] A Wesleyan missionary contributed the story of a
mother with a frail child living in his compound at Vuna
Point, Taveuni. He asked her to come twice a day to his
house for fresh cow's milk, yet 'although her child was
dying of starvation, she found it irksome to apply for
milk. Her maternal affection failed under the strain of
walking 110 yards twice a day . . . she is but a type of
most Fijian mothers of delicate children.'[8] In their
final report the Commissioners also blamed the Fijian men
for treating their women 'as mere beasts of burden, and
sexual conveniences.'[9]

Fijians, too, had discussed the decrease. 'In the old
days,' mourned a village chief, 'when we were darkminded
and in a savage state we lived. Nowadays when we are
civilised and enlightened we die.'[10] A remarkable array of
remedies had been proposed of which a Kadavu Buli's was the
most effective: the Buli of Sanima prosecuted several
couples before the native magistrate of Kadavu on the
grounds of abortion. There was no evidence other than that
they were married and childless. The cases were discharged
but all the wives subsequently gave birth to healthy
children.[11] On the same island the Buli of Nakasaleka

simply ordered thirteen childless women to have children
and nine of them did so within a year, the remaining four
within two years. [12] The Roko Tui of Bua interrogated all
the married women of his province and produced the
following statistics: there were 12 per cent childless for
natural reasons or because they knew how to prevent
conception, 17 per cent who conceived but artificially
aborted the offspring, 46 per cent who had children but
neglected them until they died, and only 25 per cent who
had healthy families. For this situation the Roko blamed
the import of 'foreign ways', meaning Tongan, and the
abandonment of good old Fijian customs such as the spacing
of families by a long period of sexual abstinence after
childbirth. [13]

Despite this evidence of real interest in their own
welfare, Governor O'Brien seems to have adhered to the
familiar stereotype of the natives sunk in apathy. It was
well expressed in Basil Thomson's The Fijians: A Study of
the Decay of Custom. Fijians, we learn, if not natives
everywhere, are incapable of any routine or any moderation;
system of any kind is incompatible with their nature;
custom makes no provision for innovation. [14] What a Fijian
most wanted, agreed the Colonial Secretary in 1902, was 'to
be left alone to eat, to sleep, and to follow his own
devices . . . all forms of authority are irksome, even
those to which they have been accustomed for many
generations, though without them they would fall at once to
the level of the animals'. [15] Fijians were seen as emerging
from the physical struggle of intertribal warfare to the
'moral struggle of modern competition'. [16] It was a
difficult, perhaps fatal 'time of transition' - the phrase
that neatly sidestepped further analysis for the next fifty
years. Neither O'Brien nor any of his successors until Sir
Philip Mitchell (1942-44) doubted that the salvation of
this squalid decaying society was for Fijians to become
more like 'the sturdy yeomen' of England were romantically
understood to be: hardworking, individually self-
sufficient, thrifty farmers and artisans, loyal to their
social superiors and devoted to their families in the
privacy of picturesque, clean little cottages - with
separate bedrooms. But where to start?

Reluctantly conceding that it was 'still the day of
small things in Fiji', O'Brien felt that Fijian society
would be immediately improved by better water supplies and
medical facilities, by educating the people in sanitary
matters and the care of young children, and by tightening

up provincial administration to enforce existing regulations - 'sheeves [sic] of regulations . . . hundreds of resolutions . . . all a dead letter'. What was new in this mundane package was simply O'Brien's determination to reform Fijians whether they wanted it or not. The eager reassumption of the white man's burden implicit in this program of good and public works was underscored by O'Brien's lack of faith in the capacity of the Fijian elite to further the aims of progressive government: 'The chiefs would cheerfully agree to and verbally support any regulation or resolution whatever that the Government might desire - but always subject to the tacit reservation that they should continue to remain exactly as they were.'[17] The massive inertia of Fijian life needed shock treatment beyond the powers of government to administer, but at least a start could be made.

The system of administering through the society's own leaders should be supplanted, O'Brien advised the Colonial Office, by some agency more trustworthy and capable, in short by bringing 'the perseverance, conscientiousness and method of competent English officials into continuous and personal bearing on the details of administration of native affairs'. O'Brien regretted that his predecessors' land policy had left the Crown without revenue from realizable assets and thus dependent for district administration on the goodwill of chiefs 'utterly indifferent to the welfare of the people'. To replace them overnight with European officers would have cost over £20,000, or slightly more than the whole native tax revenue. Not to mention the resentment of the people if they saw the abolition of a system to which 'in their queer conservative fashion' they had become attached. [18]

The government decided to allocate part of its increasing revenues to the elimination of some of the worst hazards to public health, especially poor water supplies. A scheme to supply the Rewa River delta with piped water cost £11,000 to complete. Numerous smaller projects were undertaken such as the construction of concrete tanks on the dry islands of Lau, and three provincial hospitals were built, with quarters for European medical officers. These unprecedented public works for the benefit of Fijians absorbed over £21,000 between 1897 and 1900.

A further £2000 was set aside from the beginning of 1899 for a new experiment in district administration: the appointment of four Provincial Inspectors to supervise the

work of the existing Fijian officials in eight provinces.
O'Brien saw this as the first step in bringing 'the Fijian
problem' under control. From a developmental point of view
the chief weakness of the nineteenth century administration
had been its want of executive follow-up at local level.
This had been clearly perceived by men such as Walter
Carew, the experienced Commissioner of Colo East, who had
written in 1896:

> Nothing but the very strongest measures such as a
> Regulation compelling the cleaning of every
> village daily, Sundays and all, when the people
> rise in the morning, with severe penalties on all
> whether villagers, Turaga ni koros, or Bulis
> rigorously enforced, regardless of rank or
> position, will ever bring them out of their
> condition of sloth into which their failing sense
> of self-respect and patriotism is fast sinking
> them.

Thurston himself had commented that 'no native would
supervise as indicated in the Comrs minute, and yet his
suggestions are necessary'.[19] O'Brien now had the money and
the men to resolve Thurston's dilemma - in a way Thurston
would never have approved.

'The success of your appointments', the Provincial
Inspectors were told, 'will be judged entirely by its
practical results in the way of checking depopulation,
ameliorating the condition of the natives and increasing
the out-turn of native produce.'[20] They were to enforce
long-standing regulations relating to the planting of fruit
trees and crops, the freeing of women in advanced pregnancy
and after childbirth from carrying heavy burdens or
fishing, the care of the sick and of young children, and
the general health and well-being of the people. This
charter was vague in relation to their status vis-a-vis
Fijian officials with whom they were expected to work.
They had no direct magisterial powers. Each of them went
his own way to get results and left detailed accounts in
daily diaries eagerly read by O'Brien. The margins were
peppered with his 'Bravo!' or 'very nice' or 'stupid of
him'. He queries the need for a new stone fence for a
village in Bua: 'Would not a wire fence be really
cheaper?'; despatches a dozen bottles of Hepster's Extract
of Codliver Oil and some preserved milk for an Inspector's
wife to dispense; enquires anxiously whether the people
are building latrines and whether 'their habits thereat'

are improving - they were.[21]

By the end of his first year as a Provincial Inspector
(1899), Frank Spence had travelled 2896 miles up and down
the provinces of Cakaudrove and Bua. He found it effective
to take his wife with him: 'What escapes my notice is seen
by her.' Laura Spence kept her own diary. 'It is dreadful
to see how the poor little creatures are neglected', she
wrote 'Some of the women are so densely stupid. It is a
most trying and difficult work and requires a good temper
. . .' In one month, August 1900, this energetic lady
visited 43 towns, inspected 299 houses, burnt 665 dirty
mats, and treated 60 cases of ringworm. Her husband
meanwhile was having trees felled, ditches filled in,
drains dug, wells cleaned and, in some cases, villages
moved bodily to healthier sites. [22]

Spence's counterpart in charge of Ba and Nadroga,
Sydney Smith, left the best account from which to surmise
the reactions of Fijians to this unprecedented interference
in their domestic affairs. Smith saw himself at war with
the old system: 'I feel I am pulling in one direction
trying to wipe out things Fijian and substitute common
sense while there is a Roko perpetuating "the Fijian".'
When he arrived at a village he dispensed with what he
called 'the Fijian capers' - and went straight on to
inspect the drinking water, bathing places and houses: 'I
won't be bothered with their wretched presentations, and
never do accept them . . . The Roko (rotten institution)
should be made to leave these things alone, and work; work
hard. He is handsomely paid. Either that or get out of
the road. Not hinder me.'[23] Similarly in Tailevu, Islay
McOwan had very foreseeable problems with the Roko,
Ratu Epeli Nailatikau, senior son of Cakobau, the great
Vunivalu of Bau. Ratu Epeli asked O'Brien, unbelievingly:
'Did you really appoint him [McOwan] to rule the province
entirely by himself. . . he does so, and in any way he
pleases, nor is there any consultation between us. I
should know when he comes and when he goes; we should
discuss things beforehand so that I can have my say - just
as it was published in Na Mata [the Fijian language
government gazette]'. O'Brien counselled McOwan to 'humour
him a bit, and keep him au courant and not to let him feel
that he is being counted out'.[24] It was a first hint of the
practice that later developed of allowing the Rokos the
trappings and not the substance of power.

The Rokos had an opportunity to voice their anger at the Council of Chiefs of 1902 where their ill-feeling was explained by Ratu Jope Naucabalavu in a sentence: 'The cause of our trouble is that new white men without knowledge have taken charge of our affairs.'[25] They argued that if villages could be moved and Bulis dismissed without reference to themselves, then their whole way of life was threatened - and by men whose specific goals, however progressive, made no allowances for the feelings of the communities involved. As a result of these protests and of reports of unrest in the provinces, the Inspectors were withdrawn in 1903 and replaced by three Assistant Native Commissioners based in Suva and Labasa. Inspections became much less frequent, but the powers of the Commissioners clearly overrode those of the chiefs. The policy of 'closer domestic interference' introduced by O'Brien was to be pursued with varying intensity for the next forty years.

The inspectorate was not O'Brien's only instrument for improving the villages. He asked the Roman Catholic and Wesleyan missions in Fiji to mount a hygiene mission and provide the detailed instruction that no Provincial Inspector or his wife could be expected to manage single-handed. Bishop Julian Vidal released eight European and fourteen Fijian nuns to work in the vicinity of the Catholic mission stations. The Wesleyans were not much taken with the scheme, although the wives of their missionaries had done similar work before. With reason they feared that the Catholics would use the hygiene mission to infiltrate Wesleyan villages. They successfully demanded that the Governor restrict the Sisters to Catholic villages, drawing an angry reaction from some of their own adherents: 'Do you really believe that we should all die rather than a Catholic attend to us when we are sick?'[26] For the work of the Sisters was well received by the people. An enthusiastic supporter wrote in Na Mata: 'the Sisters are the enemies of dirt, they are the enemies of all foetid atmospheres, they are kindly, they are loving, they are anxious to assist us and their example is one we might very well follow.'[27]

The Sisters sallied up into the hills of Namosi and other remote areas not covered by the Provincial Inspectors to root out the accumulated filth of years. Before bonfires of old mats, grass, clothing, and trees that had been growing too close to houses, they upbraided the startled populace for their unclean ways and showed the mothers how to care for their infants. After a few months of the campaign in Serua, the European magistrate reported that hardly a house had not been turned out and thoroughly cleansed. Raised sleeping-shelves (vata) were provided for every occupant - although there was doubt that they were much used. (The vata survive to this day as the rock-hard wooden platforms of honour on which the European guest in a Fijian home is firmly condemned to sleep however much he inclines towards the comfort of a soft matted floor.) The Sisters began to grow discouraged as they realized that as soon as they were out of sight the people reverted to the habits of centuries. Fijian officials were not always cooperative. With malicious humour the Roko of Serua made his point on an inspection of the Sisters' own mission station while they were away in the hills. He had all the mats inside the church pulled out, pronounced filthy, and burnt on the spot. The hygiene mission seems to have petered out about 1903 when the Sisters resolved to confine their activities to the more congenial task of educating children.[28] It was not until the child welfare movement began in 1927 (see below) that a way was found to change the alleged attitudes and practices of Fijian mothers.

After nine months' annotating the diaries of the Provincial Inspectors and the Sisters' reports, O'Brien sadly concluded that reforms of a deeper social nature were needed if the standard of Fijian life was to improve. He was depressed by 'the almost total extinction of all incentive to individual exertion', and chose as his first target the practice of kerekere: the relatives and friends of a man could, it seemed, 'request' his personal property in the sure knowledge that he would be too ashamed (madua) to refuse. Sydney Smith had told O'Brien, who relayed the story to the Legislative Council, that in Nadroga a man would buy a new lamp with the proceeds from his bananas - and break the glass on the way home in the hope that it would then be less attractive as an object of kerekere. 'Are there any people on the face of the earth so inherently and incurably industrious that they will exert themselves more than they need, if they are not allowed personally to enjoy the fruits of their labour?'[29]

O'Brien naively hoped to abolish kerekere by the untiring moral persuasion of the missionaries and his own officials.[30] The Rokos and Commissioners were asked to bring kerekere up for discussion in the district and provincial councils, so long as resolutions on the subject were 'spontaneous and not "deferential"'.[31] Resolutions duly came forward - in Cakaudrove every tikina claimed to have

abolished it in 1898, and when other provinces followed
suit, the Governor really believed that he had achieved a
lasting reform. He told the Legislative Council that where
efforts had been made to educate the people on the evils of
kerekere, they were tending not to hide their utensils,
lamps, plates and fine mats.[32] And indeed these articles
are not usually objects of kerekere today, if they ever
were, though the general practice certainly did not succumb
to rhetoric. It had a function not perceived by O'Brien
and his men. Kerekere was not merely begging, although it
was (and is) described as such by Europeans. Granting a
favour conferred status on the giver and the right to make
a return request in his own moment of need or whimsy. 'It
is as clear as daylight', explained a Fijian in a letter to
Na Mata, 'that one cannot kerekere indiscriminately. If
you come and ask for my lantern because you are short, by
and by I will be short of clothes and I will ask you for
some. It will be in return for my lamp.' Kerekere was a
common man's lala, he added, referring to chiefly rights to
conscript goods, and it could only be done without if the
chiefs eased their demands on the people and all
transactions in Fijian society were put on a cash
basis.[33] The problem with kerekere, replied a dissenting
correspondent, was that 'The lazy man goes to kerekere the
hardworking man, but the latter has no need to ask anything
of the former ... Fiji-style they are both reduced to the
same state.' [34] The practice remained in force - an
effective levelling or distributive mechanism that has
always inhibited the accumulation of private capital and
still binds individuals closely to their kindred.

The organization of communal labour was O'Brien's
second target for reform. There was no question of its
abolition. As the chiefs had said immediately after
Cession, no man could build a house by himself to the
generous Fijian proportions requiring raised foundations,
heavy timber posts and crossbeams, and a thatched roof.
Nor could an individual drag timber for a canoe. Men had
always worked in groups under the direction of their chief
for the needs of each other and of the community.[35] The
Native Regulations took communal labour a stage further by
requiring it for roads, provincial office building,
hospitals, tax gardens or any other project approved by the
provincial councils. The self-reliance of this system
appealed greatly to a penny-pinching government, but it led
to many allegations and some instances of chiefly
oppression - just how much O'Brien wanted to know. It
appalled him, for instance, to find that the European Tax

Inspector could not provide 'even the faintest approximation to an estimate' of the work involved in tax operations. [36] It had always been left to the chiefs to call out as much labour as was needed for a particular operation, and at any time they saw fit.

Part of the solution, decided the Governor, was for the provincial councils to draw up a more specific annual program of work and allocate definite times not only for tax work but also housebuilding, planting, road clearing and especially the labour requirements of officials and chiefs. At least a month was to be set aside for 'individual betterment' - generally December. (Ironically, this seems to be the origin of the contemporary Christmas-New Year 'happy time'.) The first programs drawn up for 1900 did not reassure the Governor that Fijians saw things as he did: 'Lala to be left to the chiefs to exact when the people are free' or 'whenever a chief may really require it', coconuts 'to be planted at all times'. [37]

In time the program of work became formally more specific, but when enforced, tied the people so much to particular activities that it came to be regarded itself as one of the major obstacles to the individual betterment O'Brien had hoped to encourage.

The native taxation scheme was the one area of past Fijian policy which O'Brien still endorsed for its 'necessitating a certain though very limited amount of exertion'. Its abolition, he feared, would make Fijians 'even idler and more indolent than they are at present'. [38] At the turn of the century the scheme was still working fairly well. The average annual cash refund to the producers between 1892 and 1902 was over £12,000, or 60 per cent of the total assessment; the cost of collection was only 6 per cent. Sugar cane was grown for tax in the Rewa delta area, on the Navua River (Serua), and in Ba, Ra and Macuata. Although the average village tax field was only about 2 acres, requiring around thirty days' work a year, Fijians produced 15,447 tons of cane in 1900 worth £7432 at the five mills. [39] In the copra provinces (Cakaudrove, Bua, Kadavu, Lau, Lomaiviti, Yasawas) the work varied greatly with the fluctuations in price. With copra around £9 a ton in 1902 a man needed to contribute about 3 hundredweight or 900 nuts towards the assessment, three days' work at the most if the nuts were easily accessible in a clean plantation. Where tobacco was the allocated crop, each man might tend 200-300 plants. [40] Though cotton and rice had been tried, as well as coffee, the only other significant crops now were yaqona (kava) and maize. Fifteen tons of yaqona were sold in 1901 at 9 1/2d per pound, and 28,000 bushels of maize at 2s 1d per bushel. The only villagers exempt from payment in kind were 270 men who lived close to Suva and Levuka and who were accustomed to selling their produce at the markets for cash, providing a useful service to the townspeople.

It was left to the chiefs to make the actual division of labour - the point that most worried O'Brien. European magistrates sometimes acted as tax inspectors to coordinate the work between villages and especially to supervise the heavier aspects of cane harvesting in the sugar areas. Cane always gave the most problems. Fijians found its cultivation alien to their subsistence techniques and resented the distances they often had to travel to reach the cane fields - over 20 miles in some areas. They shirked the work whenever possible: 'Growing cane is a nightmare to the natives and to the Inspectors', wrote McOwan from Navua, 'until absenteeism can be quashed'.[41] Another magistrate had to hold special monthly provincial courts to deal with offenders. It needed a tough brand of personal leadership to make the scheme work. The Colonial Secretary, W. L. Allardyce, recalled how he once had the whole of Serua province out cutting cane, several hundred people, and kept the Deuba mill supplied unaided. Ten days' work was enough to meet the provincial assessment, but only because he slept with them in the rough shelters on the field, roused them at daylight, and worked with them till dusk.[42] After the death of Thurston, who expected this kind of leadership of his subordinates and gave it himself, there were few men of Allardyce's calibre really prepared to make the scheme work. Their fellow countrymen had always been loud in its condemnation and now the Fijians themselves, unaware of the consequences, were tempted by what seemed the easier alternative of paying taxes in cash.

From Macuata came the most detailed account of how the system was breaking down under less able men - or if the opinion of magistrate Nathaniel Chalmers is preferred, it was 'entirely owing from first to last to the utter carelessness and indifference of the Bulis and the people'.[43] CSR Company officers prepared the Labasa tax field and provided £60 worth of first-class cane tops for planting. Chalmers himself, an old sugar hand and a notoriously bad manager of men, laid them out on the field and showed the Buli and his men how to cut the tops, lay them in sets, and space them in the rows. The weather was exceptionally dry, so he instructed them to tread down about 6 inches of soil over each set. With the planting under way he left the Buli in charge and returned to his office. The next day he heard that all 48 acres had been completed. Gratified, he rode out to inspect. The men had already gone home. To his disgust he found that the cane tops had been thrown anywhere into the furrows, uncut, and with a foot or two exposed to the scorching sun. He galloped to the house of the Buli and demanded that the entire field be replanted immediately. This time he supervised the work for a few hours, but the moment he was on his way back to Labasa to hold a court the cane was 'shoved in anyhow' with the result that not 1 set in 500 vegetated. And CSR had no more tops to spare. The field was planted a third time with tops from other districts and finally yielded a miserable 8 tons per acre: 'I respectfully submit that it is utterly hopeless and a most heart-breaking business to cultivate cane under the present system.' Would it not be more efficient, Chalmers suggested, to have one large plantation for several districts combined and work it systematically with teams of good workers drawn in rotation from each tikina? O'Brien gladly approved, hoping that the more regular work would also teach 'habits of continuous industry'.[44]

The experiment, like most experiments in Fiji, began well. The conscripts lived in the field in temporary huts and grew their own food crops on the side. Then a drought in 1900 destroyed the crop and discouragement tailed into indifference. Although 1901 was a better year and the crop was expected to realize £1200 (2400 tons from 191 acres), the Provincial Council of Macuata unanimously requested permission to abandon cane growing for the more leisurely routine of copra cutting. The reaction of the Receiver General expressed the newly ambivalent attitude of the government towards the taxation scheme. How far should the wishes of the people be allowed to undermine 'their own good'? 'Macuata is a very backward province and unless the Govt. made it a duty for them to do something more than work up their nuts they are not likely to show any enterprise. I therefore think for their own good they should fish beche de mer or grow a crop of maize so as to get money to increase their comfort.'[45] But what if the people felt they were comfortable enough? It was not a question the progressive administrator could ask.

Macuata was allowed to relinquish cane, and other
provinces were anxious to follow. The Roko of Serua, who
had never interested himself in tax work except to
exaggerate the grievances of his people, complained that
workers had little to eat, the cane fields were too far
from the villages, and women and children were left alone
for days on end.[46] That cane had done well in Serua was no
consideration. The neighbouring chiefs of Namosi, on a
similar theme, showed awareness of the new pieties when
they suggested that if they abandoned cane they would have
'so much more time for individual betterment'.[47] No one in
Suva believed them - though they had their way in the end.
The only 'terrible waste of labour', Allardyce had often
argued, was the time they would spend in their villages,
'sitting, sleeping, malingering, loitering, gossiping,
smoking and laughing'.[48]

The copra areas had their own sets of problems. For
months before the assessment date a tabu on gathering nuts
deprived the people, especially newly weaned infants, of a
valuable food and oil. Copra productivity was low. The
villagers could not be persuaded that it was worthwhile to
thin out their plantations (cut down good trees?), tend the
young saplings or plant for the future. Fijian plantations
could be identified by their dense tangle of undergrowth,
as if the palms were growing wild and their fruit a
gratuitous windfall. To meet a small quota was often
difficult, ana yams were substituted at 50s and 60s a ton
or logs at about 1s each. Another solution was for one
district to proceed en masse to another and kerekere for
all their wants. The Matuku islanders sailed one year to
Nakasaleka in Kadavu and requested food. After several
days of lavish hospitality they sailed away with 10,400
taro (£50), fourteen large kava roots (£2 16s) and one
bullock (£5). Some time later the Kadavu people made a
return visit to Matuku where they presented twenty-seven
tabua (whales' teeth). On the way their cutter nearly came
to grief on a reef and later cost £27 to repair. They were
reimbursed with 1000 coconuts, enough for only £11 worth of
copra:[49] a typically Fijian transaction in which the social
context was far more important than the economic disparity
revealed in these irrelevant calculations of a hostile
official.

Wherever possible Fijians were trying to subvert, so
to speak, the economic goals of the colony by subsuming
them into more congenial and traditional ways of meeting
their needs. Whereas in the nineteenth century the

government valued the stability this state of affairs gave
to the colony and recognized the satisfactions of Fijian
social life as good in themselves, in the twentieth century
the proponents of more material progress were to become
impatient with a society that showed such disrespect for
individual profit. These people had to be educated out of
their 'malaise' and learn the values of honest work for
private advantage: the common good would look after
itself.

In his final effort to foster individualism in Fijian
society, O'Brien instructed the magistrates and Bulis in
1900 to apportion the cash refund according to the
contribution of each individual. Where it was enforced,
the order had unexpected consequences, at least in the case
of copra. Whereas previously a district had met its quota
by pooling the resources of its landowners - those who had
no land in production cut their neighbours' copra - now the
owners began to demand payment in pigs or mats or cash to
compensate for the diminution of their share in the refund.
Some districts went a step further and began to sub-assess
individuals from the start for a fixed quantity of copra.
For the first time taxes became a problem for the landless.
The Roko Tui of Lau, the province most affected, pleaded
for individuals to be allowed to pay in cash.[50] The absurd
situation had arisen in his and other provinces where
individuals were selling produce to storekeepers to raise
cash to buy the particular produce required for taxation in
kind. The Council of Chiefs in 1902 asked therefore that
it be left to the provinces to decide in what form they
should pay their taxes.

O'Brien rightly feared that to grant exceptions would
bring down the scheme altogether. In 1900 when the tobacco
crop failed in Colo West he had allowed the people to go to
the coast and work for a few weeks, but 'strictly as an
exceptional case and not to form a precedent'.[51] But under
his successors frequent exceptions were made. By 1906
Namosi, Serua and the interior Colo provinces had abandoned
their tax fields. Almost alone of the provinces Ba - or
rather its energetic Roko, Ratu Joni Madraiwiwi - resisted
the trend to cash payments. Ratu Joni allowed the people
to have individual gardens and kept a strict tally of each
man's contribution. In 1908 the people despatched produce
that realized £2500 in excess of the assessment of £647
19s. Some individuals received a refund of up to £10.[52]

Ratu Joni had been trained by Thurston, and like his old friend and chief he must have feared the social consequences of the taxation scheme's imminent destruction. By 1912 there were so few districts paying in kind that it was decided to make cash payments obligatory from the following year. 'I look upon the change as final', wrote the Native Commissioner, adding no regrets.[53] The mood of government had changed. They knew well that Fijians would mortgage their coconut groves to the nearest trader who would himself have the nuts collected and the copra cut, with the net result that the owners would receive less than half the value of their produce. They also knew that the loss of the central marketing organization provided by the old scheme would relegate Fijians to the edges of an ever more alien-dominated colonial economy. They hardly bargained perhaps for the enormous amount of petty prosecution in the courts that would be necessary to hound villagers into exercising their new-found individuality and so extract cash taxes that were scarcely more than would have been given back to them under the Gordon system by way of refund. The changes were seen as the inevitable price of an ill-defined concept of general progress through the 'time of transition' to a more western way of life.

Sir George O'Brien had loosened the skewers, his successors began to pull them out. Would the whole Gordon-Thurston legacy disintegrate with the native taxation scheme, would Fijian society collapse within and the colony become a proper British dominion run in the European interest? The next assault was led by an able and well-meaning Governor who enjoyed a reputation in the Colonial Office as one 'whose whole interest wherever he has been has rested in and through the natives . . .'[54]

Chapter 2

The assault on land rights

On 11 October 1904, the day after he arrived in Fiji,
Everard im Thurn was installed as Supreme Chief of the
Fijians with ceremonies he acknowledged in his diary as
'extraordinarily interesting'. On the evening of the same
day he was recovering in his office when he noticed

> something that seemed a great dog creeping up and
> licking my boots. It was a magnificent Fijian,
> an officer of the Armed Native Constabulary, who
> had crept on all fours vaka Viti to take the
> earliest opportunity to prefer some request. I
> was startled - and . . . gave him to understand
> that he was never to do such a thing again.[1]

Vakaviti, Fiji-style, is a word im Thurn was to use often
in the following six years. Applied to individuals it
never lost the connotations it has here of unmanly
behaviour that ill became the dignity of full British
subjects. Applied to land rights, vakaviti was synonymous
with chaotic.

From his diaries it seems that im Thurn came to his
views on the state of Fijian society after talking to Chief
Justice Sir Charles Major, Attorney General Albert
Erdhardt, and a few other government officials of
comparatively short-term experience in the colony. They
had one thing in common: they agreed with the long-held
view of the European settlers that the Gordon-Thurston
system, or 'the communal system' as it was now called, had
outlived whatever usefulness it might have possessed in the
early years. It was hampering the natural development of
the colony and destroying the moral fibre of the Fijians
themselves. The new Governor was easily persuaded to the
popular view that the Fijians had lost the will to live and
were doomed to extinction.

By April 1905 im Thurn was confident enough to speak
to the Council of Chiefs in perhaps the most unpleasant
language they had ever heard. The chiefs, he charged, were
'killing' the people who 'do not even care for the trouble
of living and of raising children for a race which is dying
out so fast that unless a change comes soon, there will not

be one of you left in forty years . . . The Fijian people
are perishing chiefly because they are not allowed any
liberty to think and act for themselves.' He appealed to
the chiefs to help their people become 'more like real
men . . . fit and willing to do men's work' so that with
the gradual substitution of British laws for the backward
Native Regulations the people would eventually be on the
same level 'as white British subjects are'. As a grand,
but in the context boorish gesture, he announced that he
was abandoning forthwith his personal rights as Supreme
Chief to isevu, first fruits. These were voluntary tokens
of goodwill from the provinces, a pleasant reminder also of
Fijian expectations that the Governor would act towards
them as a true chief. To Sir Everard it was all vakaviti,
unprogressive sentimentality: 'In future I do not want
anyone of you Fijians to offer me anything for which you
will not let me pay.'[2]

Having prepared the chiefs for radical change,
im Thurn set about laying the foundations for a future
whose prosperity would be assured by a large European
population with the capital and skills to bring into
production the vast tracts of fertile land a dying and
indolent race could never hope to use. He reawakened the
vision of building a strong outpost of the British Empire
in the South Seas, moving the Fiji Times to hail him, quite
accurately, as 'the first Governor of Fiji to make any
public recognition of the fact that the colony may have a
British future; that the lands of the colony are necessary
to that future; and that the present conditions of land
tenure are untenable'.[3]

Whereas Gordon had argued that the alienation of land
had already gone to the 'very verge' of what should be
permitted if the Fijians were not to be lorded over by
white settlers, im Thurn saw the European development of
the 4,250,000 uncultivated acres of the colony as his first
priority.[4] It was then he confronted the implications of
the Fijian myth interpreting the Deed of Cession as a
personal covenant between the chiefs and their Queen,
reflecting their retrospective satisfaction with the way
their first Governor had articulated British respect for
their rights and privileges.[5] Had not Gordon, and his
successors too, outraged the European community by
enthusiastically treating with them as Supreme Chief to
brother chiefs, even to the details of Fijian ceremonial
etiquette? The proof of the wisdom of Cession was that the
people had been given a secure legal title to the lands

remaining to them. Alienation had been halted. From the Fijian language compendium of Native Regulations they could invoke Commodore Goodenough's response to the offer of Cession made on 12 March 1874: 'It is clear to me that you are not ceding the land itself or your people. That is good.'[6] In the Fijian popular mind the lands had been given by the chiefs to the Queen vakaturaga, that is, by way of a chiefly presentation which entitled them to expect that the Queen in her reciprocal generosity would return the lands to be shared and used by the people. Gordon did nothing to disabuse them of this notion; he encouraged the myth to secure their loyalty - despite the plain provisions of article IV of the Deed of Cession vesting in the Crown all lands not actually used by a tribe or chief nor needed for their 'probable future support'. Ordinance XXI of 1880 had established a Native Lands Commission to give legal recognition to Fijian ownership of all lands not already alienated, and to implement Gordon's personal pledge that what Fijians then held would be confirmed to them. In 1908 the former Governor wrote to Lord Elgin at the Colonial Office: 'I do not only think, I know, that I must have repeated the assurance at least 30 times.'[7]

Im Thurn made a determined attack on the Gordon-Fijian viewpoint, suspecting a cosy conspiracy to defraud the Crown of its legitimate assets. He reviewed the history of Fijian land transactions as 'one great blunder from the beginning . . . from 1875 we have again and again failed to claim the lands but even ostentatiously pretended to recognise . . . the natives' imaginary rights as real'.[8] On solid historical grounds im Thurn argued that pre-Cession Fijians had lived in a constant state of petty war and that their boundaries shifted frequently: it was pure invention to speak of ancestral rights to pieces of land or to say, as Gordon and others did, that every inch of Fiji had its owner. There were large tracts of land unoccupied at Cession which should have been marked off immediately as Crown land and kept for future European settlement.[9]

To im Thurn the work of the Native Lands Commission had been conceived on false premises. It was attempting to codify and standardize customary situations that varied from one district to another, situations that were of their essence uncodifiable. In his first year of office he also observed that the NLC hearings in Tailevu province seemed themselves to bring to a head or even cause serious disputes. He suspected the ageing David Wilkinson, who had

served the government off and on since Cession, was
mentally incapable of effecting reasonable settlements, but
in any case he was impatient for the 'impenetrable
obscurity' of Fijian custom eventually to give way to 'the
clear light of the Real Property Ordinance'.[10] Im Thurn's
analysis of the problems of codifying custom was
brilliantly done and has won him the respect of modern
scholars, although few have thought through the political
consequences of his determination to get Fijian land into
the open market.

The only move towards rational management of the
Fijian estate had been the unanimous consent of the Council
of Chiefs in 1903 to the suggestion that the government
should have the entire control of the leasing of 'waste'
lands or those lying idle.[11] By March 1905 some four
hundred vaguely described blocks had been nominated for
leasing by the provincial councils, most so truly waste or
inaccessible as to be useless for settlement. Im Thurn
suggested to his subordinates that alienation would have to
be made easier. The Chief Justice was enthusiastic, urging
that the time had come for the government to take unused
lands 'say the owners yea or nay'. The Native
Commissioner, Francis Baxendale, 'as representing the
natives' assured the Governor that drastic reforms would be
'welcomed with pleasure' by Fijians.[12] Without consulting a
single chief, im Thurn had his first reforms passed by the
Legislative Council in May 1905. Fijian lands became
alienable with the consent of the Governor-in-Council, the
twenty-one year limit to leases no longer applied, and the
Native Lands Commission was restricted to the hearing of
actual disputes. The European settlers could hardly
believe that a simple ordinance could strike at the heart
of Fijian polity so long sustained by the official
majorities in the undemocratic legislature. Over the next
three years 104,142 acres of Fijian land were quietly sold
and became freehold. The Council of Chiefs was never
convoked to give the Fijians their opportunity to assess
what was happening and write their thoughts to the King.
But they were not without vigilant friends abroad who soon
became aware that things in Fiji were not what they used to
be.

The land sales attracted little attention in London
until a former Governor, Sir William des Voeux, sent the
Colonial Office a cutting from the Fiji Times of 27 June
1906 describing the purchase of a Rewa riverfront property,
'Navuso', for £1500. Under a lease that still had seven

years to run the Fijian owners had received an annual
rental of £415. The purchaser, prominent Suva lawyer
H. M. Scott, had made quite a bargain. The Governor
defended the transaction (which had only been approved in
Executive Council by his own casting vote) on the grounds
that the land was exhausted, the real rental value was only
£200, and that even if the deal was a bit dubious then 'a
few experiences of such a character are likely to teach
more self-reliance than years of leading strings'.[13]
    Im Thurn had on another occasion put his dilemma in terms
that should have alerted the Colonial Office to a
fundamental shift in the position of the Fijians: 'The
social and political status of the Fijian native in this
British colony is so extraordinary and anomalous that it is
a matter of very great difficulty to hold the scales evenly
when the interests of the natives and Europeans are weighed
against each other . . . '[14] Two years after taking office
im Thurn forwarded for approval an ordinance (XVI of 1906)
to empower the government to resume land for 'any
undertaking proposal or policy which may appear to the
Governor in Council desirable as directly benefiting the
Colony'. One of the situations im Thurn had in mind was
the possibility that Fijians at some future date would
refuse to accept in the remote districts prices lower than
they were demanding and receiving in the sugar centres.[15]

    Although Sir Everard never admitted to the connection,
this ordinance came after months of frustrating
negotiations by CSR and government officers to obtain about
10,500 acres of unused swamp lands lying between Nausori
and Wainibokasi on the Rewa River. The proposals involved
moving five villages of 352 people. Ratu Joni Madraiwiwi,
now Roko Tui of Ra, was called in to gain their support.
The chief was foiled by the agents of two Suva lawyers who
encouraged the owners, the Nakelo people, to hold out for
the high rentals they were used to receiving from Indians
for small blocks. 'The real trouble', said Ratu Joni in a
moment of chiefly exasperation, 'is that they have never
had anything to decide before and it's only in the time of
the Government that they are allowed to have
any.'[16] Im Thurn could not have agreed more.

    David Wilkinson had another view of the matter and
wrote a strong letter of protest, with a copy to Gordon,
now Lord Stanmore, alleging that the Nakelo people had been
bullied and insulted and had a 'deep-seated
dread . . . that in some way or another they [were] to be
deprived of their ancestral lands . . . A native said to me

the other day "has our Governor ceased to be our High Chief?"' [17]

Im Thurn dismissed Wilkinson's views as 'hysterical' but on the whole the old man had better reason for his fears than did the Governor for holding optimistically to a contrary opinion. Sure of the rightness of his cause, and encouraged by the enthusiasm of the European community and the apparent acquiescence of the Fijians, im Thurn introduced in June 1907 a third ordinance (IX of 1907) providing for the sale or lease of native land to Fijians and its conversion thereby to freehold title. It also allowed for the devolution of the powers of the Native Lands Commission to magistrates or others so that they could settle disputes on the spot, with appeals against their decisions lying to the Supreme Court rather than the Governor-in-Council.[18] Thus was another safeguard of Fijian interests, direct appeal to their supreme chief, quietly removed.

The Colonial Office, by now thoroughly alerted to im Thurn's real intentions, sharply enquired whether the ordinance was 'merely a device under which land held individually by a native Fijian may be disposed of to a non-native' and whether Fijian opinion ahd been sought on the matter through the Council of Chiefs.[19] In his reply the Governor ignored the last suggestion and confirmed that there would be no restrictions on individuals selling their land, but that it was not likely to happen very often. In a long review of the whole land situation he suggested that the time had also come for a special commission to assess the position of Fijian natives 'as affected by special legislation and by that legally recognised, but yet formless, law of "Fijian custom" ("vaka viti") and their consequent partial exclusion from the rights and obligations of ordinary British subjects'.[20] Although nothing came immediately of the last suggestion, it reveals the true context of his land reforms as the major item on a much larger agenda: the reformation of the whole Fijian system.

Meanwhile government officers and one or two Fijian Rokos were attempting to circumvent the problem of alienation by obtaining large tracts of land for leasing. Resistance was strong in provinces where the best lands had already been alienated, as in Ba and Cakaudrove. The fifteen inhabitants of Nanuca in the latter province, for instance, had 3000-4000 acres of land but regarded none of it as surplus, even though 30 acres would have sufficed for their subsistence planting. Land in the Rewa delta was also hard to obtain as the owners could get quite high rents from Indians and saw no reason why they should subsidize either CSR or the government. In the province of Bua, however, Ratu Joni Madraiwiwi spent ten weeks in 1906 inspecting surplus lands and obtained for the government 51,000 acres for ninety-nine years at the rate of £10 per 1000 acres. In 1907 he obtained another 12,000 acres. The Macuata people surrendered 50,000 acres at £1 per 100 acres from 1 January 1908. About the same time 60,000 acres of good grazing land were obtained in Colo West.[21]

It needs recalling at this point that the eyes of the original Fijian lands, especially the river flats, had been picked before Cession, and that Fijian ownership of 83 per cent of the lands, while tremendously important in the larger sweep of history, is not as impressive in economic terms as it may sound. After the second wave of selling just described there remained in Fijian control (July 1909) only one large area of first-class flat land, the Waidalici and Sawakasa flats in northern Tailevu, some 50 miles north of Suva. In the course of a routine inspection by Ratu Kadavulevu and Assistant Native Commissioner W. A. Scott, the proposal was put before the District (Tikina) Councils of Namalata and Sawakasa that the government should assume the entire control of these lands. The signatures of the owners were obtained without difficulty on the understanding that planting reserves would be set aside and none of the lands would be leased to Indians, who, the people claimed, 'taught them bad customs and polluted their water courses'. The land surrendered included 5000 acres immediately suitable for cane, bananas or tobacco and a further 2000 acres that needed draining. There were 30,000 acres suitable for grazing.[22]

Before the end of the year the people reconsidered. The old Sawakasa chief, Ratu Kamenieli Bituvatu, with all the original signatories alleged duress and tried to repudiate the agreement: 'We did not hand over our lands, you spoke of it first. We did not ask for this.'[23] Im Thurn, of course, had little sympathy and made an ill-conceived appeal to Fijian precedent: 'Vakaviti, Cakobau would, if he had known that there were people [Europeans] ready to use and pay for this land, have given over this land to those people. I quite as much vakaviti' . . . am prepared to lease to those people.'[24] The people were held to a miserable deal, and regretted it ever after.

With varying degrees of grace, then, Fijians did hand
over considerable areas of land to the government, far more
than could be taken up by prospective settlers. Refusals
to lease, even if applications were totally unreasonable
and required the removal of a whole village, were blown up
by   the   Europeans   as   further   evidence   of Fijian
intransigence, while the generous concessions just noted
received scant publicity. It did not suit the Fiji Times
to attack the European speculators who were tying up 8000
acres on the Dreketi and Sigatoka Rivers, or to admit that
there were greater problems than the availability of land
for the colony's agricultural development. In January 1908
the Planters Association commissioned the Suva lawyer
R. Crompton to prepare a long petition to the Secretary of
State for the Colonies demanding that the 'Crown should
take   such [unused] lands and open up the same for
cultivation by planters'.[25] The petition was based on the
rights of the Crown under article IV of the Deed of Cession
and its interpretation of the events since Cession closely
followed that of im Thurn, whom the planters now saw as
their champion. In his supporting arguments to the
Colonial Office, im Thurn was careful to avoid the
appearance of sectional bias and to profess great interest
in the welfare of 'these interesting natives'. But he
agreed with the planters that Fijian landlords were
objectionable; they could perform none of the duties of
the position. They had neither knowledge nor capital;
they just received rents and appropriated improvements.
Europeans with freehold titles would at once ensure that
the property did not deteriorate, and usually they were
able to raise capital for development. Believing that the
Crown had a clear right to surplus lands in any case, he
was resigned 'as a matter of grace' to allowing Fijians a
price for their lands but insisted that the first aim of
the government was that the lands be developed and 'the
exorbitant demands of the Natives for their more or less
imaginary rights' should be firmly resisted.[26]

The Planters' Petition, and the knowledge that it had
the support of the Supreme Chief, sent waves of distrust
deep into a Fijian community now thoroughly aroused.   The
chiefs within reach of Suva met one evening at the home of
their would-be champion and lawyer Humphrey Berkeley.   The
chairman of the Methodist church was present, and he
reported that the chiefs were convinced a supreme effort
was being made secretly by the Europeans to deprive them of

their lands.[27] Ratu Peni Tanoa, leading chief of Naitasiri, and several others said in a letter to the Native Commissioner that they feared a terrible reversal 'as happened in New Zealand - and like the Maoris we too could be reduced to slavery'. They asked that the full petition be translated so that they could study it themselves. Im Thurn was willing: 'It seems at least fair to put it into the power of Fijians to understand what is going on.'[28] The final decision lay with the Colonial Office, of course, and an outraged Lord Stanmore used both his private connections there and his seat in the House of Lords to defend his original land policies with passion. Stanmore achieved just the right elder statesman's blend of allusions to arcane knowledge of Fijian complexities and his record of integrity and experience with withering scorn for the intellectual confusion of a tactless successor - an upstart who thought planters a better judge of Fijian problems than the Scottish lord who, in winning the love of the people for British rule, had himself acquired 'the heart of a Fijian'.[29]

Stanmore carried the day. The Colonial Office rejected the Planters' Petition and im Thurn's arguments and upheld the noble lord's view that no distinction could be drawn between waste lands and occupied lands - what im Thurn had called 'true Crown' and 'true native' respectively. All lands were to be regarded as Fijian property and not to be leased or sold without the consent of the owners.[30]

The defeat of im Thurn's reforms has been persuasively explained by Peter France in The Charter of the Land as the victory of orthodoxy, a return to the misleading dogmas about Fijian society proclaimed by Gordon to justify his policy.[31] In another sense, though, it was a victory for Fijians, the defeat of a vision of the colony's future which identified 'the real interests of the natives' with the denigration of everything in Fijian society that offended current British ideas of progress, democracy, manliness or self-respect. What would have happened if im Thurn's land reforms had gone through? Was not individualization of land tenure the classic colonial device for achieving a rapid transfer of native land to European settlers? There could be little doubt that if Fiji had been able to attract several thousand more settlers from New Zealand and Australia they would in time have gained self-government, abolished the Fijian Administration, and built on im Thurn's arguments and his legal precedents to justify easier ways of alienating the best lands. Im Thurn's Fiji of the future was a more prosperous Fiji, perhaps, but it offered no hope for Fijian autonomy and success only for those Fijians with whom the Europeans chose to share their skills. Equal British citizens in theory, they would have become fringe-dwellers in fact; at best a picturesque background, at worst a broken society of migratory labourers and leaderless peasant farmers devoid of influence at the national level.

The land controversy overshadowed other elements in im Thurn's program of reform. He particularly chafed at the need to subsidize chiefly officials. Was there not some way of eroding their privileges and fostering the emergence of better-educated men with more progressive goals?

Chapter 3

The erosion of hereditary privilege

When a newcomer such as Sir Everard im Thurn observed
Fijian society from the outside, it was easy to conclude,
as he did, that Fijian chiefs were bleeding their people
pale.   For the person of the chief was still hedged with
elaborate ceremonial, deferential modes of indirect and
plural address, courtly euphemisms, crouching low when he
passed, the tabu attached to his clothing and food, and
above all the dread fear of incurring his ancestors' curse
by even unwitting breaches of his sacredness. (Even half a
century later when customary modes of respect were said to
be breaking down, there was no more common story in
folklore and personal reminiscence than the evils that
befell a man who went against his chief.)

It was a mistake, though, to perceive Fijian
chieftainship in the twentieth century simply as a system
of despotism. So much of the chief's style, dignity,
income and power depended on the practical goodwill of a
people no longer dependent on him for their land or
physical security. They gave food, property and labour to
the chief with the clear understanding that he represented
the honour of their group in its dealings with other groups
and that he would bear the main burden of hospitality to
visitors. He was helped, then, to maintain a certain
'state' but expected to exercise liberality to all. Fijian
expectations of the chiefly order were well expressed by
Epeli Rokowaqa in the Wesleyan newspaper Ai Tukutuku
Vakalotu in 1932:

> The Ratu or Tui or Rokotui: it is his heavy
> burden to rule the land . . . the installing
> groups entrust the land to him because they rely
> on him to be their source of life, prosperity and
> increase. [1]

The people expected chiefs in government positions to
use the perquisites of office to maintain a greater state
and incur greater liabilities. There is little evidence to
suggest that Fijian chiefs amassed fortunes in office, but
much to show that they lived beyond their means to meet the
reciprocal obligations attached to their privileges.

38

Im Thurn saw it otherwise. He was concerned about the extent to which the Native Regulations protected the lala rights of chiefs to make levies on the people for their personal needs: housebuilding, garden planting, supplying visitors with food, cutting and building canoes, supplying turtle, and making mats, masi cloth and other articles.

Without lala, the Council of Chiefs had declared in 1892, their social organization would be destroyed.[2] In one form or another lala entered into all relationships between the people and their chiefs. In 1875 David Wilkinson echoed chiefly experience when he wrote: 'in fact it is the keystone of the Chief's government and authority over his people, the channel through which comes his "sinews of war" in times of trouble; and his "ways and means" in times of peace'.[3] In 1898 he reaffirmed that there was nothing so 'natural familiar or so effective to keep up the peoples industry', but he regretted that lala had been brought into disrepute by 'young bumtious, covetious, impecunious, indolent chiefs who impose upon the people simply because they are of the family who have the . . . fudule right over many tribes or peoples'.[4]

Im Thurn based his assessment of lala primarily on detailed reports from Kadavu, where the chiefs either retained more power over their people than in any other province, or had to exercise it more openly because their people were so turbulent. 'Of course the custom of lala is objectionable in our eyes', confided Francis Baxendale of the Native Department to im Thurn, marking well his reader's prejudices, 'especially as the chiefs have for some time, in many places, given up doing their part of custom, but vested rights cannot be disposed of off hand.'[5] He was commenting on a complaint of a Kadavu man: 'The chiefs' lala is our trouble - our taxes a mere bagatelle . . . Never a day passes without some exaction - 10 yams here - 10 there, a root of grog, a fowl, a pig. We work and produce copra - the Chief sells it for money - get nothing: he levies yams which he sells for money.'[6]

On one inspection of Kadavu, it was learned that the Roko Tui had levied 5000 yams on Nabukelevu and sent the Sanima people to cut buabua and vesi trees for his new house. It was not of course registered on the program of work. The Methodist mission in Kadavu - as in every province - asked for contributions in kind, say, twelve yams for each man, woman and child every three months, and arranged a highly successful annual vakamisioneri collection along the competitive lines of customary exchange, with district vying against district to keep a continuous procession of contributors taking coins to swell the collection plate by which their district's honour would be measured. In 1905 vakamisioneri collections totalled over £5000.

These facts built up in im Thurn's mind the impression of a people continually being discouraged and impoverished by greedy chiefs and missionaries: 'practically all the rights are to the chiefs and not to the "commoners"'.[7] After the Governor had assailed the Council of Chiefs in 1905 (see previous chapter), his speech was published in the government newspaper Na Mata and some villagera wrote to thank him for launching a new era: 'We will be free to give our attention to other things for the benefit of our wives and children'.[8] Im Thurn undoubtedly believed he had a vast silent majority behind him. He was encouraged in June 1905 to make the death of Cakaudrove's high chief, the Tui Cakau, an opportunity to ban 'these burdensome funeral ceremonies' and begin lightening the load on the people - though this particular decision, to ban the burua or mourning ceremonies, was more likely to have shocked the people: it robbed them of one of the great occasions in Fijian life.[9] And it was only spectacular inter-provincial gatherings such as this that the government had a chance of regulating. A letter to Na Mata in September 1906 described a small exchange (solevu) that had just taken place between some of the ladies of Bau and Vuci village, Tokatoka. The ladies brought only three snakes and traditional clothes, the writer claimed, and exchanged them for sixty mats. They received three days of hospitality during which were consumed a cow, thirty pigs, 800 yams, 910 puddings, countless taro and £2 worth of tea. The ladies then returned to Bau with 133 mats, eighty tins of biscuits, and piles of yams and dalo for their chiefs.[10]

If it offended government that these kinds of exchanges continued to absorb so much of the productive energies of the people, it concerned Fijians more when they did not take place with the customary sense of proportion and reciprocity, or when the Bauan chiefs (the main culprits) and others failed in their return obligations. Another writer in Na Mata added a further dimension to the lala question: 'At this time it seems to me that our chiefs are ruining or perverting the custom of lala for they exercise lala on the whole province according to their government appointments.'[11] Although this complaint was

answered by others who pointed out how much greater lala
exactions were in the old days, the real question in the
Fijian mind seems not to have been the actual extent of
lala but the ease with which chiefly Rokos and Bulis
dispensed with the customary ways of making requests and
treated lala as a form of renumeration.

The problem of accommodating traditional lala rights
within the colonial order can be best illustrated in
Tailevu. From many decades before Cession and until
Thurston called a halt in 1894, the Bauan chiefs had
exercised wholesale lala rights on those island communities
of Lomaiviti known as qalivakabau, subject-to-Bau, and also
on certain groups in Tailevu known as the kai vali,
household servants of the Bauans. In the rest of Tailevu
and Lomaiviti the lala rights of the Bauan chiefs were more
circumscribed. Levies were contributed either voluntarily
or were requested through properly appointed mata, envoys
or intermediaries. According to Ratu Joni Madraiwiwi, who
grew up in Cakobau's household, mata from the nearby
districts of Namata, Namara, Dravo, Buretu, and Kiuva lived
permanently on Bau. The mata would on occasion be sent to
their towns with some request to be made vakaveiwekani, 'as
if from relatives', for all these people were counted as
true Bauans (kai Bau dina). Then in the north of the
province there were the towns of the kai Waimaro Dri (the
districts of Namalata, Sawakasa, Wailotua and Naloto) who
were allies or borderers (bati) required to send aid to the
Bauans in time of war. Other districts still further north
- Namena, Dawasama, and Nakorotubu in Ra - contributed to
Bauan trading exchanges (solevu), as did certain parts of
Naitasiri province and the original inhabitants of Suva.
First fruits, isevu, were not presented to the Vunivalu of
Bau but to the temple Navatanitawake. In a good year
offerings (roverove) of yams might be made from the bati
towns and others, but they were, claimed Ratu Joni,
voluntary tokens of friendship. [12]

Given the military might of Bau before Cession, the
voluntary nature of tribute from Tailevu should not be
overemphasized. Ratu Joni's more important observation was
that the bureaucratic operations of the Fijian
Administration had effectively levelled away these nice
distinctions between the status of each vanua or district
and the roles of particular villages. Though traditional
ranking continued to be preserved in seating arrangements
and the details of etiquette and oratory within the
procedures of the councils, no village or district could

claim a special exemption from meeting the needs of the province on the grounds that Bau had first to approach them in the proper way.[13] It was all too simple a matter for the Roko Tui of Tailevu to decide that every man in the province was to bring, say, ten yams to Bau as the Roko's official lala - it was no longer relevant to inquire what was the Vunivalu's customary entitlement. As a Native Lands Commission inquiry showed in 1917 to an embarrassing degree, the Bauan chiefs were losing touch with the old order and were confused about their exact relationships with particular communities and their rights and privileges at custom.[14]

To deal with the Fijian Administration, then, is to deal with an ambiguous amalgam of old and new. The imposition of colonial rule and appointments deriving from the Crown intruded radically new principles of organization with accountability to the top, yet in many ways the chiefs were trying to lead their people as they had always done and felt much the same obligation to ensure their prosperity. Provincial and district councils operated in the customary style and really bore little resemblance to western institutions of local government. On the other hand, the more official duties such as tax collecting and road making deviated from the customary ways of using men and resources (to satisfy the minimum demands of colonial rule), the more need there was for the apparatus of a developed state, especially the system of courts and punishments. Conflicts of loyalty and confusion of rules were thus built into the Fijian Administration. Yet perhaps these same conflicts and ambiguities were its fundamental strength in that they arose from the interlocking of bureaucratic and customary processes, giving to one the advantages of the other. Allegiance to chiefly officials was total: 'there was no situation where a chief was not a chief'.[15]

Some of the younger Rokos were sensitive to the government's preoccupation with lala and moved of their own accord to restrict it. Thus Ratu A. Finau, Roko Tui Lau, who had unsuccessfully tried to levy property in 1901 to take to Bau in honour of the deceased Ratu Epeli Nailatikau, announced at the end of 1905 that he had abolished lala except for housebuilding and plantations. He was much praised.[16] In 1909 the new Roko of notorious Kadavu, Ratu Ifereimi Qasevakatini, suggested that all 'official' lala attached to the office of Buli and his own be abolished and that each chief limit the exercise of lala to his own people and adhere strictly to local custom. The response was unexpected. The Bulis protested that their people were not prepared to let the Roko of their province be entirely dependent on his own people for his lala:

> They desired to do their share, in fact they objected to be left out, especially as oco [a feast] was to be provided. They desired to assist the Roko of the Province as had always been the custom in Kadavu. Buli Sanima sd. 'We are Fijians - not Indians, let us act always as Fijians in accordance with the custom of our lands.' 17

Whereupon it was resolved that each man of five districts would give the Roko ten yams and four districts would plant his gardens as desired. The Bulis' lala was set as two days' work in July, August and September. It is a nice glimpse of the tendency of Fijians to come to rapid terms with congenial aspects of the Fijian Administration and hallow them as chiefly customs - indispensable to the Fijian way of life. 18

Nevertheless in 1911 the Council of Chiefs finally resolved to forgo the Roko's official lala. 19 Lala exercised on behalf of other Fijian officials, usually the magistrates, provincial scribes and Native Medical Practitioners (NMPs), was also abolished. The officials were given a small increase in their salaries and told to rely on them. Only the Bulis retained lala rights attached to their government position. (Usually the men of a district worked a day or two each month in the Buli's garden.)

A revised code of Native Regulations issued in 1912 abolished the original regulation (III of 1877) regarding chiefs so that it was no longer an offence for Fijians to disobey their chiefs 'in all things lawful according to their customs'. A new and dubious distinction was made between 'personal' and 'communal' lala rights with the obvious intention of isolating and defining a set of chiefly privileges that could be gradually whittled away. In the meantime personal lala was still authorized for housebuilding, garden planting, supplying visitors with food, cutting and building canoes, supplying turtle and making mats, masi cloth or other traditional manufactures. Chiefs were obliged - as they were by custom - to feed or pay those performing services. A village could arrange for

the commutation of personal services by making an annual
payment in cash or kind. This provision was never acted
upon, which suggests perhaps that personal lala was still
accepted by the people as part of the customary order of
things and not found over-burdensome.

The cornerstone of the 'communal system' remained -
redefined in the Communal Services Regulation (7 of 1912).
Individualism was fine as a slogan but when it came to the
provision of essential day-to-day services such as the
clearing of bush tracks between villages or of land for
planting, the constant repairing of thatched houses, the
housing of newly married couples, or the supplying of
visitors (not least colonial officials) with food, the
villages needed the cooperation of its able-bodied men for
at least two or three days a week. The government
accepted, for want of a practical alternative, that if
village leaders were deprived of physical sanctions against
the lazy, they needed the support of this regulation. With
less justification, communal services were later extended
to include the transport of government officers on duty,
the carriage of official letters, and the assistance of
Native Lands Commission surveyors.

The concentration of coercive power behind 'government
work' and the reduced emphasis on hereditary privilege were
keenly felt by chiefs of the old school, especially those
who lacked administrative jobs. In 1912 Ratu Joni
Maitatini of Rewa complained that the position of chiefs
had become 'a pitiable one indeed. The privileges of the
chiefs have been gradually withdrawn and to put it plainly
in the English language he has become the "laughing stock"
of the community. Surely those high chiefs need protection
and support at the hands of the Government.'[20] Later
instances of old-time personal lala on the grand scale are
rare. On 7 April 1919, Ro Tuisawau of Rewa arrived in true
chiefly style at Vabea in Kadavu and blew the conch shell
for the Ono people to come together. He demanded that they
give him over 4 tons of copra for which he had obligingly
brought seventy empty bags. Lala vakavanua, traditional
lala, Tuisawau called it - 'stealing', translated the
European magistrate of Rewa, although he added that the
chief would undoubtedly have been within his rights in
years now gone.[21]

Ro Tuisawau was representative of many individual
chiefs whose stars were in the descendant, whose lives did
not fuse conveniently with the colonial ethos, who for lack

of education, or inclination, or a certain kind of personality, did not seize on the new possibilities for advancement and power in the Fijian Administration. Foremost amongst these chiefs were the 'dissidents of Bau', as they were known in government circles, a large group comprising the unemployed members of the four chiefly divisions (mataqali) on the island. They were led by Ratu Etuate Wainiu, eldest but lowborn son of Ratu Epeli Nailatikau, thus a grandson of Cakobau. Wainiu had made a short career in the Armed Native Constabulary; likewise some of the others, including Ratu Joni Colata, Ratu Tevita Raivalita and Ratu Tevita Wilikinisoni Tuivanuavou, had held and lost government appointments.

These men were the sons of chiefs who had lived a life of violence and abundance, and who even after Cession had sailed their great canoes to collect tribute from most of the Lomaiviti group and many parts of Viti Levu - exactly which parts was already a matter of dispute. Wholesale abuse of their lala rights led Thurston to bar access to Lomaiviti by Ratu Epeli Nailatikau and the Bauan chiefs in 1894, and although for several years tribute continued to come on a voluntary basis, the Bauan chiefs found themselves chronically short of food.[22] They had little land of their own, having at best indirect or secondary rights to lands occupied by their traditional vassals and allies. None of these rights was upheld by the Native Lands Commission. The Bauan chiefs were particularly embittered by their failure to gain part of the Namata lands directly opposite the island, a decision made in 1894.[23] The Namata people, originally from Namalata further north, occupied their lands at the pleasure of the Bauans, the chiefs argued, as did most of their neighbours in southern Tailevu. When some of these lands were sold between 1905 and 1907 the Bauans received nothing.

Ratu Joni Colata led a large delegation to the Native Commissioner in 1907 to put their grievances:

> At the present day we see very many commoners coming to Suva to receive the rents of lands. We receive no portion of this money . . . Our position at Bau is an impossible one. At present nothing is brought to us with which to clothe ourselves or to provide oil for our lamps . . . Wherever we go we are the laughing stock of the people who receive money. They say, 'They are Chiefs - they have no lands.'[24]

The chiefs were told that if they had particular claims to lands not yet registered by the NLC, they would be heard at the appropriate time but that past decisions were absolutely final. In 1908 the chiefs sent three strong letters in Ratu Etuate Wainiu's handwriting direct to im Thurn and advanced their general claims further: the disposal of the lands and of the commoners themselves was in the hands of the chiefs and the Bauans had inviolable rights particularly to lands in Tailevu and Lomaiviti. The present occupiers, they said, were not the true owners but tenants-at-will, 'squatting on the lands of us Bauans . . . visitors on our soil'.[25]

On 14 May 1909 the chiefs set out these claims at great length in the first of several memorials to the Secretary of State for the Colonies, detailing the migration histories of the various 'squatters' of Tailevu to prove that their true lands lay elsewhere, and alleging a gross miscarriage of justice in the early hearings of the NLC. They made great play of the fact that their arch-enemy Ratu Marika Toroca, the hereditary Roko Tui Namata, had been a Native Lands Commissioner and a favourite of white officials. Had they realized at the time that Cession would bring an end to their rights and impoverish them, they would never have consented so readily. They had been misled, robbed of legitimate privileges.[26]

If the details of their case were weak, the general thrust of the argument was strong enough for the government and the Colonial Office to consider privately the possibility of some compensation. A Downing Street official conceded: 'There can be no doubt that at the time of Cession, neither the chiefs of Bau (including Thakombau) nor the British Government had any intention of impoverishing the chiefs or of allowing the people to omit their customary payments.'[27] The chiefs sensed this chink in the armour and pursued the question with a persistence and bluntness that exasperated the government: 'These people will clutch at any straw to gain their ends and a little sympathy. Ratu Wainiu told me yesterday he would never stop agitating the question and that he had many more bullets to fire.'[28]

The chiefs were doubtless aware that it was unlikely their literal claims would be accepted, but they hoped to secure a 5 per cent share of lease monies in all the Bauan dominions, which Wainiu maintained were the whole of Fiji.

In 1912 the government appointed a committee to discuss the distribution of rents. It was decided that the Bauans undoubtedly had rights of a general character over whole communities and districts such as the qalivakabau, 'vassals to Bau', on Ovalau, Koro and Moturiki, but that these were sovereign rights and did not proceed from proprietorship of the soil, rights that had become meaningless when the colonial government assumed the protective role the more powerful chiefs had once played.[29] No change was recommended in the formula governing the distribution of rents by which the turaga i taukei, who received one-twentieth, was defined as the district chief of a vanua, not the high chiefs to whom most of the former owed allegiance.[30] However several witnesses from Lomaiviti were prepared to give the Vunivalu of Bau some share in the rents. 'We are related by blood to the Bau people', said the Buli Nairai, 'I would give 2s [a tenth share] to the Vunivalu' - likewise the Buli Nasinu (Ovalau), who acknowledged that the Vunivalu had the right to order them 'to do anything he wished'.[31]

The ownership of Lomaiviti lands was finally decided by the NLC in 1915.[32] The chiefs made strenuous but unsuccessful attempts to salvage their rights by seeking co-ownership of the disputed lands. Finally in February 1917 a commission was appointed to ascertain which Bauan chiefs could properly require lala and from which people, and whether it was 'possible to arrange for the commutation of such personal services by a lump sum payment or by an annuity'.[33] A notice in Na Mata, January 1917, required Bauan chiefs to fill in a written claim form. This was done by Ratu Pope Seniloli, E. Wainiu, and five of the latter's supporters. The commission gathered some interesting evidence on past Bauan relationships but never completed its work. Wainiu predictably made claim to 'vakatadumata to the whole of Fiji', that is, to send envoys with requests to those parts of the group Bau was unable to rule directly.[34]

The question of compensation remained unresolved until a further memorial from the Bauan chiefs to the Secretary of State in 1921 provoked Governor Sir Cecil Rodwell to suggest that the issues be shelved for all time by a 'final and more or less arbitrary settlement by the Governor'.[35] Several hundred acres of Crown land on Koro - valued at about £4000 - was the pay-off, 'our final gift to the Bauans', formally given over by Rodwell at Bau on 13 November 1922.[36] At a meeting with the chiefs on Koro in

48

January 1923, A. L. Armstrong on behalf of the government
felt the need to remind them that the Governor had the
whole of Fiji to control and

> could not devote his time exclusively to Bau.
> The Secretary of State had under his control many
> millions of people and territories so vast that
> they could not even imagine them. To think that
> he would reconsider a question already settled
> concerning a tiny island which could not even be
> found on a map . . . showed a very false
> conception of the relative importance of the
> Bauans.[37]

The chiefs agreed that in accepting the lands they
relinquished all claims to compensation for the loss of
rights or privileges formerly enjoyed. Ratu Wainiu and two
others (Ratu Tuisavura and Ratu Rusiate Busa) declined to
accept the agreement. Wainiu, defiant to the end, lived to
a great age and on the death of Ratu Pope Seniloli in 1936
he was chosen to act as Vunivalu, a position he held for
nearly twenty years. In 1937 he made a further appeal to a
new Governor (Sir Arthur Richards) suggesting he receive 5s
in the £ from all the lands leased in Fiji.

> I am Edward Wainiu a direct descendant of
> Ratu Cakobau . . .
> I pray that you will have pity on me and do your
> utmost to see that a just and fair portion of the
> Fiji Government money will be given to me
> annually that I may rightfully enjoy the rest of
> my days as befitting a grandson of Ratu Cakobau.[38]

The Bauans, he said, had been 'left in poverty like a lot
of drifting people' but it was only true of those Bauans
and other chiefs who could not turn the colonial situation
to their own advantage.

Chapter 4

The new politics of chiefly power

The more able Fijian chiefs did not need to fetch up
the glory of their ancestors to maintain leadership of
their people: they exploited a variety of opportunities
open to them within the Fijian Administration. Ultimately
colonial rule itself rested on the loyalty chosen chiefs
could still command from their people, and day-to-day
village governance, it has been seen, totally depended on
them. Far from degenerating into a decadent elite, these
chiefs devised a mode of leadership that was neither
traditional, for it needed appointment from the Crown, nor
purely administrative. Its material rewards came from
salary and fringe benefits; its larger satisfactions from
the extent to which the people rallied to their leadership
and voluntarily participated in the great celebrations of
Fijian life, the traditional-type festivals of dance, food
and ceremony that proclaimed to all: the people and the
chief and the land are one. 'Government-work' had its
place, but for chiefs and people there were always 'higher'
preoccupations growing out of the refined cultural legacy
of the past (albeit the attenuated past) which gave them
all that was still distinctively Fijian in their threatened
way of life. This chapter will illuminate the ambiguous
mix of constraint and opportunity for chiefly leadership in
the colonial context as exercised prior to World War II by
some powerful personalities from different status levels in
the neotraditional order.

Thurston's enthusiastic tax gatherer, Ratu Joni
Madraiwiwi, was perhaps the most able of them, and in his
happier days was generally esteemed as one of the finest of
'the old school' of chiefs. His father was the feared
sea-marauder Ratu Mara Kapaiwai, Cakobau's cousin and
greatest domestic rival. With the blessing of Wesleyan
missionaries, the recently converted <u>Vunivalu</u> sent Ratu
Mara to the gallows on Bau, 6 August 1859.[1] Legend has it
that before his execution Ratu Mara pleaded for the safety
of his 10-day-old son Joni, promising Cakobau that one day
the child's descendants would 'bear Fiji up'. And that
night Cakobau dreamed that he himself was falling with the
noose around his neck when from the sea flew a huge
flying-fish - the fish named in Mara's battle cry - and
swept up between his legs to take his weight and prevent
the noose from tightening. Then the fish flew on and
looked back and there was the head of Mara Kapaiwai;

49

whereupon Cakobau resolved to take good care of the infant.

It is certain that Ratu Joni spent much of his youth in Cakobau's household; in later years he liked to claim to speak on Bauan affairs with special authority. After the death of Cakobau's son, Ratu Epeli Nailatikau, in 1901, he was the senior of his generation and vigorously opposed the claim of Ratu Epeli's son, Ratu Kadavulevu, to inherit Cakobau's defunct title of Vunivalu of Bau. 'I am wholly of the clan Vunivalu', Ratu Joni claimed in 1913, 'the highest chief by birth in this town.'[2] According to the accompanying genealogy (his own version), his claims were strongest on the maternal side. His mother was Adi Lolokubou, the daughter and first born child of Tanoa Visawaqa, the former Vunivalu of Bau and father of Cakobau, by his highest-ranking wife Adi Talatoka - herself the sister of the Tui Cakau of Cakaudrove but installed on Bau, so Ratu Joni claimed, as Ranadi Levuka, one of the titles of the Vunivalu's senior wife or consort. He also claimed that before Cakobau had died the old chief had appointed him to follow Ratu Epeli Nailatikau - but not in the title of Vunivalu:

> None of you will drink the cup of installation as Vunivalu when I die as I gave Fiji to the Great Queen Victoria and her heirs forever, together with the right to be consecrated and installed as Vunivalu - that is why I offered yaqona to the Governor, that he might drink the installation cup, for he is the representative of the Queen in Fiji for all time.[3]

The old chief would only promise that 'if the Vunivalu's children or relations were well behaved and loyal they would get government appointments and emoluments - otherwise nothing'.[4]

Ratu Joni, for one, threw in his lot with colonial government. After some years' schooling at the central Methodist training college at Navuloa, he took a job in the Audit Office where he first earned his reputation for competence, reliability and hard work. Thurston chose Ratu Joni to be his deputy in Ra in 1889. His regular Monday reports to the Governor revealed his thorough grasp of the aims and procedures of government. Authority came naturally to him. At the same time he had a shrewd eye to his own advancement, an awareness of the considerable opportunities government office gave him to consolidate his

Rewa lady = ——————— BANUVE ——————— = Lakeba lady

Bauan lady = TANOA = Talatoka   Lakeba lady = BUISAVULU VUIBURETA

Samanunu = SERU CAKOBAU Lolokubou =   MARA KAPAIWAI

EPELI NAILATIKAU = Nanise   JONI MADRAIWIWI = Litiana Maopa

KADAVULEVU   J.L.V. SUKUNA

GENEALOGY OF Ratu Joni Madraiwiwi (Source CSO 14/1745)

hereditary standing and the position of his descendants - as well as a clear perception of what the Governor did not need to know. Determined to give his children the best possible education, he used 'prisoners' to maintain extensive food gardens and raise cattle to sell to the sugar mill at Penang. For his eldest son Ratu Sukuna he retained as a member of his household at Nanukuloa an Anglican priest and science graduate from Melbourne, the Rev. Charles Andrew. Ratu Sukuna was proficient in English and mathematics even before he went on to secondary schooling in New Zealand to become the first Fijian to matriculate to university. A daughter, Adi Vasemaca, was sent to the Seventh Day Adventist school at Cooranbong, New South Wales, and another son, Ratu Tiale W. T. Vuiyasawa, went to Wesley College in Melbourne in 1911. [5]

Ratu Joni's reputation as Roko Tui of Ra was such that in 1904 he was given Bua to rule conjointly, holding it for four years. He was then in a better position geographically to exploit his maternal connections in Cakaudrove and somehow secured from the Somosomo chiefs in 1907 a grant of over 2000 acres at Nalovo in Cakaudrove on the Vanua Levu side. [6] By 1912 he had spent £2000 improving the land and converted it to a Crown Grant that year. The adroit official's security was threatened however on another flank. Ratu Kadavulevu, who succeeded his father Ratu Epeli Nailatikau as Roko Tui of Tailevu in 1901, was pressing his claims to be regarded as Vunivalu of Bau.

Kadavulevu had been educated in Sydney and was greatly popular with Suva's European community as a fine cricketer and merry host. As Roko he aroused rather less enthusiasm, at least with the Native Commissioner William Sutherland who once remarked that 'it would pay the Province to allow him his full salary to stay away and play cricket all the time'. [7] On 1 March 1907, before any of the preliminary consultations had taken place, and without summoning from Kaba, Lakeba and Koro the people who were traditionally involved in the installation ceremony of the Vunivalu of Bau, Ratu Kadavulevu was offered yaqona by his hereditary spokesman (matanivanua), Ratu Aisea Komaitai, with the intention of 'drinking him in' to Cakobau's chiefly title. Im Thurn saw the ceremony as 'pure farce, probably due to the drinking of liquor other than yaqona', and William Sutherland wrote to tell Kadavulevu that the so-called installation was 'a childish thing' and could never be recognized by the government. Kadavulevu protested that it was an old Bauan custom, and nothing to do with the government.[8] Ratu Joni disagreed. Normally he had preferred to keep his family affairs apart from government, but clearly in this case his defence rested as much on Cakobau's bequest of his title to the Sovereign as it did on the breach of custom. Furthermore he argued that if the title of Vunivalu was to be restored, then his own claims were better than those of Kadavulevu whose aping of western ways and ignorance of custom Ratu Joni despised.

The ill-feeling between these two chiefs was not widely known until Ratu Kadavulevu was forced to retire on half salary in 1912 because of some £300 he had taken from the Tailevu provincial funds. Ratu Joni, who had been Roko Tui of Ba since 1910, was transferred to take his cousin's place. Bau was not big enough for both of them and the island was soon split into two factions. For reasons that are not clear from the records, but probably out of jealousy of his higher born brother, Ratu Etuate Wainiu and his followers weighed in behind the new Roko.[9] The Rokos of the other provinces feared the effects of a public humiliation of Ratu Kadavulevu and successfully appealed against his prosecution. The Bulis of Tailevu begged for his reinstatement, as did a delegation of his European friends. Ratu Joni's claims, then, were far from being universally admitted. Many Bauans would have held against him the taint of his father's rebellion and have regarded him as a usurper.

Ratu Joni's first moves on Bau were characteristically practical. The island was chronically short of food. The new Roko imported yams from his gardens in Ba and led the planting himself. He expected the Bauans to become self-supporting for the first time, while Wainiu tried to make sure that the first fruits came to the Roko, not to his predecessor:

> It is right that all customary presentations should be made to Ratu Joni Madraiwiwi, the Roko Tui Tailevu, since he has taken up his chiefly place in Bau, that is to say, isevu of yams or dalo or the fruits of the land: he is the eldest in our chiefly rank . . . when people bring things today they are not ordered to do so, but come voluntarily and give generously . . . he loves all the people and feeds them . . . his kindness would break a man's heart.[10]

Wainiu, the supporter of lost causes, was perhaps not the

best advocate Ratu Joni might have employed to answer the
accusations of his enemies that he was oppressing the
people and overbearing to his fellow chiefs.

Governor Sir Ernest Biokham Sweet Escott visited Bau
in October 1913 expressly to support Ratu Joni's authority.
The districts of Dravo and Tokatoka brought their
contributions for the welcoming ceremonies directly to
Kadavulevu - probably, as Sutherland suggested, relishing
the opportunity 'to fly one off against the other'. [11] When
the Roko's welcoming ceremonies for Escott were under way,
Kadavulevu strolled nonchalantly across the rara, the open
space where the various contingents were sitting
respectfully in their hundreds not daring to lift their
heads above those of the Roko and the Supreme Chief. In
his remarks Escott referred once again to Kadavulevu's
claims to be Vunivalu: 'You old chiefs know full well that
there can be no successor to Cakobau . . . no pretensions
in that direction will be recognized. The Roko is my
deputy in this Province . . . '[12] The Council of Chiefs
discussed the feud at their meeting in May 1914 and
prevailed on the two men to bury their differences. Both
signed a solemn convenant, prepared by Ratu Rabici, the Tui
Cakau (highest chief of Cakaudrove), that henceforward they
would be of one mind and live in friendship and love.[13] And
both kept their promises until Ratu Kadavulevu died on 12
December 1914.

Ratu Joni's preoccupation with traditional politics
was by no means over. He was persuaded to lend his name to
the campaign for the restoration of Bauan privileges and
was implicated in an elaborate plot to maintain Bauan land
rights on Ovalau.[14] Thereafter G.V. Maxwell, who found in
favour of Cakobau's grandson, Ratu Pope Seniloli, as
Vunivalu of Bau, did much to try and discredit Ratu Joni
and questioned his loyalty during World War I, even though
two of his sons privately joined allied armies and were the
first Fijians to experience European military
combat.[15] Governor Sir Cecil Rodwell was unwilling to force
a bitter end to a distinguished career and apart from
issuing Ratu Joni with severe warnings in private,
procrastinated until at the end of 1920 he was relieved of
the problem by the old chief's death. The career of Ratu
Joni Madraiwiwi was soured towards its close by the absence
of a man like Thurston who would have understood the
difficulties a Roko faced in reconciling government
objectives with the realities of Fijian politics.

Im Thurn hoped that the high chiefly style of Ratu Joni and his peers would die with them. A new class of purely civil servant Rokos was in the making, men who would have less stake in high chiefly politics. Deve Toganivalu, of a second-ranking Bauan mataqali, was one such self-made man. He had begun his career at Levuka in 1880 as a boy clerk. After several minor provincial postings he served diligently in the Native Department until in 1908 he asked for and received the post of Roko Tui of Bua. At his installation ceremony, however, he made it perfectly clear that he saw himself elevated both as Roko and chief, and he was always accorded thereafter full chiefly honours.[16] The personal honorific Ratu began to appear before his name and passed on to his distinguished son and grandsons in the civil service. Under Toganivalu's rule and that of his son George who succeeded him in 1928, Bua had the reputation for being the best-run province in Fiji, but also one of the most traditional.

A more striking example of an experimental 'career appointment' to head a province was that of a tough police officer, Ratu Ifereimi Qasevakatini, described by his commander as 'the most trustworthy native official' with whom he had ever had to deal.[17] He had served twenty years in the Armed Native Constabulary, worked in New Guinea with Sir William MacGregor and been overseas on two other occasions. By 1908 Ratu Ifereimi was restless in the service and discontented with his annual salary of £60. He let it be known to the Governor that he wanted a Rokoship. On the very day in November 1908 he heard of the death of the Roko Tui of his home province of Kadavu, he penned an application to be considered for the position ahead of the ex-Roko, Ratu Asesala Robarobalavu, who had long been seeking reinstatement.[18] The latter was chief of Tavuki, one of seven districts (vanua) of Kadavu but with some claim for a primacy of honour - Tavuki had always provided Kadavu with its Roko Tui and Ratu Ifereimi, as chief of lower-ranking Yale, was small beer indeed.

The Tavuki chiefs lost no time in rallying to Ratu Asesala's cause. They regarded the Rokoship as their private possession, the means by which they had been able to dominate the province since Cession:

> Tavuki, Your Excellency, is the foundation of law; here was established the entire work of British Government in the province of Kadavu and it was the great chiefs of Tavuki who began,

established, promoted and guaranteed this work.[19]

At the funeral of the deceased Roko, Buli Naceva urged the appointment of Ratu Asesala on behalf of his fellow chiefs. The eight Bulis of Kadavu petitioned the Governor in writing on the same day.[20] As four of them were Tavuki chiefs, Ratu Ifereimi had anticipated their appeal in his letter of application:

> I truly believe that you know and the government knows my long, faithful and diligent service. It is true perhaps that some of the Kadavu people will want Ratu Asesala Robarobalavu to be Roko again but that, I believe, is only true of the chiefly yavusa itself and does not represent the real desires of the bulk of the people [na lewe ni vanua]. For the [Tavuki] chiefs fear that an outsider will be appointed who will abolish or suppress their long-established exactions on the people, and it is as clear as the noonday sun to me that they have no regard at all for the real welfare of the people, their country and the needs of the modern day.[21]

The letter reveals a calculated appeal to European sensibilities; it won him the appointment. A protest delegation that came to Suva in December 1908 was firmly turned away. The jubilant people of Yale set to and built their long lost chief-turned-Roko a splendid house at Gasele where he and his highborn wife, Adi Seinimili Rokolewasau, entertained on a lavish scale. In a thinly disguised slight to Tavuki, the usurper arranged for the meeting of the Provincial Council to be held at Yale in 1910.[22] In a more direct attack he then arranged with Suva to have the large chiefly district of Tavuki cut in half. The newly-created tikina of Ravitaki had been the main source of labour and food for the Tavuki chiefs' lala, and Ratu Ifereimi forbade them to make any demands on the district. The chiefs began to feel as bitter as the 'dissidents of Bau' did when their flow of goods and services had been similarly interrupted: 'Ratu Ifereimi ignores us and brings us into disrepute ... It seems as though he is trying to wipe out the true chiefly seat of Kadavu, to destroy the foundation of law in Kadavu and the true chiefly line still living in Tavuki today'.[23]

The Roko was an impetuous man who brooked no opposition. On one occasion he wrote to Buli Tavuki with measured insolence: 'I am the <u>Roko Tui</u>. I am the only chief in Kadavu ... I do not know any man in Kadavu who counts for more than the <u>Roko Tui</u>. I am the only man who decides things for you.'[24] The outraged Tavuki chiefs drew up a list of charges to present to Native Commissioner William Sutherland at the Kadavu Provincial Council of 1911 - most of them so trivial and personal that the complainants began to be embarrassed by having to read them aloud, especially when it came to charges that he had maltreated the people. One chief said bluntly that the charges were not really meant to be taken in detail, but as general complaint against the Roko: 'The Roko treats his own people very generously and is greatly liked by them', he admitted.[25]

Shortly after this confrontation Ratu Ifereimi fell ill with pulmonary tuberculosis and was forced to resign office in November 1912. Before he died in the hospital at Vunisea on 25 March 1913, he requested that his two young sons at the Queen Victoria School, Ratu William MacGregor and Ratu Henry Berkeley, should be found 'a chiefly work'.[26] One became a police officer, the other a doctor. There was certainly no chance of their continuing their father's challenge to hereditary authority on Kadavu: the Tavuki chiefs regained the Rokoship and retained it to 1960. This interlude was regarded in Tavuki as an aberration. Ratu Ifereimi's fate is a reminder that presumption (<u>viavialevu</u>) in the Fijian cosmos has all the connotation of hubris in the Greek; overweening pride brings a fell stroke from heaven. As one chiefly informant insisted, the minds of the protagonists in these obscure dramas were still steeped in a world that goes 'deep down to Bulu', the world of the vengeful ancestral spirits who do battle for their stock and are gratified to come forth from their rightful seats in the assemblies of the land.

The honour of their ancestors was a driving force in the lives of many chiefs who bucked against the petty legalities of colonial administration and strove to win greatness for their people. Ratu Aseri Latianara's career in Serua is a vivid example of the complexity and challenge of the purely local politics that preoccupied these men. From his father and uncle Ratu Aseri inherited the leadership of the Korolevu, a powerful and numerous people who lived in three main divisions along the southern coastline of Viti Levu. Bfore Cession it was one of the least stable areas in the group - in David Wilkinson's Native Lands Commission findings the people were 'perplexingly mixed up both in their tribal and Mataqali distinctions'; their lands had been a battleground for the armies of the Korolevu and their arch-enemies from Namosi.[27] At the first NLC hearing at the end of the century the Korolevu were recognized as paramount only in their own immediate district, the tikina of Serua. The administrative overlordship which their chiefs had enjoyed since 1877 as Roko ruling the many fragmented groups in the whole province of Serua could only have been endorsed in customary terms by describing Serua in the official records as a matanitu, one of the large-scale federations existing before Cession. It is quite certain that Serua had never been organized in that way.

Yet three decades later when the NLC reopened its hearings in Serua, the province emerged in remarkably tidy shape as a single matanitu. Ratu Aseri Latianara is listed as Vunivalu of an enormous eleven-village 'vanua of Serua' (90 per cent of the population of the province) federated with one much smaller one and another in Colo West. Chief after chief went before the NLC headed by Ratu Joni Madraiwiwi's son Ratu Sukuna (with Ratu Aseri himself as Assessor) to acknowledge that they now 'went to' Serua acknowledging Ratu Aseri and his successors as overlord with the title Vunivalu. While Serua must provide the most extraordinary example of the lengths taken by the NLC to completely reorganize 'traditional' Fijian polities, no European in higher circles of the government seems to have appreciated at the time (nor did Ratu Sukuna choose to enlighten anyone) that the outcome was the personal victory Ratu Aseri had been trying to achieve since his installation as Vunivalu of the Korolevu in 1912.[28]

Five years before this ceremony Ratu Aseri had been allowed to take over his ailing father's government duties as Roko Tui; he was confirmed in the post in 1909. A powerfully built, intimidating man of little education, given to ungovernable rages followed by contrite and generous compensation, the young Roko soon fell foul of a local European storekeeper, George Barrow. This neurotic ex-journalist compensated for the poverty of his operations by composing verbose memorials to the Governor, and, if that failed, to the Secretary of State in London, regarding the evils of 'the communal system' as demonstrated more particularly in the cruel excesses of chiefly power in Serua. The Korolevu chiefs despised him, and he knew it.

A few months after Ratu Aseri took office, Barrow sent Suva a lurid account of a terrible beating the Roko was said to have given his pretty young wife aboard his yacht as it was coming into Suva harbour. She jumped overboard to escape, was recaptured and trussed up with rope to prevent her jumping again. In Barrow's version Ratu Aseri had trolled her behind his yacht as shark bait until she was half drowned. Though the woman herself declined to cooperate at the inevitable inquiry (she said she had deserved the beating and still loved her lord), Ratu Aseri was found guilty of assault and the Governor angrily dismissed him from office.[29] The chairman of the Wesleyan mission wrote to a colleague that the chief was 'writhing in agony over the humiliation' and he was 'justly suffering'.[30]

More likely the humiliation was for his province, for Ratu Aseri was replaced by a Bauan chief - Serua's first 'foreign' Roko. A second Bauan succeeded in 1910 and ruled until he was virtually driven out in 1913 and replaced by a local man. Ratu Aseri was finally reappointed in 1916, only to face the secession of some of his own people from Serua to Colo West.

The details of the story, insignificant perhaps in themselves, reveal some of the character of chiefly politics at village level. For when Komave district had petitioned from the turn of the century to be attached to Colo West, the inconvenience of travelling to the Roko's quarters on Serua Island or the European magistrate's at Navua was the alleged but not the real issue. Although the Komave people, the Noi Vuso, had occupied their lands for over fifty years at the time of the 1899 Native Lands Commission, the previous occupiers (the Lutuya) who were loyal Serua dependants (qali) now living just inside Komave at Navutulevu, were recognized by the Commission as the 'true owners' (itaukei dina) with joint tenancy of the Noi Vuso lands and the right of reversion. Thereafter the Noi Vuso chafed at the lala demands of the Serua chiefs. With the help of Barrow, they petitioned for either a European Commissioner in Serua or for transfer to Colo West.[31] Finally in December 1916 Governor Sir Ernest Bickham Sweet Escott, impressed perhaps with the perseverance of the petitioners, ignored the advice of his subordinates and ordered the transfer of the whole Komave tikina to Colo West.

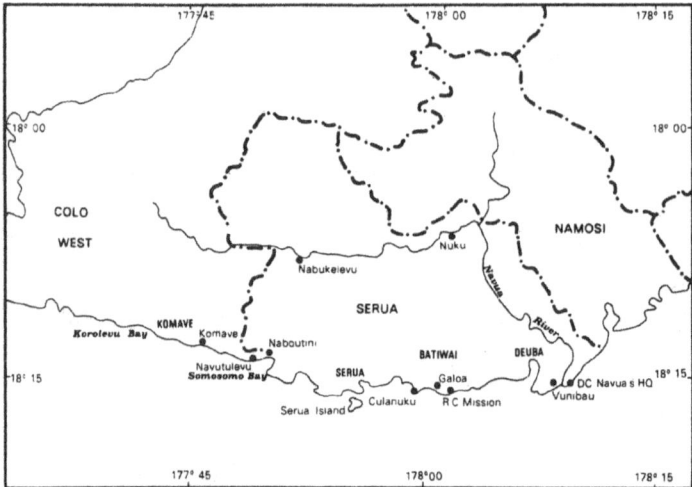

Map 2   Serua

This decision was hailed by the Noi Vuso as a triumph
over Ratu Aseri and a body blow to the prestige of the
Serua chiefs: 'for although it refers to government
administration only, <u>natives do not appreciate that
distinction</u> and take it as a complete severance of all
relationships - tribal or otherwise'.[32] Ratu Aseri tried
hard to have the decision reversed: 'The attachment of
Komave to this province is not just a recent thing but very
ancient . . . and to me it seems a drastic thing that
suddenly they should be cut off from our province
when . . . it was approved that we should be one province
in accordance with our ancient boundaries.'[33]

The Komave chiefs rubbed salt in the wounds by
frustrating Ratu Aseri's attempts to make traditional calls
on the members of Korolevu residing in Komave. In 1921, to
give an example of the petty irritations which enraged Ratu
Aseri, the Buli Komave forbade the Navutulevu people to
supply their chief with an <u>oco ni vale</u>, a customary
presentation of food needed to pay off some housebuilders.
'Ratu Aseri is very indignant', commented the Provincial
Commissioner of Colo West, 'and accuses Buli Komave of
secretly working against him and attempting to undermine
his powers as chief among his own people.'[34]

At the second inquiry of the NLC in 1932 the Noi Vuso
people appealed against the right of the <u>Vunivalu</u> of Serua
to call himself their supreme chief: 'Rogiano Duwailea our

chief', said their spokesman, 'is known is <u>Tanivuso</u>. He is politically independent and owes allegiance to no one.' The <u>Tanivuso</u> himself wrote that they had had 'nothing to do with Serua' ever since they had been separated from the province administratively in 1916. In a highly didactic judgment Ratu Sukuna denied the possibility, except in the interior of Viti Levu, of having a <u>vanua</u> that was not directly under or at least protected by a Supreme Overlord; he ruled that the <u>Vunivalu</u> of Serua was without doubt 'that Superior Overlord or Paramount Chief' for all Komave.[35] (Later with the reorganization of 1944 - the issue still much alive - Nabukelevu, Naboutini and Navutulevu villages were returned to their rightful province but the rest of Komave remained outside in the new province of Nadroga and Navosa. Komave was reluctant ever afterwards to acknowledge that it owed any allegiance to Serua.) It seems then that the drawing of administrative boundaries was re-stated by the people, so to speak, as the seal of independence and dignity in traditional politics as well. In other words, by the manipulation of its decision-making processes the Fijian Administration had become a new battleground for the resolution of traditional rivalries and the pursuit of local political ascendancy.

Oral traditions give a glimpse of how hard Ratu Aseri worked to win the loyalty of the province. He is remembered above all as 'a strong chief, strong in the government, in the <u>vanua</u> and in his words'.[36] On his <u>raikoro</u>, village inspections, he would enter a house at random, call the family together and regale them with stories until they rocked with laughter. Starting at the topmost village on the Navua River he would progress slowly downstream staying overnight several times en route and at each stop swelling his entourage with chiefs and elders until he arrived back at Serua Island with a great crowd in festival mood. He fed the throng with fish and 'true food' for up to a week and then sent them home with more fish for their families. Sometimes, it is said, he took people to Suva on his handsome yacht (which some years consumed a quarter of the provincial revenues) and bought them beer at the Club Hotel. He gave each of them a hibiscus to produce as their liquor permit, assuring them that the mention of his name would suffice for the law. And if any became drunk he sent them home in taxis: 'Ratu Aseri was our greatest chief of all.'[37]

Such stories, which are legion, make it clear that Ratu Aseri used his government position to create a new feeling of unity in Serua. The chiefs who declared for him at the NLC hearings in 1932 had been impressed by his years of service and hospitality and, as one informant explained, Ratu Aseri had convinced them that there was no use every little _vanua_ district standing on its historic independence. They overlooked the legal fact that they were also signing away the share of the rents reserved for the head of the _vanua_. Some lived to regret their decisions. (Four decades of rising land values later, one of the surviving chiefs swore that he must have been light in the head after Ratu Aseri's alcoholic hospitality the night before the hearing.)

Much of Ratu Aseri's unifying work began to fall apart after his death in 1940. Nevertheless if successors can be installed to lead Serua again, they can take heart from Ratu Aseri's demonstration that nothing in Fiji's history can quite match the combination of chiefly power and natural leadership to build community. His achievements were not such as would impress development-minded colonial officials. Ratu Aseri belonged to a world where what mattered most was the prestige of his people, ceremonial celebrations of their corporate pride, and the functioning of his chiefly titles to secure their peace and prosperity.

From the same world came his friend on the Native Lands Commission, Ratu Josefa Lalabalavu Vanaalialia Sukuna, who in the 1920s and 1930s was emerging as the one chief who had a foot in both the colonial and neotraditional orders.[38] His father Ratu Joni Madraiwiwi's effort to equip him to meet the Europeans on their own terms had paid handsome dividends, not in happiness perhaps, but at least in experience and skill. From school in New Zealand Ratu Sukuna had returned to clerical work in the Colonial Secretariat and schoolteaching at the Lau Provincial School, then resumed his education at Wadham College, Oxford, in 1913. With the outbreak of war he was unable to enlist with a British regiment, for no coloured colonials, and certainly not the grandsons of cannibals, were eligible to fight alongside Englishmen. The French were glad to receive him into the French Foreign Legion, where he served nine months in the trenches. He was decorated with the Croix de Guerre and Medaille Militaire for 'superb zeal and courage' and wounded in September 1915.

Embarrassed by his success, the colonial government had him recalled to Fiji where he received a hero's welcome. As a sop to his conviction, shared universally by the chiefs and people, that Fijians would bear arms with pride and should be allowed to fight, Ratu Sukuna was allowed to drill a Fijian platoon and then accompany a labour contingent of 100 men finally allowed to serve (uneventfully) in France in 1917.

After the war, Ratu Sukuna returned to Wadham and read for the Bar at the Middle Temple, then returned in 1921 to his first major post as Native Lands Commissioner in January 1922. This position enabled him to build up an encyclopedic knowledge of Fijian traditions and customs. His conservative views of Fijian society were already established and did not change significantly for the rest of his life. Ratu Sukuna saw the individual as feeling instinctively that 'not only his services but also his life belonged to the family and ultimately to the tribe of which he was a part, and so he devoted himself to the will of custom and to the commands of the elders without so much as a thought for abstract rights'. In return a Fijian had a definite share in the life and well-being of the tribe. There was nothing in his experience to develop 'self-regarding qualities' or a sense of personal responsibility. Loyalty, obedience and respect for authority were the keystone of the Fijian ethical sense - ideas which the Communal Services Regulation had wisely kept functional. No Fijian would work for work's sake or to develop himself. 'The native mind' had not yet lost its dependence and inertia, and little had been done to broaden it. Fijians then would do best to remain within their fundamental groups, provided they were given strong and enlightened leadership by their chiefs.[39] Of Ratu Sukuna's personal leadership at national level much more will be seen. His faith in Fijian community life rested on a keen sense of the alternatives that had been weighed and rejected. For a long time to come, so he believed in the 1920s, and still believed in the 1950s, the quality of most Fijians' lives would depend on good village and district organization.

Chapter 5

The continuities of village life and politics

Until World War II more than eight out of ten Fijians were in villages - not haphazard hamlets strewn through the countryside but hierarchically structured groups of villages organized within and without by interlocking administrative, political and customary arrangements. The lines of official authority were clear and hinged on the office of Buli, the government-appointed district chief usually in charge of 200-600 people in about three or four villages. After twenty years' experience in charge of the Colo provinces, Walter Carew had argued in 1896 that the Rokos 'could be dispensed with any day without any evil results' - and in the decades following they often were - but 'if there is one thing more certain than another in Native Politics it is that we must not wilfully run counter to the Bulis but must support them and their dignity all we can.'[1]

It is tempting to suggest that in fact the only reason the Bulis did survive so long in the twentieth century (to the 1960s) was because no one could devise a cheaper system of local government. Bulis were given little support and recognition. Conversely they were comparatively free to rule their districts much as they liked, and rural life had long developed its own momentum. Just as the traditional model of vanua (federation) with its preoccupations, loyalties and emotions infused the government district or tikina, so the chiefly model of the head of a vanua - usually styled Tui in modern times (Tui Nadi, Tui Bua, etc.) - governed the role expectations of the Buli. In practice it was not feasible for a commoner to hold the post. If he did so, on the appointment of a European official, then he had to give his orders legitimacy by seeking the approval of the acknowledged leaders of the vanua. The appointment of a man who was both an outsider and a commoner was an outrage that seems to have occurred only once - Colo West in 1909 - and the man died within a month of taking office. The ancestors had a way of looking after these things.[2]

By regulation, if not also by custom, the Buli enjoyed the chiefly privileges of lala, although this seldom amounted to more than a day's desultory work in his garden each month. He also received 5 per cent share in lease monies, an amount that was significant (more than £50) in about six sugar-cane tikina (Nailaga, Bulu, and Sekituru in Ba; Labasa, Naitasiri, and Nausori). Elsewhere it was a few shillings to a few pounds, no real compensation for an annual salary that was £6 to £12 at the beginning of the century and £18 to £24 after 1927. The lowest clerk in the civil service was twice as well paid as the man generally acknowledged to be the lynchpin of the Fijian Administration.

Apparently then the Buli was not in the first instance a civil servant so much as a subsidized chief. He was already at the apex of a self-sufficient little world that provided its own rewards: style, the power of keeping the peace, the dignity of presiding over the eternal flow of goods and services. If he chose not to conform to the chiefly expectations of his role, then he was depriving himself of the only rewards offered him. And yet, the same man was responsible for the implementation of all the orders of the Roko, the magistrates, the provincial council, and the entire body of Native Regulations.

Of all the Buli's government duties the most onerous and most important was the collection of his district's tax assessment and provincial rate (a total of some £35,000 from all the provinces). Ratu Sukuna once wrote a sensitive account of the Buli's dilemma:

> Unlike his Biblical prototype who waxed fat on taxes and not on the love of Jews, the Buli fattens rather on the goodwill of his people, taxes for him being nothing but a temptation leading to ruin. Hence all that any of his brethren has to say to him to delay payment is au sa leqa, which is being interpreted, I can't pay. Knowing that the anger of authority is far away, but the displeasure of the people at his door, the Buli being one of them construes the saying liberally and replies, sa vinaka which means, all right. And so it goes on, a perfectly natural and intelligible proceeding.[3]

In the district or tikina, the Buli presided over a thoroughly ambiguous institution. Legally the Bulis and their district councils were responsible to the Rokos and the provincial councils, the European magistrates and finally the Governor (through his deputy, the Secretary for Native Affairs or Talai). The Native Regulations gave the district councils at first sight minimal direct

66

responsibility.   The areas listed read as though they were
the wishful thinking of a sanitary inspector:

> There shall be in each district a Council called
> the District Council . . . consisting of the Buli
> of the district, the chiefs of towns, and the
> chiefs of qalis and mataqalis in the district and
> any other person or persons directed to attend by
> the Buli . . .
> The Council may make rules affecting any or all
> of the following matters:
>
> 1.   public bathing places;
>
> 2.   keeping the villages clean and the planting
>   of couch grass therein;
>
> 3.   the removal of rubbish;
>
> 4.   the planting of gardens;
>
> 5.   village paths and bridges;
>
> 6.   house building;
>
> 7.   any other matter concerning the health and
>   good government of the district; and these
>   rules shall be submitted to the Roko of the
>   province for his approval. [4]

It was of course the 'any other matter' of the last
clause that gave the council significance in the lives of
the people. Tikina councils did not eagerly assemble to
discuss village trash problems but primarily to arrange
'the affairs of the land', na ka vakavanua. And even the
routine items of the official agenda would be coloured by
local personalities and kinship politics:

> The resignation and appointment of Turaga ni
> Koros, concealing discussion on suitability and
> status;   the planting of food crops, which
> doubtless produced arguments about season and
> quantity;   the need for better water supplies,
> involving the decision to break such and such
> family ties; the renovation of village drains,
> which brought up the complicated subject of
> providing food for all communal workers;   the

tabu on nuts for the payment of the [Provincial] Rate, where compromises were proposed and considered; applications for exemption from communal services, in which the characters of the applicants were lauded and attacked. Clearly then these Councils play a large part in the life of villagers. [5]

At no stage was there an attempt to regulate the procedures followed in these councils. The idiom was that of local custom. The chiefs and their spokesmen (matanivanua) sat on fine mats at the innermost end of an ordinary village dwelling facing down to the customary yaqona bowl and its attendants. The village elders sat facing the chiefs from the other sides of the room, ranged according to the local table of precedence. The meeting was begun with a yaqona ceremony with its implicit invocation of the ancestral spirits, though hallowed by a prayer to the God of the Sabbath. Conventions of etiquette and oratory applied as much to the tikina councils as they did to any other assembly of the land.

Provincial councils by contrast were more formal affairs, held only once a year and usually attended by a European officer from the Native Department. They were heavily dominated by the routine requirements of government work, mainly the raising of taxes and the allocation of provincial resources to public works. But the gathering of so many people in one place, up to two hundred delegates and their attendants, made the provincial councils the major social event of the year, a festival of the people with much exchange of property, mekes and feasts on the side.

A typical report of the Provincial Council of Colo East gives some glimpse of the priorities of the people on these occasions.

The proceedings were opened with the usual ceremonies followed by a huge magiti [feast] for the two thousand odd people present. After four hours of keen discussion, Council adjourned for further feasting and mekes and after the second session of Council, the proceedings closed with a well-practised meke from the women of Muaira, followed by the dividing of the spoils and all districts' veisau [exchange]. [6]

Only in this social context did the provincial
councils match the importance of the monthly <u>tikina</u>
councils as a liturgy, so to speak, a celebration of
corporate identity and common ideals on the one hand, a
reaffirmation of the dignity and status of each constituent
group on the other. The district and provincial councils
provided a congenial forum for making decisions required by
the colonial government without doing violence to
traditional decision-making processes and preferred forms
of social intercourse and collaboration. It would be a
pointless exercise to attempt, as scholars have done with
colonial institutions affecting land, to filter out those
activities of the councils which were 'authentically'
Fijian from those which were pseudo-customary colonial
innovations. It is more to the point to argue that the
very success of the original Gordon-Thurston design in
maintaining a strong rural Fijian corporate life preserved
also the capacity and inclination of the people to assert
their own priorities and modify the instrusions of the
western economic order espoused by the European and Indian
communities.

Much of Fijian village life was governed by day-to-day
subsistence tasks and communal labour obligations.
Fortunately there were many 'great occasions' such as the
marriages and deaths of high chiefs to enliven the year
with expectation and a heightened sense of living. Some
festivities involved weeks of preparation. The Wesleyan
missionary at Lakeba reported in June 1918 that Lau had
been 'holding high festival for a month' to lift the
mourning for Ratu Epeli Nailatikau (died 1901):

> It has been continual round of 'magitis'
> [feasts], mekes, boses [councils],
> sports . . . Surely not less than 500 visitors
> and possibly nearly 1000, were here from every
> island in Lau. Not one buli, n.m. [native
> minister], catechist or chief worth the name was
> absent. As many as 17 cutters were in the
> harbour at any one time . . . Dalo by the 10
> thousands, yams and nearly a score of bullocks,
> etc., pigs and turtles in even larger numbers.
> The goods [for the <u>solevu</u>, exchange] consisted of
> three large canoes, gatu [snakes], mats,
> magimagi, [sinnet, braided cordage of coconut
> fibre] . . . [7]

The quarterly and annual circuit meetings of the Wesleyan church, to which four out of five Fijians belonged, were often accompanied by spectacular exchanges and gifts of property with district vying with district not to be disgraced by a poor showing. A wooden slit drum (lali) would announce the beginning of a procession into the village green. As the women danced and sang, glistening warriors might carry on their shoulders a fully rigged canoe bearing in the prow a muscular youth blowing into a conch shell to herald 'the approach to land'. The canoe would be lowered to reveal a wealth of fruits and marine delicacies, while others brought in young bullocks, pigs, turtles and crabs. Long lines of women would follow with seamless fathoms of painted masi cloth and beautiful mats, lay them before the chiefs and join the seated chorus. Men would enter with bunches of bananas and coconuts to pile in mounds before taking up club or spear for their war meke. The appreciative semi-circle of spectators and rivals vastly enjoyed the music, pageantry and general air of munificence on these occasions.[8] Only the presence of a gratified missionary or occasionally a European official amongst the chiefs reminded the people of the chill colonial order that discounted such manifestations of corporate pride. At best they were tolerated as pleasant but unproductive echoes of the glories of older Fijian economic and social life.

Apart from the festivals of church and state, there endured well into the 1920s and 1930s traditional trading networks that supplied from the surplus of one region the deficiencies of another. At Lomaiwai in Nadroga the people made salt in the mangrove flats and smoked it in cylinders of fibre so that it could be transported to Rewa and traded for pots, to Vatulele for choice masi, Kadavu for mats, Lau for rope-fibre or wooden bowls, Colo for yaqona, timber and bamboos, upper Serua for kauri gum (makadre) used for glazing pots and making torches. Apparently the specialties of each region were well known and in the predominantly social context of customary exchanges there was no incentive, even if the resources were present, for one region to challenge the monopoly of another. It was never the object of trade to make a profit in the commercial sense:

The important thing is not that the exchange is trade, but that the framework within which it takes place is primarily social, not economic. The economic relationship is brought about

> because of the social relationship; the economic
> need is solved through a social mechanism; the
> economic transaction gives expression to an
> already existing social relationship part of
> whose function is to satisfy this type of
> need . . . [9]

Even if the quality of district life prior to World
War II eludes documentation other than the repeated verbal
eulogies of old people pining for the good old days of
ordered life and simple plenty, it seems that the <u>tikina</u>
was an institution ideally suited to give Fijians effective
direction of their own local affairs and satisfaction of
their material and social needs. It was still strong
enough in 1939 for the Secretary for Native Affairs to
claim that not a single Fijian was destitute or homeless, a
situation simply taken for granted at the time but one
which takes on retrospective interest with the recent
recognition of rural destitution as a serious problem in
some parts of contemporary Fiji.[10] In Ratu Sukuna's words
spoken in 1944 after 11,000 Fijians had passed through the
armed services:

> There can be nothing spiritually very wrong with
> a system that maintains the old and the sick
> without resort to homes for the aged and schemes
> of social security, that despite discouragement
> and discrimination comes forward in times of
> stress and danger to help the larger community of
> which it forms a part.[11]

Secondly, there was throughout the inter-war period a
remarkable absence of serious crime in the provinces.
Between 1930 and 1939 in Lau, times of acute depression for
the copra industry, the annual reports of the District
Commissioner mention up to a dozen major cases a year but
nothing more serious than adultery, larceny or assault. In
1936 and 1937 not a single serious offence such as
aggravated assault came before the courts.[12] Again, such a
situation was taken for granted, though there was a great
deal of minor court work, mainly for failure to pay rates
and taxes. Even if the court statistics concealed the real
level of crime in the community, they testify to the
efficacy of a social system able to dispense with the
assistance of the courts in maintaining peace and achieving
reconciliation.

That is not to say social harmony precluded a vigorous political life, but district politics interacted rather little with wider colonial affairs and could often be withheld from effective official surveillance. Or when the Fijian Administration did become formally involved, the real issues were frequently misunderstood in Suva. The success of some of the Nadrau people in the centre of Viti Levu, for instance, in breaking away in 1920 to form a new tikina of their own - a process of subdivision that occurred elsewhere one hundred times between 1875 and 1944 - grew out of eight formal petitions, fourteen years of passive resistance to the chiefs of Nadrau, and memories of local wars that went back well before Gordon's 'Little War' of 1876 in the interior. (Nadrau had been rewarded for its 'loyalty to the Crown' with enlarged district boundaries.)[13]

Local hostilities and rivalries, ever a feature of Fijian life, generated intense feelings, though as Nation observed of Fiji in the 1970s, parochialism had a paradoxical community-building function as well.[14] The relative rigidity of the Fijian Administration, the lack of arms, and eventual invocation of colonial law ensured a compromise or at least a stalemate in the end - though not without periods of paralysis which underlined both the dependence of chiefly leadership on administrative support and the frustrations of alternative leaders.

Ratu Penioni Ravoka, the hereditary chief styled Ratu mai Verata, was one such leader who could not bear the constraints of colonial order. In ancient times (not so long ago to the Ratu), Verata or Ucunivanua had headed a powerful confederation (matanitu) of tribes and enjoyed extensive lands and a large population. The chief's village lay some 26 miles north of Bau, with whom common ancestors were recognized. Early in the nineteenth century Bau challenged Verata's hegemony. Naulivou, the Vunivalu of Bau, defeated Verata in battle. Verata retaliated some years later with a massacre of a party of Bauans visiting Waimaro, whereupon Cakobau forced the unwilling allies of Bau to join forces and lay siege to Verata.

In colonial times the power of Verata was a memory kept alive by their resentment of the prominence of Bauans in the Fijian Administration, and especially in Tailevu province. Shackled by the pax britannica, the Verata chiefs and people resorted to the arts of petty annoyance and impudence. In 1890 Ratu Epeli Nailatikau (Roko Tui of Tailevu) complained that the Verata people had cut up the

nets of his fishermen, the Lasakau; and when he had gaoled
a Verata man on Bau island, 'instead of making use of the
gaol water closet he used to go to the one belonging to the
Lasakau people and pull parts of the thatch out for his own
convenience'. When provincial taxes were due from Verata
the young men set sail for the Yasawas or Koro; when they
were at home they drank yaqona day and night and brawled at
will.[15]

This reputation for lawlessness continued down to the
1930s. Ratu Penioni Ravoka was a wild eccentric man. In
1915, it was later alleged by the chiefs of Tailevu, he
declared himself completely independent 'even as regards
the King'. When accused by Buli Nakelo and twenty-four
other chiefs in 1921 of trying to divide the province of
Tailevu into two, the Ratu countered that it would be a
good thing: 'I want a separate province to prove my zeal
for the government, for it is a long time that we have been
relying on Bau and our hearts are not in it.' In July of
the same year, Ratu Peni fired several shots in dubious
salute as the Roko lay off the reef at Verata waiting for
the turn of the tide.[16]

Apenisa Lawenitotoka, the Bauan appointed to replace
the rebellious chief as Buli, was powerless in Verata; on
one occasion he was threatened and ordered to leave the
town when he requested food for workers on Bau. Verata
made no contribution to the feasts and the meke dances of
the Tailevu Provincial Council in June 1922. Apenisa
confessed to the government in April 1923 that his
instructions were ignored in Verata: if Suva did not
intervene then the Ratu might as well be reinstated as
Buli. Apenisa was removed and a higher-ranking Bauan, Ratu
Waqalevu, appointed Buli Verata from 1 July 1923. The
people refused to build him a house and he retreated to
Bau. Then Ratu Peni began to intimidate the Vunivalu of
Bau's servants (kai vale) at nearby Kumi. All Fiji was
talking about the dispute.[17]

Bau felt that its prestige was at stake. The Rokos of
Cakaudrove, Bau, Ra, Macuata and Lau were prevailed on to
appeal to the Governor for his 'chiefly ruling' (lewa
vakaturaga): 'The people of Verata are steeped in
insolence and scorn our traditional customs of courteous
dealing . . . [Unless punished] the spirit of foolishness
and the spirit of discord will grow amongst the people of
the land and they will come to despise their chiefs.'[18] At
the Council of Chiefs in 1923 it was suggested that the old

Ratu was insane and ought to be locked up. However when the European magistrate of Rewa visited Verata in March 1924, he was hospitably received and was able to arrange for the Bauan Buli to retire in favour of a second ranking chief of Verata (Laitia Drevuata).[19]

The Veratan example was, as the high chiefs had feared, infectious. In 1925 the Tailevu Provincial Council representatives revolted against the 'customary' demands of the chiefs of Bau to have the repair of their houses put on the provincial program of work. When Ratu Pope Seniloli, the Vunivalu of Bau, appealed to them to remember their old customs, 'there was no response and it was quite obvious from the attitude of the people that they were unwilling even to consider the proposal'. Although there were fifty-six houses on Bau in a bad way, only seven of the 200 delegates would agree to include the building in the program of work. The whole burden fell to the home tikina of Bau with the result that the chiefly island became more and more decrepit. (The Provincial Council partly relented in 1929 and offered to repair one house for each tikina.)[20]

In 1930 Verata took to the attack again. The Buli defended his tikina against another charge of non-compliance with the Provincial Council resolutions on housebuilding: 'Verata did not owe allegiance (vakarorogo) to Bau in ancient times nor does it now'. The practice of using government institutions to achieve housebuilding on Bau was corrupt, he argued; there was a customary way of sending envoys (mata) with such requests, and a customary way of complying which had better regard for the dignity of the parties than did the threat of prosecution. Who were the Bauans to talk of upholding ancient customs?[21]

The Veratan challenge was taken seriously by Bau and the whole chiefly order. Ratu Sukuna regarded it as a conflict that 'had repercussions through the whole length and breadth of the Fijian Social System'.[22] The government of the day had little interest in Fijian politics and was glad to delegate to Ratu Sukuna the resolution of this dispute (and several similar disputes). A special hearing of the Native Lands Commission was held on 7 September 1933 at Naimasimasi, half-way between the contending seats. Both sides attended in force, and with much ceremonial skirmishing. Proceedings began with a 'fine conciliatory speech' by Ratu Aseri Latianara of Serua (sitting as Assessor) and both sides gave evidence 'without rancour', perhaps because Ratu Peni declined to appear personally.

Ratu Sukuna ruled in favour of Bau.[23] Ratu Peni had one last moment of glory in October 1935 when he ordered the Roman Catholic and Wesleyan mission staff to leave their houses and gardens. He was arrested and committed to the Lunatic Asylum in Suva.[24] For it is written in the hearts of Fijians that those who defy chiefly authority will become sick or insane.

If the issues and preoccupations of the chiefs and people in these affairs seem excessively parochial, the scale minute, and the general orientation towards past glory or old grievances rather than colonialist desiderata such as economic prosperity or the national interest, then it is a true reflection of the nature of Fijian societies prior to World War II - and the background for understanding the failure of alien concepts of progress to take root amongst the people. And yet Fiji was to produce at least one man who tried to inspire the people to transcend local parochialism and grasp a vision of progress larger than Ratu Sukuna and his peers were willing to countenance.

Chapter 6

Apolosi R. Nawai and the Viti Company

If Ratu Sukuna was to become the statesman of Fiji,
Apolosi R. Nawai was its underworld hero - the only man
from the ranks of ordinary villagers who rivalled the
statesman for eloquence, personal mana, and a compelling
vision of the future of Fijians in their own country. Ratu
Sukuna's claims to leadership rested not only on his noble
blood lines, but on his Oxford-given ability to hold his
own amongst the most educated men in the colonial service
and yet articulate a coherent philosophy of Fijian values
dear to himself and inherent - so he said - in the
psychology of individual Fijians and in the dynamics of
Fijian community life. Apolosi's forebears in the Yasawas
and in Narewa, Nadi (where he was born about 1876) were so
insignificant that he went to fantastic lengths later in
his life to invent for himself a lost line of chiefs. His
followers, including many chiefs, did not dispute his claim
to be descended from the ulumatua, first-born, of a
legendary canoe of ancestral heroes supposed to have landed
at Vuda Point in western Viti Levu.

Perhaps Apolosi's true spiritual ancestors were rooted
less in the world of chiefly power than in the dark
substratum of Fijian life, the forces of the occult. No
account of the Fijian colonial experience can avoid some
confrontation with the enduring beliefs of Fijians in
supernatural intervention by the ancestral spirits and some
of the old gods such as the great shark Dakuwaqa.
Draunikau, sorcery, survived as an adjunct to personal
malice and political ambition: it remained a phenomenon of
perennial interest and fear in the lives of the people. In
the popular mind any man who rose to great power and
influence had unseen hosts, as it were, at his personal
command. Belief in the occult forces of the spirit world
was implicit in the mana of the chiefs (for Christian
preaching had done little to undermine the aura of
'legitimate authority'). Certain groups such as the
world-famous firewalkers of Beqa and the little-known
turtle-callers of Nacamaki on Koro openly celebrated their
obligations to the spirits. And occasionally the same
forces were focused in the leadership claims of prophets
without honour in their colonial homes.

Apolosi grew up around Nadi on the western side of
Viti Levu - Yasayasa Ra - and in his early career called
himself, when he wanted his admirers to ponder the anomaly
of his ostensibly humble origins, na kai Ra, the man from
Ra. The phrase would also remind his audience of the
long-standing but repressed hostility the speakers of
Fiji's western dialects - often incomprehensible to
easterners - felt towards the domination of the Fijian
Administration by Bauan chiefs and their allies. The
appointment of men such as Ratu Joni Madraiwiwi to be Roko
Tui of Ba and the Yasawas had lowered the national prestige
of the province; the difficulty of governing Ba and rapid
increase of its Indian cane-growing population led to its
subdivision in 1920 into the small provinces of Ba, Nadi
and Lautoka, all under direct European rule.

In the popular mind, these provinces, and the
adjoining ones of Colo North and Ra, were indisputably the
home not only of ancestral heroes but of wild and defiant
men. Drauniivi on the northwest boundary of Ra province
was the home of Navosavakadua's Tuka cult in the colony's
first decades. When Apolosi was a village lad in Nadi,
'Navosa' had proclaimed the imminent return of the twin
gods, Nacirikaumoli and Nakausabaria, the authentic
originals of the deceitful Wesleyans' substitutes, Jehovah
and Jesus. They were to usher in a new age when Fijians
would rule their own land again and the whiteskins would be
driven into the sea. Believers were promised nothing less
than Tuka, immortal life or eternal youth; unbelievers
would be annihilated.[1]

Although Navosa died in exile in 1897, his followers
kept the movement alive in the interior, where there were
few signs of government power, little education, and men
not at all unwilling to be identified as bete, priests -
though perhaps not on Sunday, when as in every village of
Fiji the population went to church and sang praises to the
Lord God of Hosts Who knows all things but Who truly
blesses the Fijian people, a villager might explain, with
great mana.

Doubtless the young Apolosi was steeped in this
accommodating theology of village life, and surely he heard
the miracle stories of the prophet - how the British had
put Navosa through the rollers of a mill without extracting
a drop of his blood, then bound him in weighted ropes and
buried him alive at sea en route to Rotuma only to find him
on arrival dangling his legs over the end of the wharf

waiting to greet his captors.[2] When Apolosi joined the
lucky few to progress beyond a few years of village
education and enter the Wesleyan central school at Navuloa
(at the mouth of the Rewa), he was already thoroughly
versed in the pre-scientific psychology of his people, and
later revealed a remarkable capacity to validate his
leadership ambitions by arcane references to both scriptual
and traditional symbols. Where Ratu Sukuna relied on
hereditary status, western education, prestige in the
colonial establishment and closely reasoned appeals to
history, anthropology and natural justice to advance his
conceptions of the needs of the Fijian people, Apolosi
spoke directly to the heart; he addressed the actual
perceptions of the people in the language they understood.

In the first decade of the century those perceptions
often were that Fijians were coming to occupy an inferior
place in the colony's economy, that the future lay with the
Europeans and, to a growing extent, the Indians, and that
the chiefs of the land, more especially those who sheltered
their privileges within the ranks of the Fijian
Administration, were unequal to the task of satisfying the
material aspirations of their people.

The collapse of Thurston's taxation scheme and
marketing organization had bound Fijians hand and foot to
European and Chinese traders buying produce in small lots
and selling merchandise at atrocious prices. The Planters'
Petition of 1908 seeking the confiscation of 'unused'
Fijian lands and the knowledge that it had the support of
their Supreme Chief Sir Everard im Thurn had created - in
Ratu Sukuna's own words - 'an atmosphere of troubled
suspicion . . . for the first time perhaps since
Cession'.[3] The European magistrates were successfully
striving to increase their direct executive authority at
the expense of Fijian officials. Sydney Smith, one time
Provincial Inspector in western Viti Levu, was at large in
Macuata openly contemptuous of those 'very useless
officials' the Bulis: when they came to 'squat' in his
office he told them they were an avaricious lot, greedy for
Indian rents while deservedly rotting as a result of 'their
own laziness'.[4] In 1913 the magistrates were restyled
District Commissioners (Provincial Commissioners if there
was no Roko) and assigned the duties of any government
department, including for the first time direct oversight
of Fijian affairs.[5] New Rokos were styled Native
Assistants, on about half the salary of a senior Roko Tui,
and with no share of rent monies. Young Englishmen or

local Europeans, 'often completely ignorant of native customs and modes of thought', were given broad discretionary power.[6] All correspondence had to pass through them, an insult to chiefs like Ratu Aseri Latianara or Ratu Pope Seniloli, the Vunivalu of Bau.

In the same year, 1913, Apolosi emerged into the public eye. He and a minor chief from Bau, Ratu J. Tabaiwalu, had for some time been leaders of a team of carpenters based at the new mission training institute at Davuilevu, outside Suva. They took contracts to build those capacious wooden churches which had become, along with sailing cutters for coastal villages, a status symbol of communal pride and an incessant drain on the meagre capital resources of the villagers. Oral traditions on the Wainibuka River have it that the team was building a church at Korovatu near Vunidawa in 1911 or 1912 when Apolosi first began to canvass village meetings with his scheme to start a Fiji company. He was then in his early thirties, young for a Fijian to assert leadership, and he had to be careful to avoid showing his disrespect for the established order.

Was it a perception of the senseless capital waste in oversized churches, or the procession of European-owned punts taking Fiji's bananas down the Rewa tributaries to Suva, or was it compassion for the villagers hammering up banana cases for a pittance that finally inspired Apolosi, with eloquence still remembered in those parts, to transcend all bounds of etiquette and make a bold plea for innovation? He said later he had lived in blindness for years until he suddenly realized that the only way the itaukei could get a fair deal was to compete directly in the economy and keep the export and import of food and produce in their own hands. First they could cut out the white buyers who controlled the river trade, then the agents in Suva, then perhaps the shipping lines . . . Why could not Fijians pool their capital in one vast company, learn the skills, invest the profits, and above all enjoy the dividends that flowed from their land and their labour straight into a few whitemen's pockets as surely as the Rewa River emptied into the sea? His countrymen lived like the Hebrews weeping beside the river of Babylon longing for their land to be restored to them. They should steel themselves, be strong and determined (yalo qaqa). Or would they forever be content to let foreigners develop their lands and employ them casually for 2s a day - less, he noted, then a whiteman in Suva spent on feeding his horse.[7]

These were powerful themes that spoke to a people's pride, challenged their submissiveness to the whole framework of their lives, and compounded their anxiety about the future of the race.

When Apolosi said 'We Fijians' to people with whom he had no connection or status, he was speaking a new language, cutting across the intense parochial bonds that kept the constituent groups at every level of Fijian society and administration dependent on chiefs for leadership and initiative. His stroke of genius was to avoid an overt challenge to the chiefs and find a new basis for legitimacy in the western model of a company of shareholders united solely on the basis of their capital contribution and the specific aims of modern enterprise, and delegating control of all operations to a managing director. Undoubtedly he had heard of a similar Tongan company and the rumoured prosperity of its members. Apolosi neither understood nor cared for the legal details of company organization - he gambled that the symbols of status, the business titles, an impressive office, the company letterhead and above all the shareholders' meetings would validate his scheme in the eyes of the people. It was still essential, though, to create the impression that the powers of the land were at least tacitly in support, giving the Company, as Ratu Sukuna later explained, 'the chiefly authority it would have otherwise lacked'.[8] Many chiefs who were without government appointments, or had lost them, notably the 'dissidents of Bau', Ro Tuisawau (a high chief of Rewa), and the hereditary chief styled Ratu mai Verata at various times lent their prestige to Company 'committees' and 'boards' or attended meetings in the early years.

Government only became aware of the Viti Company at the end of 1913 when Apolosi's agents began to solicit 'share' subscriptions from chiefs and people in nearly every part of the group. The promoters claimed government approval, prompting an official warning to the people in Na Mata not to be duped by a company that was not known to the government.[9] Shareholders were asked to sell produce only to their Company and be content with a lower price until its offices were properly established in Suva. The people of Lutu and most of their neighbours on the tributaries of the Rewa River gave their bananas without payment to Apolosi's agents; the islanders of Nayau in Lau province gave him their copra, and one district in Ra province handed over its entire tax money. The Company aroused

great excitement in all parts of the group and was widely
attributed to the inspiration of the twin gods
Nacirikaumoli and Nakausabaria, a suggestion Apolosi did
nothing to dispel. In January 1914 Joni Kuruduadua, an old
Fijian servant of the government in the interior, roused
himself from retirement to warn that the Company's objects
were said to be the return of the lands alienated to
Europeans before Cession, the takeover of all European and
Indian stores by Fijians with some to be sent to establish
markets overseas, the abolition of government taxes and the
eventual expulsion of all Europeans from Fiji - not to
mention 'other reports which it is not seemly to relate'.[10]

Kuruduadua's reticence almost certainly alludes to the
revival in the highlands of obscene meke performed for the
old gods, with some rather disturbing new lyrics:

Fijian prepare for battle!
Close in with bayonets drawn.
Apolosi and his boys will win;
Wait for his word of command.
Hurl the whiteskins out to sea
Or make them cook and wash
And carry away our trash
Their feet will be posts for our
houses;
Sew up their tongues for our sails;
Gouge out their eyes for inkwells.
Hail Apolosi, firstborn king!
Lead our land to freedom
Lead us to happiness.[11]

Apolosi issued orders to the Bulis of eastern Viti
Levu to assemble with their people at Draubuta village in
the Rewa delta for the hoisting of the Company flag on 29
April 1914. When the Secretary for Native Affairs, K.J.
Allardyce, told the Bulis by circular letter that in no
circumstances were they to take their orders from the Viti
Company, Apolosi and Ratu J. Tabaiwalu countered with a
circular of their own, impressively typed, saying that
Allardyce's letter was 'foolish indeed' as there was no law
to prevent the collection of money or the formation of a
company. Allardyce urged that Apolosi be exiled forthwith
under the Confining Ordinance (III of 1887) originally
designed to remove Navosavakadua to Rotuma without trial.
Governor Sir Ernest Bickham Sweet Escott, fatally ignorant
of the interpretation Fijians would place on his caution,
allowed the meeting to go ahead. He feared 'a false step'.

Was not the government now anxious that 'the communal
system with its paralysing influence on individual effort
and ambition should be broken down'? Apolosi's Viti
Company could herald a healthy new phase in the Fijians'
transition from simple subsistence to a liberal economy.
The protests of the threatened European banana interest had
to be balanced against the government tradition of strong
protection for the legitimate aspirations of the Fijians.[12]

That certainly was not the view of the traditional
leaders of the Fijians, the high chiefs. The Tui Nayau
(Roko Tui of Lau in his government capacity) was one of the
first to try and discredit the Company. Apolosi, he
reported, had arrived in state at the island of Nayau with
£70 worth of gifts to exchange for women. At a district
church meeting (polotu) Apolosi boasted that he did not
honour anyone in Fiji, neither white, red nor black, nor
any Governor, Roko or magistrate. To dramatize the point
he tore up summonses issued by the European magistrate at
Lomaloma. Finally, warned the Roko, Apolosi was advising
the people not to pay their debts to the Europeans.[13] The
other chiefs had their first opportunity to discuss the
Company at the Council of Chiefs in May 1914. They were
assured by the Buli of Nadi that Apolosi and his brother
Kiniviliame were 'people of no position' and that they had
both been driven out of Nadi. The Viti Company was the
work of young upstarts, an affront to chiefly prerogatives.
The Council urged the government to prohibit the collection
of money for an unregistered company and to prosecute the
promoters. A shrewd chief of Kadavu added that as long as
Apolosi and his followers were allowed to make their boasts
with impunity, the people would assume tacit government
approval for the venture. The chiefs were acutely aware of
Apolosi's need to give the Company the aura of their
authority before the people would rally to its flag.[14]

In a predicament created by its own mood of
liberalism, the government replied that only the misuse of
money was unlawful. Apolosi must be legally convicted of
an offence before the Viti Company's activities could be
constrained. As no one could be found who would testify in
court to his squandering of money held in trust, the man
from Ra had free rein to develop his organization. To
heighten the impression of a great chiefly enterprise he
appointed a large number of Company officials with
authoritative-sounding titles. Almost every Buli in the
District Administration was flanked by a 'Manager' while
the government village chiefs, the turaga ni koro, were in

many places virtually replaced with Company nominees
bearing the same title. Similarly he appointed <u>ovisa</u> to
correspond with provincial constables, and threatened to
fine or imprison the enemies of the Company. It was as
though there were two governments in Fiji, complained the
<u>Roko Tui</u> of Macuata. [15]

Promoters of the Company carried its messages and
instructions from village to village, stirring up
enthusiasm and collecting funds. Apolosi was later to
claim, and it was doubtless the case, that he had little
control over what they said and did in the name of the Viti
Company. Nor was there much that a handful of overworked
magistrates could do to monitor their movements. In August
a levy of £10 was demanded from every district and the
membership fee fixed at £1. In the banana-rich villages of
the Rewa delta Apolosi proclaimed that anyone selling to
Europeans would be prosecuted by the Company and
imprisoned. The Provincial Commissioner of Colo East
reported that rather than sell to European buyers offering
cash on the spot, the people were burying their bananas.
The government began to realize that intervention would
soon be necessary: it was simply a question of the length
of the rope. [16]

When it came to the disposal of bananas, copra, and
other produce, Apolosi was compelled to work with Europeans
already in the business. Although the details of his
dealing are not documented, it seems the Viti Company had
its own inter-island cutters and river punts - essential
status symbols - but used established firms to handle
overseas shipments. Seeing a chance to capitalize on
Fijian patriotism, five Suva businessmen went ahead without
Apolosi and legally incorporated a company called the Viti
Company with a capital of 10,000 shares at £1 each, 5 per
cent on allotment. A certificate to commence business was
issued on 16 January 1915. The memorandum of association
provided for all the business activities Apolosi had urged
Fijians to take on themselves: the marketing of Fijian
produce and traditional manufactures, the management of
wholesale and retail stores, importing and exporting,
shipbuilding, insurance, banking and auctioneering.
However the board was always to have five of its seven
members Europeans and in the first instance no Fijians were
appointed. [17]

In letters to the Governor and the press the European directors denounced the use of the Company's name by Apolosi or anyone else to collect funds. For his part, Apolosi seized on this parasitical Viti Company's legal standing to impress or confuse the people with the legality of the original Viti Company in its diffuse semi-political form. In January 1915 he brought some 3000-4000 people back to Draubuta for meetings and celebrations lasting nearly a month. (In oral traditions this meeting is often telescoped into the first and regarded as the real inauguration of the Company.) Apolosi addressed the crowd from a high stage hung with a hundred tabua (whales' teeth). Ro Tuisawau, dissident high chief of Rewa, is said to have presented Apolosi with a large tabua, to confer on him a chiefly mandate to ensure the prosperity of the whole country. Many minor chiefs and ex-government officials were present, as well as five Bulis of Colo East expressly forbidden to attend. The meeting is poorly documented but apparently Apolosi used it to bolster his claim to be the true leader of the Viti Company, for shortly afterwards he warned the Bulis of Nadroga they should cease their hostility to the company 'lest you incur serious trouble'. Did they not understand that the Viti Company had been duly registered and had legal authority?[18]

In March 1915 Apolosi faced a crisis. The first annual general meeting of the legal Viti Company in the Suva Town Hall was to be held on the 27th; hundreds of Viti Company shareholders (of both companies) were expected to attend and they would learn for the first time that Apolosi was not the Managing Director - one A.J. Mackay was. Apolosi met the problem head on. He called his own meeting for the evening of the same day to follow Mackay's, which went badly enough. Mackay warned of 'certain Fijians . . . who can only be called Germans' collecting money illegally in the name of the Viti Company. Then the Tui Nausori took two tabua to the directors, begging them to take no notice of Apolosi and his agitators: 'Europeans were the only people who could run their Company properly'. At night hundreds of Fijians and a few curious European observers or officials packed the hall to hear what Apolosi would have to say in reply.[19]

The man from Ra drove up outside in a gleaming black car and attired in a well-fitting tussore silk suit made for him by Peapes of Sydney. The Fijians in the audience received him as if he had been the Governor himself, but Apolosi was careful to begin on the self-deprecating note demanded by both his sense of dramatic contrast and Fijian chiefly etiquette:

> Chiefs of all Fiji and chiefs of _Papalagi_ present here today. I am one who has not been long in this world, I am but a child [he was about 39] . . . it is not my prerogative to summon you chiefs together that you should leave your chiefly lands and put aside your chiefly rank to attend a meeting called in my name. Why then did you come? To see me? Is it not rather that you endorse this work of cleanliness to achieve our prosperity and increase in the present time . . .

Then after outlining the history of the Viti Company from the time his blindness was lifted to realize that only a company could give the _itaukei_ a fair deal, he criticized the opposition he had received from Europeans, including the directors of the legal company. He asked the meeting why he had been excluded from the board: 'Someone tell me. Am I a thief? Do I oppose the Government?' He paused for a minute or two to search the faces of his audience. No one said a word. Then he went on to say how sad he was to hear that the afternoon meeting had gone badly for them. Could someone tell him why? One Felipe volunteered that they were angry to see Fijians had been excluded from the board. If it was really a Fijian company then surely Fijians should be in control. Apolosi asked the meeting to raise their hands if they agreed. There were no dissenters.[20]

Much encouraged no doubt, Apolosi stepped up his fund raising for a variety of schemes called 'Life Insurance on Native Towns,' 'A Fijian Club,' 'Entrance to the Viti Company' and others more or less under his direction. European settlers were more alarmed by the political undertones of the movement. Viti Levu was alive with rumour. In one cable the District Commissioner of Ra reported that a young girl had been killed, cooked and partly eaten in Colo West. Settlers at Tavua, near the old seat of the _Tuka_ cult at Drauniivi, demanded ammunition. George Barrow took time off from his little vendettas in Serua to warn that the European population was in real danger. He had heard heathen songs and dances gleefully representing the whites as swimming for their lives: 'Everything seems to point to an approaching conflict between black and white.'[21]

In May 1915 Apolosi was touring the Yasawa group collecting copra when a Fijian constable sent from Suva arrived at Yaqeta with a warrant for his arrest on a charge of embezzlement in Rewa. When Apolosi flatly refused to go, the constable returned to the mainland for reinforcement. On 17 May, the police arrived at dusk to find Apolosi standing on the beach between two fires with about thirty men seated in a circle around him. Apolosi said in English, 'Stand up, boys.' Tense and sweating, his protectors rose and stood shoulder to shoulder in silence. Light from the fire illumined their 3 foot pile of stout batons, and flickered up to faces blackened as if for war. Police Inspector Scott-Young read firmly from his warrant. Apolosi raised one arm and replied: 'I swear by Jesus Christ that I won't be taken alive. You may take my dead body. I don't care if you have 2,000 warrants. I will not go.' For an hour and a half Scott-Young stood there reasoning and threatening into the darkness. Then fearing bloodshed - his own - he retreated to his boat.[22]

Two days later the Inspector-General of Constabulary, Colonel Islay McOwan, sailed from Lautoka with an armed party. At the mouth of the Ba River they intercepted a little fleet of cutters manned by Apolosi and his followers. The leader and twenty-four of his men were apprehended easily and charged with resisting a police officer in the execution of his duty. There were rumours, but as always no convicting evidence, that Apolosi and his men were on their way to Natutu in Ba to raise open rebellion and that if those people refused, then he was to go up into the mountains of Colo East. Apolosi was tried in Suva and sentenced to eighteen months with hard labour. His brother Kiniviliame and six others received shorter sentences, but there were many others to carry on his work under the name 'Fiji Produce Agency'. Their leader was one Joeli Cava of Vuce, Tokatoka, who reasserted the legitimate business aims of the Company and curried favour with the government. At the same time a meeting of the FPA at Sabeto in December 1915 drew up a protest against the government's attempts to control leasing arrangements and urged that Fijians themselves should cultivate their idle lands and market the produce. The Governor received a large delegation led by Joeli at Government House on Christmas Eve, 1915, discussed their objections and cautiously approved their projects. For the colonial authorities were still prepared to encourage Fijian commercial ambitions provided they did not 'interfere with the social organization necessary for the good life of the majority of the people . . . the only life possible at this stage' for Fijians.[23]

Four weeks after his release on 30 September 1916, Apolosi was back at Draubuta for a hero's welcome and to tell how much he had suffered for the Company cause. He inspected a guard of honour of 120 schoolchildren neatly dressed in the European clothes prescribed by the Company as the outward sign of progress towards a modern way of life. A surprise visitor was A.J. Mackay who announced that he had sold his 200 shares in the legal company to Apolosi. The board was now short of its required number and proportion of European blood; or rather the title director ceased to have any more meaning than the other titles in the original Company's pantheon. Books were kept spasmodically, and recorded only a fraction of the Company's transactions, most of which were handled by Apolosi personally. Thousands of pounds were unaccounted for. While some trading activities continued to be attributed to the registered company, an astute official warned 'the future historian of Fiji' not to be puzzled by the 'Company's' notoriety relative to

'the very evident unimportance of the registered company trading under that name . . . It is perhaps most intelligible if it is understood to denote the general body of native opinion dissatisfied with the present condition of native life and government, of which body of opinion the trading company is only a minor manifestation.'[24]

In November the district of Lutu constructed a meeting house for the Company, 96 feet long, 36 feet wide. (The foundations are still visible.) Meanwhile Apolosi and Joeli were making a new bid for respectability. They called on Governor Sir Ernest Bickham Sweet Escott to leave a donation of £30 for Lady Escott's fund for wounded soldiers, and implored His Excellency not to believe evil stories that might be spread about them. They also called in at Davuilevu, Apolosi's alma mater, and talked with the Principal, the Reverend C.O. Lelean, about their plans for Fijians. Apolosi enquired after his young relative Lucy and begged Lelean not to allow her to be sent to the hospital for training as an obstetric nurse - the 'moral danger' of the place distressed him. Lucy should go to his school at Draubuta where the Company's own teacher, Tikiko Tuwai, would give her a modern education that included (it later eventuated) nightly classes for the girls in 'massage'. Apolosi impressed Lelean, as he had the Governor, with his sincerity and enthusiasm.[25]

On 7 December 1916 the real Apolosi with his harem and a large entourage travelled in a flotilla of boats up the Wainibuka River to Lutu for the opening of the Bose Ko Viti, the Council of Fiji, as the meeting was not inaptly called. As he came ashore with Ro Tuisawau beside him the assembly of 5449 people from every part of Fiji gave him the muted roar of the high chiefly tama: duo! o! The high chiefly presentations of tabua, and the full kava ceremony (yaqona vakaturaga) were performed just as they would have been for the Supreme Chief or a member of the Royal Family.

Wherever the man from Ra moved, a body of ovisa with red armbands cleared the way; when he was inside a house or sleeping, they mounted guard on the doorways. His eight 'doves' took it in turns to roll cigarettes and put them in his mouth, or cool him with fans. At short meetings held daily for a week Apolosi and the Company officials were dressed in white shirts, white trousers, golf stockings and tennis shoes. Physically Apolosi (like Navosavakadua) was not impressive. He was neither tall nor, by Fijian standards, powerfully built. His dark full face was dominated by wide-set eyes under heavy eyebrows and a nose that flared out around cavernous nostrils. Fijians remember him for his resonant voice and the way his eyes focused hypnotically to seal his message. 'When he spoke', recalled one, 'it was like a bullet hitting your brain - whack!' Or in the words of a man of Matacawalevu village, Yasawas: 'Once Apolosi opened his mouth your mind was no longer your own.'[26]

At Lutu he compensated for his lack of physical stature by sitting in an elaborate pulpit-like wooden throne ornamented with the flags of many nations, his bodyguard to either side, and at the lower level in front of him two men with typewriters to take the minutes of the meetings like the Hansard reporters in the Legislative Council. Could anyone doubt that a great chiefly council was now in progress?

> Lutu, 7th December 1916, 12 noon. I now open our meeting house. The Government has ordered that as I am the promoter of the Company, I should be the Manager . . . if there be anyone here who is an enemy of the Company . . . I shall send to Suva for Constables to arrest him . . . God has

appointed me to be your comforter in bodily and spiritual things. Many chiefs of Fiji now dead and many still alive are not equal to me . . .Before I was born God predestined me to be your chief and to bring into being a new scheme by which Fiji would be independent in future and free from Government control . . .

In the words of a Fijian constable, 'It was exactly like a government meeting. There were Chief Constables, Magistrates, Doctors, just as if Apolosi was founding a government that might become something terrible . . . one question I wish to ask about Apolosi, if everybody salutes him as they do what is the use of the Government?'[27]

A vast program was agreed upon. The Company would have ships and shipyards, stores and storehouses, a soap factory, its own school system. A Committee of Chiefs was formed under Ro Tuisawau, once Roko Tui Rewa, most of them harbouring some grievance against the colonial government. Company officers, managers, town chiefs and clerks were appointed for every province except Macuata and possibly Bua. Apolosi's own salary was fixed at £100 a month. The meeting closed on 20 December, in an atmosphere of celebration and hope.

The first signs that the euphoria was not to last came from some Colo East banana growers who received no payment for five shipments of bananas. Hitherto they had willingly accepted half the market price or less, for the cause, but their patience and loyalty did not extend indefinitely. They refused to send further shipments. Nevertheless they also refused to sell to Europeans and in the latter half of 1917 thousands of bananas rotted on the trees. Not a single man could be found to testify against the Company in court. Between January and April 1917 Apolosi received in his own name over £3000 in bananas and copra. After examining the chaotic books of the Company an accountant found there was no way of knowing the real extent of its operations or what happended to the proceeds. Since government was powerless to act under the existing Companies Ordinance until the shareholders petitioned for redress, it proposed to the Colonial Office a Native Company Ordinance giving the Registrar of Companies draconian powers of supervision over any company with a single Fijian member. The Secretary of State thought it difficult to believe such a measure could be contemplated seriously, and there the matter rested.[28]

Intoxicated with his wealth and often with alcohol,
Apolosi had begun to make extraordinary claims for his
personal status. At Lutu the Colo West people had hailed
him in song as king, and on one occasion he stopped a fight
by raising himself on the shoulders of some men, saying:
'Please understand I will not have the least trouble in my
presence for I alone rule [lewai] Fiji and if I say "let
Fiji go to ruin", it will go to ruin.'[29] Similarly in the
New Year of 1917, at the wedding of a Suva friend's
daughter, he brandished two bottles of liquor he had waved
under the noses of policemen en route, and then launched
into a tirade against the chiefs present and absent:

> I alone am the chief of Fiji: it is the will of
> God. These other chiefs only work for
> themselves; they don't spare a thought for you
> or your welfare. Just look at those two chiefs
> who went to the Great Council of Chiefs: they
> did nothing for our prosperity and I say they are
> scum (kaisi), all of them. You know who I am,
> Apolosi R. Nawai na kai Ra. In times past I was
> not known while the states of Bau and Rewa were
> renowned, but wait and you will see . . .

Summoned to a meeting with Ratu Sukuna - back from the war
in France - and other officials of the Colonial Secretariat
in March 1917, Apolosi solemnly promised that henceforth he
would not encourage chiefly ceremonies in his honour and
that he would abandon the use of official-sounding titles
for Company agents.[30]

Ratu Sukuna wrote an impassioned appeal the same month
for much more drastic government intervention to bring
Apolosi's 'sordid and unpatriotic' doings to a halt.
Deportation was the only solution, he said:

> Thinking Fijians look to the Government for help,
> vaguely wondering, with their autocratic views of
> government, why Apolosi and his followers have
> not been suppressed. His utterances and letters
> have been shown to be clearly against constituted
> authority and yet nothing is done . . . Apolosi
> is trafficking with racial feelings for position
> and gain . . . It is crime of the worst kind. It
> is an example of life unthinkably vile.[31]

But again government decided to wait for hard evidence of
sedition.

About June 1917 Apolosi finally found a European businessman he could trust, an American named Walter Jago. Jago, it seems, tried hard to restrain Apolosi and establish the Viti Company on sound business lines. But it was too late. The settlers were after Apolosi's head for telling the Fijians that it was folly to lease lands to Europeans for 5s or 10s an acre and watch them reap £10 and £15 an acre in cane. If Indians were prepared to find £1 an acre or more, Apolosi was saying, why should Europeans or sugar companies get land for less? Two Europeans attended one of Apolosi's rallies at Nakorovou, Tavua, on 31 August 1917. Afterwards one of them made a statutory declaration that Apolosi had said, <u>Koi au na meca ni matanitu, au na tamata kaukauwa</u>: 'I am the enemy of the government, I am the strong man'. This, and a similar declaration by the other, provided the Governor and Executive Council with the sure evidence they needed. They issued another Confining Order (without trial) exiling Apolosi to Rotuma for seven years.[32]

In an impassioned letter to the Executive Council after his arrest at Votua on 19 November 1917, Apolosi begged to be allowed to kiss the Bible in their presence and swear before God and King that he had not said anything of the sort: 'I humbly beg that you will hear me and permit those natives who were present on the 31st August 1917 at the meeting at Tavua to testify to what they heard at that meeting'. It is indeed unlikely that Apolosi would have been foolish enough to say the words attributed to him in the presence of hostile Europeans. The crude phraseology is inconsistent with his desire to give the company the trappings of legality, and the phrase 'strong man' is not typical of the dignities he claimed in his more extravagant moments. In short he was probably framed. The shoddiness of the confinement proceedings did not escape the Colonial Office: 'in the absence of judicial proceedings we really have to rely on the Governor's opinion'. The Governor was asked to review the case after a year.[33]

Apolosi's own reaction is evident in his apologia: 'I cannot turn left, right, forward or backward, up or down, with the crowd of enemies that are about me.' He also offered a psychological analysis of himself and his past:

> There are two great things that influence my body and my mind; firstly physical and mental foolishness; secondly, ignorance . . . Their

influence over me is due to my childish
instability and bad upbringing . . . My mother
and father were foolish and ignorant people.
They had no wisdom or enlightenment, and
therefore I inherited none from them whereby to
be guided in my walk through life. Any knowledge
or enlightenment that I have been able to gain
has been through my own personal efforts . . . I
have had no one to take an interest in me or hold
me up or lead me out of the black
darkness . . . it was as though I were covered
with worms and everything repulsive. Many saw
me, laughed at me, and mocked me. It was as
though they sucked my blood and wrung the water
out of my soul . . . [34]

The scriptural allusions to the Suffering Servant, a
theme Apolosi instinctively invoked at each reverse, were
both an abject admission of defeat and a clue to his forced
retreat into messianism. For the rest of his days he tried
to keep a hold over his followers - and their money - with
feverish dreams of a New Era (Gauna Vou) in which he would
be king of the world, and his leprous brother, Josevata,
king of heaven or vicar of Jesus Christ.[35] After his
release from Rotuma in 1924 he wandered restlessly through
Viti Levu and the Yasawas, ever more extravagant in his
claims, and perfecting his hypnotic rhetorical power. A
brief resurgence of excitement in the Nadi area at the
beginning of 1930, when Apolosi was predicting England's
demise and a great depression, gave the authorities cause
to exile him again for ten years. And finally when he
resumed his 'work' while on probation in Suva in 1940, he
was exiled again, transferred to New Zealand in case he
fancied himself as a Quisling for the Japanese, and brought
back to Yacata to die in 1946.

Apolosi was more corrupt entrepreneur than millenarian
prophet. Yet in his own way he was a great patriot tapping
the roots of Fijian pride by urging the people and chiefs
to cut across the parochial limitations of their existing
institutions. Even if he lacked a real set of
alternatives, he could feel what was wrong in the Fijian
Administration: there was no room for innovation and
initiative from below. Economically Fijians were in a
straightjacket. 'Very few people', he said, 'are in a bad
plight because of their own decisions about
themselves.' Apolosi died knowing that he had opened a
deep vein of discontent; he had permanently injected the

rhetoric of Fijian politics with a demand for <u>toro</u> <u>cake</u>, that is, progress, improvement, and a better return on their labour and resources.

Chapter 7

The vein of discontent

The failure of Apolosi's Viti Company to galvanize the rural economy and his own retreat into messianic delusions left something of a vacuum in ordinary village life, a loss in some places of a feeling of purpose and direction. Discontent and restlessness found several outlets: village absenteeism to escape the present, secret supernatural societies to overturn it, and modern associations to turn the existing order to greater advantage.

Colonial authorities were poorly equipped to respond to all these phenomena, but especially the underground movements they rather too easily dismissed as transient relapses into superstition. Witchcraft was of course proscribed by the Native Regulations if there was 'intent to cause fear or death', but the government trusted vaguely to the advance of education and the work of the missions to eradicate the evil gradually.[1] There was no great alarm, for instance, when a report came from Nabukelevu, Kadavu, that an occult society met regularly to prepare a special feast called the madrali, half of which was carried out to sea and offered to Dakuwaqa. And at night by the light of the mystic moon they danced naked and free - orgies of lust and abandon in the shadows of Wesley's churches though never, so far as the records allow, on Sundays.[2] There had always been isolated instances of individuals who openly exhibited signs of demonic possession and who attracted a devoted clientele. Ratu A. Finau, the Roko Tui of Lau, was disturbed in 1906 by the activities of a Cakaudrove man, Tevita Toga, at Vakano on Lakeba. Timing his performance by the throb of the lali drum for the people to assemble in church, Tevita would roll uci leaves between his palms and on his legs, then begin to shiver and tremble starting from his toes and convulsing upwards till his whole body shook violently while he leapt about shrieking horribly or forcing incoherent words through his teeth. His attendants meanwhile calmly chewed yaqona for mixing in the old way. When it was ready Tevita would drink three times then eat a firebrand three times: 'The women all believe in him, a good many men believe in him, and very few went to church in the evening . . . The people have been flocking to him.'[3] The missionary on Lakeba, the Reverend Colin Bleazard, was shocked that there had been 'some most heathenish devil-worship . . . on the island that has done so much for Christianity in other parts of Fiji &

94

elsewhere'. Some of Bleazard's own teachers were involved.[4]

In 1914 there was a similar case of 'shaking' in Ra (Tukaimalo district) - a father and son together. Four men testified to the District Commissioner that the son bit off live embers and ate them. The men were possessed by the luveniwai, 'children of the water', said the informants.[5] Luveniwai were the small gods who lived upon the coasts and rocky parts. Some were boisterous, some mild and gentle when they took possession. It was usually the young men in some kind of fraternity who would build a bower decked out with flowers and vines. They would dress themselves in more leaves and flowers and rub their bodies with perfumed oil. They then prepared a parcel of sweet flowers and fruits cooked on coals, and a small feast for themselves and the presiding priest or Vuniduvu. One portion was taken to the bush for the incoming luveniwai. Finally a sacred meke for the meeting with the gods was performed, a libation of yaqona poured and the Vuniduvu became possessed, followed by the youths until all quivered and shook: 'Isa! Isa! Ratagane [Lord Man], Isa!' After a period of hysteria, or if the spirits were slow to leave, the Vuniduvu would feed the youths live coals or beat them with clubs or throw spears at them. Possession gave them immunity from injury - but not always it seems. There was a case at Mali, Labasa, in 1905 where a youth was seriously injured by a Vuniduvu's spear.[6] Early observers such as Thomas Williams had taken a lenient view of luveniwai as a not quite innocent pastime, a diversion of youth. David Wilkinson had insisted it was not seditious: 'I feel sure no punishment will restrain, but probably promote, in some more clandestine way, manner, and place. A moral, general disapproval will be much more effective in putting down the practice.'[7]

Although specific details were hard to come by, it seems that up in the interior of Viti Levu luveniwai practices became mingled with aspects of the earlier Tuka cult, causing the government some alarm. The long-serving Governor's Commissioner in Colo, A.B. Joske, started cricket clubs in the villages to divert the energies of the young, only to find that they were used as a cloak for clandestine rituals involving an elaborate hierarchy of officials with fantastic titles. Usually there had to be some personal or political intrigue before the occult came before the courts. The wronged wife of a Vuniduvu near Nadrau informed on him to the Buli in 1907 who laid charges

against thirteen men and nine women for practising <u>Tuka</u>.
They had made offerings to a <u>Vuniduvu</u>, giving part to the
<u>Vuki</u>, the official who would supervise the turning upside
down (<u>vuki</u>) of the world decreed by Navosavakadua, after
which his votaries would rule the nations and live forever.
There were also officers styled Sergeants and <u>Kalasia</u>,
meaning scribes. (The government had just created three
classes of scribes.) Ten men were sentenced by Joske to two
months in goal. He saw it as his duty to suppress
<u>Tuka</u>-related ceremonies as leading always to larceny,
immorality and resistance to the authority of the old men
and the government. He recognized that <u>Tuka</u> was a
superstition that lent itself strongly to Fijians with its
prayers to the ancestral spirits and its promise of the
re-establishment of the prestige of the tribes that
professed it.[8] There was always the fear, though, in the
light of the earlier disturbances, that the non-advent of
<u>Tuka</u> would be explained by its priests as the lack of
propitiation with human sacrifice and that serious revolt
would ensue.[9]

It was not until 1914 that the government learned that
quite apart from the isolated cases reported by Joske, <u>Tuka</u>
had survived within a highly organized secret society
embracing all the leading chiefs and nearly all the men of
Qaliyalatina district with members in Toge on the Ba River
and in three towns of Colo West (Namoli, Nakuilau and
Vatubalavu). Ironically the high priest of the cult, Osea
Tamanikoro, the <u>turaga ni koro</u> of Batimaoli, had obtained
his commission by sending ten whales' teeth to
Navosavakadua's town of Drauniivi in 1892, shortly before
the whole village had been deported by Thurston to Kadavu,
and the same year that the hill station at Nadarivatu had
been established with a garrison of Armed Constabulary to
keep <u>Tuka</u> from breaking out in the interior. It went
underground. Little did Joske realize that Osea had
quietly been recruiting the very men who cooperated so
willingly in his heavy program of road building and other
provincial works. The Buli of Qaliyalatina, Joseva Tube,
and the <u>turaga ni koro</u> of the other Qaliyalatina towns
(Cuvu, Navala and Nakoroboya) were Osea's accomplices.[10]

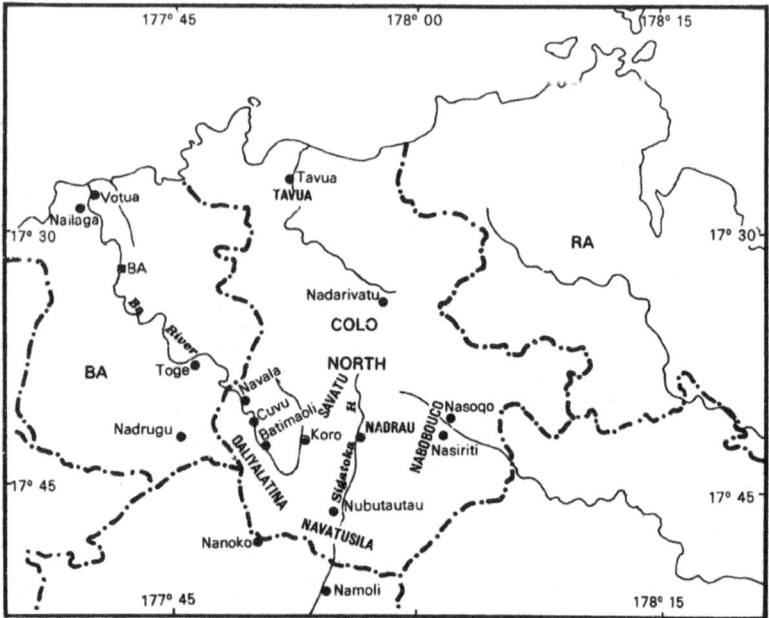

Map 3 Colo North

Each recruit was taken by a priest in the dead of night to present a root of <u>yaqona</u> to Osea and seek admission to the <u>Bai Tabua</u>, the sacred society of the twin gods Nacirikaumoli and Nakausabaria. On one occasion when Joseva Tube accepted the <u>yaqona</u> he offered the following prayer:

> I accept this <u>yaqona</u> the <u>yaqona</u> of the Two Gods, the <u>yaqona</u> of life. Extend ye your favour to us the <u>Bai Tabua</u> so that our land may prosper. This land is made over to Burotukula. Let the fact be known to the Vale Dina; let it be known to Vale Kurukuruya; let it be known as far as Ului Bua; let it be known to Vale Lawa; let it be known to Cautoka, let it be known to Naiyalayala. This is the prayer of the <u>Bai Tabua</u>.[11]

Burotukula is one of the spirit-lands where the twin gods are in hiding. The Bai Tabua dedicated all their lands to Burotukula as to the new heaven and the new earth. Some of the other names referred to sacred places in the Nakauvadra range, home of the gods. Normally in the yaqona ritual the ceremonial names of the chiefly lines of the participants are invoked with great respect and care. Here the implication is clear: the Bai Tabua are of the gods; they will live forever; they do not belong to the ordinary run of chiefly houses. While the yaqona was being chewed a chant such as the following was sung:

Me ra Yavala na Bai Tabua
Era taubale ki Ulu ni Vanua
Kele na Vale ko Nacoukula
Vakarewa na Droti ni Bula.
[Let the Bai Tabua bestir themselves
They walk to the Mountain
Solid stands the house 'Nacoukula'
Hoist the banner of Immortality.][12]

'Nacoukula' was the name of Osea's house. It was his audacious plans in 1914 for a huge new house that led to the exposure of the whole movement. The Provincial Commissioner of Colo North, W.E. Russell, became suspicious in May and June when Joseva Tube asked the district magistrate not to hold a court circuit in those months because there were no complaints. Rumours came to Russell on a visit to Nadrau that a heathen temple was under construction. Unusual quantities of sinnet had been ordered from Namoli in Colo West. Then the Buli himself visited Russell in Nadrau to ask permission to employ the whole district on Osea's house. Russell subsequently visited Cuvu and found the turaga ni koro's house hung around with a great number of clubs and traditional bark garments with strings of flowers - in preparation for rehearsals for a missionary meeting, said the people, but Russell was not so sure.

The Buli of Navatusila meanwhile made inquiries in the town of Nanoko near the borders of his district with Qaliyalatina and there obtained a man prepared to testify in court that his neighbours were engaged in a Tuka cult. Another willing witness was found in the Wesleyan teacher at Batimaoli. With these and three other informants available, Russell charged the Buli, Osea and fifteen others with practices similar to luveniwai (the word Tuka not actually occurring in the regulation). They were remanded in custody to allow them to retain a lawyer from Ba. The convictions obtained at the subsequent legal proceedings were quashed by the Supreme Court on technical grounds, but the trials brought further details of Osea's scheme. His house was to be entirely of _vesi_ logs dragged, not carried, from the forest and hoisted into position by block and tackle so that no part would be touched by hands. There were to be no openings apart from two glass doors or windows through which he promised they would be able to see the twin gods when they returned to inaugurate a new era and install Osea himself as ruler of all Fiji. The whites would be their slaves; some would be killed. The church and the government would be driven out. Then all the world would contribute to a vast new house to be built above Batimaoli at Vatukoro, the place where their fathers had massacred a force of Bauans sent in 1868 to avenge the death of the Reverend Thomas Baker in the previous year.[13]

Pending the outcome of the court hearings, Joseva Tube was dismissed as Buli and the _tikina_ of Qaliyalatina was abolished. Joseva, Osea and his followers then converted en masse to Roman Catholicism. If they sensed that the French priest at Ba would be a good advocate, their confidence was shrewdly placed. Père Picherit S.M. immediately began protesting their innocence and loyalty. When Russell reported in December 1914 that he had met with stubborn resistance in Qaliyalatina and urged the deportation of Osea, Joseva and three other ringleaders, Picherit obtained a copy of the letter and vigorously denied the various charges, mentioning in passing that 172 out of the 179 inhabitants of Cuvu, Navala and Batimaoli were devout Catholics. When the Provincial Commissioner had come to inspect their district it was no discourtesy that the villages were nearly empty - they had all been to the opening of a new church at Ba by Bishop Julian Vidal of Suva: 'I must say that in my opinion the danger of opposition to the Government of His Most Gracious Majesty by the natives of this district is imaginary and has no foundation in fact.'[14]

His unction and ignorance of the facts aside, the priest was surely right in questioning the need for the harsh action the government took at Russell's request. Osea was confined to Oneata for ten years, Joseva Tube and three others were confined for five years to parts of Lau and Kadavu. The people petitioned at least three times for their release and Picherit wrote on their behalf again in

1918. Finally their sentences expired in 1920 and a year later Osea also was allowed to return home. If he ever reactivated the Bai Tabua, the government did not get to hear of it. [15]

One other movement at this time deserves brief notice, that of the half-mad Sailosi Nagusolevu alias Ratu, and Aisake Sivo. Sailosi told a meeting of 700-800 Fijians at Tavua on 25 March 1918 that Navosavakadua had gone from Nadarivatu to England to kill Queen Victoria. And now Britain had surrendered to Germany, the Governor was deposed and all the white magistrates were powerless. The Viti Company would take their place. There would be no taxes and no more vakamisioneri collections; as a sign of the new order they should celebrate the sabbath on Saturday. The movement spread rapidly inland down the Sigatoka and the Rewa tributaries. The new sabbath was celebrated in Nadrau and from there two men took it to Nasoqo, Nabobouco, in April. For a short period the people were openly defiant of the orders of the Provincial Commissioner of Colo North. The religion was dubbed 'Number Eight', the last religion to have come to Fiji being Seventh Day Adventism known to Fijians in short form as the 'seventh church', Lotu ikavitu. Sailosi was confined to the asylum before he could get very far and Aisake Sivo exiled to Yanuca for seven years. [16]

The Number Eight movement had some lasting repercussions on the Wesleyan church in a few inland areas. Teachers and church officials who had desecrated the sabbath were publicly humiliated and expelled by meetings of their circuits. The Seventh Day Adventists stepped into the breach. Their Fijian agent, one Pauliasi, toured the interior with the Adventist formula for making Saturday Sunday. He saved the face of the 'Sailosiites' and established the first significant SDA congregations on the Wainibuka, in Nadrau and some towns of Colo East, where they have remained strong ever since.

All was quiet in Colo North until in June 1934 Navosavakadua (died 1897) visited Atekini Ciobale of Nasoqo, and informed him that a council of the spirits chiefs at Bua had decided the time had come to inaugurate the New Era. Navosa's own task was to visit the country of the white man and bring back the Government Offices for their headquarters. Meanwhile would he, Atekini, take charge of the people along with Ameniasi Naqiomila, who was to be the prophet through whom messages would come, and

Kitione Koro who was to be the doctor charged with dispensing the water of life to the faithful.

That at least is the beginning as the District Commissioner of Colo North, Stuart Reay, reconstructed it five months afterwards. On 4 November 1934, one of Reay's trainee clerks at Nadarivatu asked permission to go to Nasiriti, over 20 miles away in Nabobouco. On being pressed for his reason the youth explained that his father had sent for him to drink the water of life. Surely Mr Reay knew that on the 5th, 15th, and 25th of the month people came from far and wide to drink the healing liquid? - and not only to drink it but (according to several informants) to see it change colours. Mr Reay was indeed interested to find that most of his staff had already inbibed but that none cared to share the good news with him. A trusty provincial constable was despatched forthwith to Nasiriti where in a village of five families he counted 321 people - 99 of them from Colo East and 25 from Ra. Buli Nabobouco was there and Buli Muarira from Colo East. A little dispensary had been built, reserved for the good doctor Kitione and his dresser. There were three notices, one saying that those who came from various districts or provinces in Fiji were to bring letters, another forbidding anyone to approach the spring without permission - signed 'Kitione P. Koro the Doctor of Fiji'. The third forbade spitting, smoking and speaking when the medicine was being drunk. The track to the spring had been neatly cut and bordered with shrubs. A sort of outpatients' register had been kept showing that over 9000 people had been treated - although as the clerk was later found to be unable to count past 1099 Reay thought the true number was probably less than 2000. The provincial constable (a chief of Nabutautau) ransacked the Buli's private papers and came back with one curious item, a letter from the Buli to Atekini Ciobale dated 19 April 1934 telling him that he had presided at a ceremony the previous day in memory of the blood that flowed at Vunawi - possibly the spot at Nasoqo where Thurston had flogged Rokoleba, one of Navosavakadua's lieutenants.

Was this another revival of that cult? Reay believed that it was, but he could get none of the above evidence sworn to in court. He obtained convictions on the charge of illegal assembly. It is not impossible that the whole connection with Navosavakadua was fabricated by Reay's private informant - possibly a man from Nasoqo who wanted to discredit Nasiriti, hitherto a very unimportant village compared to its neighbours. The Buli of Nabobuoco himself, when Reay interrogated him on 11 November, was 'obviously in a funk' - there was no doubt that he had had opportunities to report the matter to Reay who was not impressed with his excuse that many women in Nabobouco were childless and that he had wanted to give Kitione a chance to prove himself. For Reay had been with the Buli in Nasoqo on 18 August and the latter had alluded to the talk of a new cure, but not in such a way that Reay would take it seriously. Reay was convinced the Buli was smarting from a public censure the chiefs and Bulis of Colo North had (at Reay's request) delivered in Nasoqo in December 1933. A list of the crimes of Nabobouco had been read out - defiance of orders, wholesale evasion of taxes, provocative behaviour to the people of Nasau tikina, and other offences. It at least seems plausible that they should revive a cult which envisioned the overthrow of the government.[17] What is certain is that the Nasoqo and Nasiriti people have no apologies to make about the water of life. People were still going there to drink it in the 1970s and it was carried to the sick in distant places - a catalogue of cures was available for the asking. All the inquisitive outsider needs to know any further is that the people say prayers before and after drinking it: 'it is God's gift to us.'

These extraordinary events, while confined in the main to the interior of Viti Levu, were symptomatic perhaps of a general weakening of social discipline in the villages and of the inability of the established leaders to do much about it. The greatest threat to the integrity of village life was the number of men and women absent at any one time. Absenteeism was a running sore in Fijian society because it represented the indifference of individuals to the common good and the hallowed demands of traditional cooperation. A man had not been free in former times to come and go at will; nor was he free under the original Native Regulations to leave without permission for longer than sixty days. As the chiefs began to lose their grip on the Fijian Administration at the provincial level to English magistrates, there were frequent complaints from the Bulis of Tailevu, Rewa and Kadavu about their young men:

> They come to Suva and put on no end of 'side' amongst the women and wear collars and ties and smart coats, sport crook walking sticks and turn up in great force at church - the Suva Methodist

> Jubilee Church on Sundays. They all do a minimum
> of work and when any trouble arrives away back
> they go to the Mataqali or the village and so
> make sure of shelter and food.[18]

To avoid prosectuion in the district courts, many returned
home on the fifty-ninth day then left again a few days
later.

After 1912 absenteeism was no longer an offence for
men; only women needed permission of their parents or
guardians to be absent more than sixty days - a provision
very hard to enforce. In the same year a new Fijian
Employment Ordinance abolished the main safeguards of
Thurston's legislation (the Fiji Labour Ordinance of 1895
and the Masters and Servants Ordinance of 1890).
Henceforward any employer could sign on a married man
before any magistrate in the colony who could be satisfied
that the man had 'made provision' for his dependants. If
the recruit had been voluntarily absent from his village
for two years, the employer could sign him on and any
Fijian could renew his contract on expiry so long as the
employer paid his rates and taxes. (Previously an employer
had been obliged to return a man to his village.)

The way was open for recruiters to go into Fijian
villages with heavy bags of 'yagona money'. After the
cancellation of Indian indentures in January 1920, there
was a sudden demand in the sugar industry for Fijian
labour. Fijian indentured men lived under much the same
wretched conditions as had the Indians, but for shorter
periods. They were more tolerant of crowded conditions,
especially if they were without women. CSR paid Fijian
recruiters for each man they produced in Lautoka for
engagement under the Masters and Servants Ordinance (under
which no licences were required for recruiters).[19] The men
were taken without reference to the Buli of the district or
the situation of the village. Communal and family
obligations were easily evaded and at the end of the term
of indenture, usually six months or a year, the men often
returned to their villages penniless. Having planted no
garden, they had no food and depended on the strained
charity of relatives. Some did not return for months if in
lieu of a passage home they were paid a cash sum enabling
them to holiday a while in the village of their choice,
meeting no obligations of any kind. For the first time in
the history of Fiji there were reports of food shortages in
good years, while the villages entered upon a steady

physical decline from the settlements of substantial, high-built heavily thatched houses of old Fiji towards the uninsulated, ill-drained ovens of wood and iron that later decades accepted as normal. By 1927 Islay McOwan, the Secretary for Native Affairs, noting that the government considered 'a supply of labour for agricultural purposes was of greater importance than the welfare of the natives themselves', expressed his fear that the Fijian Administration could collapse.[20]

There were, as explained in Chapter 5, enough continuities in village and district life to prevent total collapse; erosion might be a better word for the effects of the policy the Colonial Office had rather meaninglessly prescribed as 'a careful regulation of the communal system accompanied by a gradual loosening of its bonds'.[21] The term 'communal system' was often used as if there were some entity superimposed and separable from Fijian society which could be modified at any time without drastic modification of the groups - the households, villages and vanua - comprising that society. The semantic comfort of such phrases as 'loosening the bonds' concealed a woolly imprecision, a cliched liberalism of 'certain certainties' about the nature of man and society. One of these certainties in twentieth century colonial Fiji was that any restriction on the personal liberty of Fijians was an 'obstacle' to their becoming 'full British subjects' in the sense that Maoris were understood to be in New Zealand. Fijian society, like all others, had to evolve through a universal sequence of stages towards the superior western model of 'monogamous, individualistic, capitalistic, "democratic" man . . . the culminating product of a natural law of inevitable progress' realized most perfectly to date by the Anglo-Saxons with their civil liberties enshrined in the common law and protected by the franchise. [22]

Theoretically, then, the Fijian Administration and the Native Regulations were regarded as temporary expedients subject to reform and modernization to bring Fijian society 'more into line with the modern world', as it was often put. Yet specific reforms, as it has been seen above in the context of hereditary privilege, had left the regulatory framework for Fijian life largely untouched by retaining the Communal Services Regulation and the program of work. At the same time, however, government condoned male absenteeism as a safety valve, an escape route for individuals.

The chiefs, fully aware of this intolerable dilemma, fought a spasmodic rearguard defence. Without directly challenging the ethos of the day, lest they appear disloyal, the provincial councils and the Council of Chiefs repeatedly urged specific measures to stem absenteeism, increase the control of the Bulis, regulate recruiting activities, and ensure the return of labourers on expiry of their contracts. In 1917 the chiefs urged the government to give Bulis the power to compel men to return home if they were living in European towns and not in regular employment. To this and similar requests the Governor replied that it was not policy to restrict any further the freedom of the individual. Nothing the chiefs could say would be interpreted other than as reactionary conservatism. In 1923 they asked permission to increase provincial rates for men absent from home longer than twelve months (an estimated 15 per cent of taxpayers or 3000 men, of whom 840 were in permanent employment), and repeated their request that no man be indentured without the approval of his Buli. Both resolutions were rejected. An official in the Secretariat added privately: 'I realize that the foundations of the "communal system" are being undermined, gradually but surely. Evolution is the natural and philosophic order of things.'[23]

Perhaps what most exasperated these all-male councils was their powerlessness to control the movement of women. Many women simply ignored the regulations. They drifted into towns, went for rides with Indian taxi drivers, and were sheltered by European and Chinese lovers. Fijian male pride was outraged. In 1926 Ratu Sukuna proposed that the regulations be tightened to compel a woman to obtain the Buli's consent before leaving her tikina for longer than twenty-eight days. He insisted that colonial authorities should defer to Fijian practice rather than more liberated western ideals of womanhood. Fijian women, he argued, had always to be in the power of a husband, parent, or guardian: 'It is undoubtedly a grave question whether the rights of civilised women accustomed to moving in over-populated cities should be allowed to native women brought up in small villages. In Suva and Levuka the experiment is proving fatal.'[24]

The chiefs had their way on some points. After much debate the Native Regulations Board resolved that the sugar mills and larger centres should become 'prohibited areas' to unchaperoned women unless they had a permit from a Buli for stays longer than a month. As this proved ineffective, the period was reduced to a week in 1932, and two days in 1935. But the government rejected a suggestion from Ba Provincial Council in 1925 that women be compelled to weed the villages and similar suggestions from other councils that women be made to do some outside work. Their obligation to feed visitors was considered sufficient. In 1933 the Council of Chiefs wanted a further regulation to prohibit married women leaving their village without permission of their husbands, but here the government finally drew the line: 'the coercion of women is not in accordance with modern principles. A standard of conduct should be enforced by public opinion rather than by Government Regulations.' The chiefs had plainly despaired of public opinion. In 1940 they even requested a regulation to fine a woman 40s for leaving a child under 3 unattended for more than half a day. A year later the Colo East Provincial Council suggested that women remaining in prohibited areas should be whipped.[25]

The missionaries had traditionally relied not only on the chiefs but on the impact of the gospel itself to preserve social discipline. In private correspondence they were often discouraged by the results: 'Thieving abounds and such fornication as would disgrace the beasts of the field', wrote one. 'Never in my life have I seen such an immoral place as this', wrote the Reverend W. Brown from Lakeba in 1913, 'and the people do not seem to care.' Fourteen years of preaching later, the Reverend A.G. Adamson wrote from the same island: 'There seems to be very little love or anything lovely in them. It makes my heart very sad when I think that the lotu had been here for nearly 100 years and yet it's mostly just on the surface.'[26] The chairman of the Methodist mission, the Reverend A.J. Small, used to urge his brethren not to flag: 'The cure is - religion at white heat, clothes, and the safeguards that surround the well-ordered European Christian house.' Calling for 'a deeper spiritual life in the hearts of our members', he lamented that first there had to be 'produced in them a keener sense of the exceeding sinfulness of sin'.[27]

By the end of the 1920s Methodist missionaries sensed that while their circuit organization had long been interlocked with the structures of district life to become an integral part of Fijian community life - and as such was not under threat - yet the church was losing control over personal behaviour and forms of social life. Choir practices (<u>vuli sere</u>) for instance, were fun, a good excuse

for a <u>Yaqona</u> party and one of the best places to arrange a
rendezvous with the opposite sex. In early 1925 a simple
dance that began as a game taught to boys and girls in
Nadroga, the <u>taralala,</u> spread like an epidemic to the
farthest parts of the group. The <u>taralala</u> brought the
sexes together for the first time in a vibrating throng, an
unprecedented liberation from the strictures of both
ancient etiquette and evangelical wowserism. The Reverend
Harold Chambers came back to his station at Niusawa on
Taveuni one day in 1933 and was horrified to hear a great
stamping and shouting and whooping from his schoolchildren.
There he found

> two big girls from Welagi Koro . . . wriggling,
> and twisting their bodies in sinuous movements,
> and shaking themselves in such a way, as to cause
> their breasts to shake from side to side and up
> and down, before the crowd of goggling boys and
> in the midst was the teacher . . . I was
> staggered and hurt beyond words . . . sailed into
> the lot, boys and girls with my qanuya cane, and
> whacked them right and left . . . expelled all
> Welagi girls over 10.[28]

The <u>taralala</u> was a poison infecting Fijian moral life, the
Catholic and Methodist missionaries agreed, and they urged
government officers to help them stamp it out.

The District Commissioners, asked their opinions in
1931, generally agreed that the <u>taralala</u> was harmless in
itself but often led to 'immoralities'. These they were
urged to try and prevent. The missionaries knew of more
than one case, though, where a DC thought it the best thing
that had happened to the villages in years and actively
encouraged the dancing to enliven the dreary round of his
village inspections. The children's teacher in Nadroga had
innocently created a minor revolution in social mores. The
European missionaries could denounce it from the pulpits,
but they put their canes away when they saw that the chiefs
and people would adopt whatever music and customs they
enjoyed.

A century of contact with Europeans, reported Ratu
Sukuna from Lau, had long established new tastes - 'for
clothes and corned beef, for cereals and finery, for tin
and iron roofing'. Even so, with the exception of 'clothes
as the symbol of Christianity and light as the effulgence
of Divine Grace', these articles of the whiteman's trade

were 'still regarded as luxuries'. Not that their absence
would go unmourned. The year 1932 was a good one for Lau.
Crops were prolific, bananas went to waste, fish and
turtles were plentiful, there were no hurricanes or storms
- 'all the conditions, in fact, that only twenty or thirty
years ago would have made the period a memorable one. The
attitude now is the reverse!' And the reason was that copra
prices were fast falling on the depressed world market:
the Lauans had less money to spend on non-essentials and
had come to think of their agricultural existence as
impoverished.[29]

Children were staying long enough in school - financed
largely by their own parents - for Fijian leaders to speak
of a rising generation who were having difficulty settling
back into village life:

> As a body they look down on productive labour
> connected with the soil. The curse that was upon
> Adam they mean to avoid. Their reasoning is
> based on experience. Looking round they see, on
> the one side, men of education clean and
> well-dressed - appearances they have been taught
> to respect - filling all the lucrative posts; on
> the other, the simple folk dirty and untidy -
> shortcomings for which they have been whipped -
> tilling the ground. They conclude that education
> (in the only form known to them) is a panacea for
> all human needs, providing for those who partake
> of it clean and well paid jobs.[30]

Young Fijians had come to associate the immaculate
white flannels of magistrates and District Commissioners
with the prestige and power of western civilization. They
looked with envy on those few of their number whose
everyday dress was the villager's Sunday best, men whose
hands were rarely to be seen grubbing out a yam or tying
thatch. These were the ordained native ministers, the
assistant masters of the better schools, the native
magistrates, scribes, medical practitioners, clerks in the
government offices in Suva and employees of the merchant
houses - not exactly a middle class yet, nor by any means
cut off from their village families, but certainly more
oriented to the status-world of the Europeans, and more
receptive to the appeal of individualism.

For the colonial system in Fiji as everywhere offered
limited but still attractive new avenues for individual
ambition. While the neotraditional status system continued
to flourish, it has been seen, some individuals needed it
less than others: they shifted ground away from the
village and the assemblies of the land to cut a name for
themselves in the church, the regular civil service, and
the business houses. While they did not move completely
from one life to another, they were certainly learning to
be part-time operators in a world where the idiom was not
that of custom. And it was a world where they could begin
to measure themselves by European standards of comfort,
expertise or power - and feel disadvantaged. For the
fifth-class clerk on £50 a year, for the Morris Hedstrom's
messenger boy, or the assistant master at the Queen
Victoria School, it was not generally pleasant to be on the
bottom rung, however great the pride of the wife or mother
who pressed the crisp white collar.

Not surprisingly the Wesleyan church was the first
institution to feel the push of upward mobility: indeed
European ministers were shocked by the force with which the
Native Ministers, almost from the beginning, resolved to
improve their position. Me da dua vata, 'let us be one',
was their platform by the late nineteenth century. With
apt appeal to the Johannine text of Christ's prayer for
unity amongst his disciples, the Fijian divines urged that
unity was better expressed in social equality immediately
than pious acknowledgments that all would be judged equally
on the Last Day. 'They object to be told to wait on the
verandah while we go to our meals', complained the Reverend
C.O. Lelean to the mission chairman in 1904; the Fijians
felt they should eat with their European colleagues at the
same table and not have to endure what Lelean himself
described as 'the many little ways we treat them as
inferiors' - such as providing tin mugs for Fijians and
glassware for whites. The missionary thought it outrageous
that Fijians should notice and comment so accurately on the
petty hallmarks of white prestige. If a delegation came to
him, he said, he would single out for ridicule one he had
'seen that very week spitting on the floor', and then tell
the group 'they must trust to us to decide as to when and
how improvement in their position was to take place'.[31] The
chairman of the mission was equally scathing:

> Me da dua vata. And now from Ba comes a lengthy
> document in which the Native Ministers put forth
> the modest request to be dua vata, i.e., on an

equality with the missionaries - sit on their chairs, eat at their tables, live in fine houses, draw more salary, have their travelling expenses paid. They also read a lecture to the missionaries on the way they should conduct themselves to the chiefs. With all seriousness they state that the adoption of these suggestions would tend to the promotion of the work of God![32]

The European missionaries particularly feared Fijian control of mission finances. 'The majority of Native Ministers', pleaded the chairman in 1923,

do NOT desire that they should be left to the tender mercies of their chiefs in regard to their stipends. Central [European] control is to them sure control . . . And you must take the NATIVE MIND into consideration when attempting to put responsibility on him. You cannot give him responsibility if he does not want it and refuses to accept it . . . The Fijian has all that he desires in the way of responsibility at the present time. [33]

A decade later, shortly after retrenchments of Europeans had finally forced the appointment of the first Fijian to be given charge of a whole circuit (in Bua), the Reverend Harold Chambers spoke for many when he warned, 'I am not convinced that the Fijian conscience has been sufficiently educated, as yet, to the absolute sacredness of a financial trust.' There was something in that, perhaps, though a greater problem was that most of the Australian ministers uncritically identified with establishment views. Just as the Indian indenture system was long condoned, so the Fijians were seen as perpetually in a state of transition: 'They will not be ready for [responsibility] 50 years yet. They must walk first, then increase their pace.'[34]

The Roman Catholic mission was profoundly committed to 'progressive' education in its school system but not within its own institutions. Whereas the Wesleyans had ordained forty teachers by 1870 and had sent many to evangelize the Solomons and New Guinea, Fijian participation in the Catholic endeavour was long limited to local catechetical work or to membership of a body founded by Bishop Vidal in 1891, 'Les Petits Frères Indigènes' and a similar religious association for women. Little Brothers and Little Sisters were given no liturgical or preaching responsibilities or any area of real initiative. They took vows of poverty, chastity and obedience to their (white) superiors under whom they lived in community - never in the villages. Until the 1960s the duties of Fijian religious seem to have been to assist in the schools and to cook, wash, and garden for the priests and nuns. In 1922 Bishop Nicholas noted that over forty Little Brothers had taken vows and that some fifteen of them had died 'de la façon la plus édifiante'.[35] Edifying in death, perhaps, but no foundation for a truly Fijian church. The general problem of Fijian educational levels, a colonialist scepticism amongst the European clergy that they could ever be replaced, and the awesome obligation of priestly celibacy, to which a dozen or more were called but few chosen, kept the church massively dependent on expatriate staff. (In 1974 over 300 Europeans were listed in the Catholic Directory.)

Outside the churches and the Fijian Administration there was only one body of educated Fijians seeking a distinct voice in colonial affairs - the Viti Cauravou, or Young Fiji Society. R.A. Derrick, influential headmaster of the Davuilevu Technical School, sponsored an old boys' society in 1922. It expanded rapidly to include any educated Fijian engaged in 'some useful, productive work as opposed to tiko wale ga [bumming around]' and was committed to broadly progressive goals.[36] Government cautiously recognized in the society 'the articulate expression of this vague groping of the younger generation towards a new social system'[37] - most evident in their trenchant criticism of the institutional constraints on individual initiative: 'It is very difficult', one of their leaders wrote, 'for the men to be free and to decide their own work to gain prosperity and wealth.'[38] Apolosi had been eloquent on the same theme for over twenty years but these elegant men were too respectable to acknowledge any debt to the man from Ra.

Viti Cauravou conferences provided an orderly but freer vehicle of Fijian opinions than the decorous provincial councils and Council of Chiefs. When the Secretary for Native Affairs, Islay McOwan, agreed to open the 1927 conference, the movement gained a formal measure of respectability and a limited right of dialogue with government. Until World War II, resolutions were forwarded to McOwan's office for comments and replies. At its peak in the mid 1930s it claimed 4000 members.[39]

In 1930 the <u>Viti Cauravou</u> sounded a more discordant
note when it presented the Governor with a petition with
5858 signatures for laws to preserve racial purity. 'Many
of our women have children by non-natives', the document
read, 'and the Chinese are the worst offenders.' As a body
they were fiercely nationalistic and not at all
conciliatory to the rights and needs of the Indian
community: 'It is our desire to remain united with the
Europeans but not with the Indians.'[40] Similarly on
questions of land rights they were generally opposed to the
considerable concessions Fijian leaders and colonial
authorities had already made in a partial effort to come to
grips with the overwhelming demographic fact of the 1930s:
the youthful Indian population, 85,000 in 1936, was only
12,000 fewer than the Fijian and soon to become a majority.
On the Indian question the <u>Viti Cauravou</u> was solidly in
accord with the traditional Fijian view that the colonial
government had created the problem to meet European
economic needs and now had to manage it in such a way that
Fijian interests would always be paramount.

Chapter 8

Compromise for a multiracial society

Prior to the 1930s Fijians had not felt unduly threatened by the presence of Indians and had been content, by and large, to leave the details of their separate management to the colonial government and the sugar industry.

From 1887, when the first indentures were expiring, until about 1910, Fijian owners were tolerant and accommodating to individual Indians who preferred to fend for themselves rather than live in the official Indian segregated settlements (on blocks of Fijian land leased for the purpose by the government or on Crown land). Ignoring government regulations altogether, it seems that Indians were able to come to free-and-easy deals directly with the owners. 'Considerable irregularity prevails', noted W.L. Allardyce in 1889, 'as natives are seldom loath to give any one a piece of land to live on for a small pecuniary consideration on a verbal understanding between lessor and lessee.'[1] The regulations required that applications had to be approved by the tikina council and forwarded through the Roko to the Governor-in-Council. In 1909 it was reported from Labasa that Indians blithely disregarded the proper channels, bribed the owners directly and settled for all kinds of loose arrangements.[2] A mutual contempt for time-consuming legal processes was a constant feature of Fijian-Indian land transactions.

One can only speculate what might have emerged had Fijians and Indians been allowed to devise their own solutions to the land problem and more Indians been allowed to scatter throughout the group and attach themselves to the edges of village society. Children would have mixed freely and easily; schools, churches and even families might have taken them in, as happened to an unknown number of part-Fijian descendants of the 'Polynesian' labourers (mainly New Hebrideans and Solomon Islanders recruited from the 1860s until 1912). It is inconceivable that racial lines would have been so sharply drawn in later decades had not the government been dedicated to keeping the communities institutionally and physically separate.

From 1910 government decided to enforce the concentration of Indians in the sugar provinces of Viti Levu and Vanua Levu and close off the outer islands and other areas of Fijian population by the simple device of refusing leases to new applicants lest they 'scatter themselves indiscriminately through the colony'.[3] Absolutely no thought was given to developing multiracial institutions of local government in the rural areas, nor to extending the jurisdiction of Fijian authorities over Indian settlements, nor to giving Indians a place in Fijian councils at any level. Where Fijians and Indians were neighbours in closely settled parts such as Navua and Ba, the hospitable inclinations of each community received no encouragement, despite the fluency some Indians acquired in Fijian and the willingness of many Fijians to learn some Hindustani pleasantries and even join in Indian festivals or sporting events. Individuals might share a bowl of 'grog' (yaqona) on occasion, borrow tools, barter foodstuffs or chat at the markets, but there was almost no intermarriage, and Indian children were not admitted to Fijian schools. Each community, then, adjusted to a pattern of quite cordial but reserved relationships neither seeking nor being educated into truly common bonds of citizenship.[4]

Both communities were preoccupied less with each other than with the hard-line dominance of Europeans in every position of economic and political power at national level. Fijian chiefs were apprehensive during World War I that government seemed set on abolishing the Native Department as a separate identity. Three senior Rokos appealed to the Governor in 1915 to try and understand how much the old system meant to them. If destroyed, they said, 'it is plain to us that we Fijians will never be known again'.[5] For there would be no section of government exclusively dealing with Fijian affairs and safeguarding Fijian rights, no Talai whom the chiefs and humblest villagers could approach personally on matters great or trivial and through him gain the ear of the Supreme Chief.

These fears were realized in 1921 when the Native Secretariat was fully merged into the Colonial Secretary's office and the Talai's position given to an Under-Secretary. In place of the official to whose Suva quarters Fijians had always been able to go in the assurance of a courteous hearing and a lively understanding of their affairs, they were referred back to the provincial headquarters of the overworked and usually inexperienced District Commissioners. Having the agency of every government department in addition to their magisterial rounds of the whole population, the DCs had little time to

attend to Fijian affairs even if they had the inclination.
Nor were they bound by any clearer Fijian policy than the
ad hoc decisions of the Colonial Secretary.

These detrimental changes coincided with the first
serious challenge to the European establishment from the
Indians. After World War I the Indians were suffering
acutely from sharp increases in the cost of imported
staples with no redress from increased wages. They were
often poorly nourished and riddled with parasitic
infections such as hookworm. Labourers in the Suva-Nausori
area, forced to the barest level of subsistence, were
encouraged by the cancellation of all indentures on 1
January 1920 and the removal of the penal sanctions which
had kept the majority of Indians disorganized and depressed
since their first arrival in 1879. On 15 January 1920
Indian labourers of the Public Works Department began a
strike that the panicky authorities regarded as having all
the potential of a race war. And in truth it was the
beginning of a long overdue struggle by Fiji's 60,000
Indians to gain an equal position of dignity and power in
the colony. Australia cheerfully sent a warship, New
Zealand sent sixty troops and Lewis guns, all Suva's
Europeans were under arms and a few hundred Fijian
auxiliaries patrolled the streets while the Indians had
angry meetings, wrote letters and sent a deputation to
Government House headed by a housewife. Some ugly
confrontations took place but the strikers were armed only
with sticks and stones when the police finally fired into a
crowd on 12 February and killed a man and wounded
several.[6] The strike collapsed, but the Indian blood on
the road at Samabula left a stain of insecurity and fear
for decades.

The following year saw a six months' strike in the
main sugar areas of Viti Levu. When the trouble began on
the Ba estates in February 1921, CSR was left without any
household or plantation labour. Hundreds of Indians moved
into Fijian towns and were sympathetically received,
especially in Sigatoka where some Fijians employed by the
Company also left work. The French missionary at Ba
reported to his Bishop that the Indians canvassed Fijian
villages for support and that many Fijians attended Indian
political meetings: 'they understand the Indians pretty
fairly'.[7] 'We white people recognized the peril', recalled
the Reverend Stanley Jarvis a year later, and he and two of
his Methodist colleagues, Wesley Amos and J.F. Long,
stomped the countryside to persuade Fijians 'not to get

entangled with the Indians and their lawlessness'. The ministers, with the support of the Provincial Commissioner of Ba, H.C. Monckton, arranged for Fijians to evict their Indian guests and feed the Company livestock instead, or weed the railway lines. Hundreds of Fijians left their villages to live in the old 'coolie' lines for 2s 6d a day and food. Jarvis was known as 'the CSR Chaplain' for his work; when the strike was broken the Company celebrated with a dinner in his honour and a gift of £100. The Manager at Ba presented engraved walking sticks to Tui Ba, Tui Nadi and a chief from Nadroga for their 'loyal support in the time of stress'.[8]

An equally grateful government reassessed the importance of Fijian political support and reaffirmed its commitment to the paramountcy of Fijian interests. The Colonial Secretariat repented of the sorry state of the Fijian Administration. The chiefs now saw their opportunity to mend some fences and regain some of the influence they had recently lost. In a letter almost certainly drafted by Ratu Sukuna, three of the chiefs protested against the control of Fijian affairs by Europeans and the abolition of the Native Secretariat as a separate department.[9] Later they expanded their case at a informal meeting with Ratu Sukuna and two officials of the Colonial Secretariat. They deplored the complete lack of coordination of Fijian policy and practice and defended the concept of a native department as a representative institution, a powerful and hitherto successful advocate of the 'special conditions' for Fijian participation in the life of the colony - conditions which had protected their autonomy and dignity in the past and would alone guarantee their future. As an example of the low priority they felt Fijian affairs were allocated in the new order, Ratu Pope Seniloli of Bau complained of young DCs who demanded full customary honours (veiqaravi vakaturaga) that Fijians wanted to reserve for high chiefs and direct emissaries from Valelevu, the house of the Supreme Chief. And few DCs who received the honours understood their significance or responded with the courtesy and warmth expected of a chiefly recipient. For the people the ceremonies were becoming a degrading routine of cold and cynical gestures. It was the same with the feasts and mekes that the DCs, harbingers of the promoters of tourism, demanded that the people put on for their private visitors. Yet if a chief was visiting the province and paid his respects to the Provincial Commissioner in lieu of a Roko, he was not accorded like hospitality or facilities.[10]

So seriously did the chiefs fear a declining voice in colonial affairs that Ratu Rabici made a rare Fijian intervention in the Legislative Council to ask in December 1923 that a Talai be appointed and his salary paid from Fijian funds. In reply the Colonial Secretary admitted that Fijian affairs were beyond him. For a start he knew no Fijian. His principal assistant, D.R. Stewart, then spoke:

> As the so-called supervisor of native affairs I more or less resemble the head of a turtle which, decapitated from the body, continues to look as if it is alive. It is dead, but its eyes continue to wink, and winking at things is not much use. The body of the turtle . . . is gradually decomposing'. [11]

The celebration for the Golden Jubilee of Cession at Levuka in 1924 gave the chiefs an opportunity to appeal yet again 'to see firmly established the principle of government in accordance with the customs of the land'. [12] They felt that the partnership established by Gordon and Thurston had been betrayed to some extent; the promises made at Cession were not being honoured. Their request for a Talai was renewed in 1925 and met the approval of the new Governor, Sir Eyre Hutson. [13] Islay McOwan was appointed Secretary for Native Affairs in 1926, but it was to be twenty years before the Rokos were relieved of close supervision by District Commissioners through whom all correspondence had to pass. In 1930 only four provinces - Cakaudrove, Ra, Macuata and Kadavu - enjoyed full control of Fijian affairs in Fijian hands, but the force of traditional chiefly leadership survived in the large number of Rokos or Native Assistants who were hereditary chiefs in the provinces to which they were appointed. It was demonstrated above in the career of Ratu Aseri Latianara (Chapter 4) how very useful these appointments remained in the pursuit of purely local political ambitions.

Similarly it was general policy to show a certain leniency towards chiefs who misappropriated provincial funds, as seen in the case of Ratu Pope Seniloli, Roko Tui of Tailevu from 1920. A great sportsman and fond of the good life, Ratu Pope entertained Fijian and European visitors to Bau on a scale commensurate with his dignity as Vunivalu of Bau but not with his official salary. In 1922 he began to draw occasionally on provincial funds, confident that his people would be understanding if he got into difficulties. As he told it:

> Well months went by and one day a chap from the Government came in a launch - rather a blighter, I thought. We had a spot of whisky and a cigar, and he said: 'Ratu, the tide's turning and I must be pushing on. I've called, you know, to take back that tax money.' I said, 'I'm rather afraid, old boy, that I can't lay my hands on it now.' He seemed a bit miffed . . . [14]

An audit revealed a deficit of £764 16s 8d. Ratu Pope made no excuses other than his heavy commitments. On 7 February 1924 the Governor cabled the Secretary of State: 'In view of high chiefly position and for political reasons do not recommend criminal proceedings. Case can scarcely be viewed in light of European ethics . . .' With London's approval the popular chief was dismissed as Roko Tui, asked to resign his seat in the Legislative Council, but not charged. Even so the Bulis and chiefs of Tailevu, assembled in provincial council, received the Governor's decision coldly and declined to acclaim it in the customary way. Later they had to apologise (soro) to the Governor at Government House. The high chiefs, most of them connected with Bau by marriage, were unanimous that Ratu Pope should be reinstated, and they petitioned for his pardon on several occasions. Meanwhile Ratu Pope himself began repaying his debt and was finally reinstated on probation as Native Assistant in 1928. [15]

In the late 1920s, then, Fijians still had a half-hearted endorsement from the colonial government of their preference for separate institutions, nor were further attacks made on their land rights. Ratu Sukuna's Native Lands Commission made steady progress towards clarifying and registering customary titles under colonial law - the failure of im Thurn's reformation and Colonial Office instructions had left the government with no other choice.[16] Some finality in communal titles was the prerequisite for rural peace, the security of the Fijian estate, and smooth leasing arrangements for non-Fijians.

The Native Lands Commission had a formidable task, for customary tenure had always been flexible, which is not to say confused: chaos lay more in the outsider's mind unable to fathom the subtle principles and historic precedents

which Fijian community leaders would bring to bear on any
decision about a piece of land, especially non-planting
land where rights were vague or subsidiary. There was much
room for political manoeuvres and ad hoc compromise;
occasionally disputes simmered for years. The changing
needs of households (as some groups increased and others
decreased), the location of a new road, or a decision to
invest in a commercial crop such as bananas, still more the
enforced move of a village to a healthier site, were the
kind of changes which led to the reallocation of land
resources. In any case as David Wilkinson once put it, 'A
Fijian has an innate objection to finality in land
questions'. [17]

Ratu Sukuna's land hearings were formal but not
awe-inspiring: at times he had to invoke legal sanctions
to achieve due decorum. His objective was to achieve
settlements that had the approval of most landowners and
gave equitable shares to minority groups such as the
refugees of former wars. Sessions were generally attended
by a large, keenly aware audience from surrounding
districts who could intervene if their own rights were
threatened. When the final classifications and boundaries
were promulgated, it was then up to the community itself as
to how far or in what respects the official version of
their society displaced the pre-existing social
organization. To the confusion of some anthropologists and
later generations of the people themselves, the one
interacted with the other. Decisions on the use of land
may have continued at one level to be made in the old way,
but then if a dispute came to litigation, the official
records were there to achieve a finality of decision not
previously available.

From the few appeals made against his decisions, it is
interesting to see how carefully the Oxford-trained chief
applied the criteria of both equity and custom to oral
evidence. He was prepared on occasion to ignore the
arrangements put up by the people and impose his own. In
one case he set aside the classificatory statements of both
parties: 'for we conceive it a higher duty to make a
reasonable settlement of your lands than to accept any
division agreed to by you which is obviously
inequitable'. [18] In another from the chiefly family of
Cakaudrove, Ratu Sukuna rejected in summary fashion an
attempt by the highest chief to enlarge his personal
holding at the expense of the other members of the chiefly
mataqali. For both custom and equity required that the

chief who already owned 1500 acres should not receive any part of the 1000 acres shared by the other 180 members of his mataqali.[19] In the same province Ratu Sukuna took the unusual step of reopening the inquiry into the lands at Vuna when it came to his notice that the chiefly mataqali had wronged the subordinate mataqali - whose lands the chiefs had sold before Cession - by not mentioning to the Commissioners that the subordinate mataqali had been given compensatory planting rights on the chief's land. Ratu Sukuna registered these rights as encumbrances on the title. In a most revealing statement, he remarked that the Vuna people being

> courteous and courtly in the presence of their chief would not consider it proper to press their claims . . . Though there is an estoppel I am of the opinion that the equity must from the administrative side be more seriously considered. Surely the Commission is not a court: so that in dealing with natives reason weighs more than legal technicalities.[20]

Ratu Sukuna's work was well done, in the Fijian view. There seems no reason to doubt his own reported statement that there would have been few or no appeals at all had he not always suggested appeal if there was any dissatisfaction.[21] Most appeals were more a record of disappointment than a serious attempt to reverse decisions. Ratu Sukuna believed that the critics of the NLC would be hard pressed to find any lasting sense of grievance against its decisions - which was just as well, because as one Governor noted, there was no one else qualified to review the evidence.[22]

Satisfaction may have been real at the time - if there were grievances they were kept 'in the family' and did not embroil the Administration. But there was no guarantee that the heirs to the parties who made certain deals at the time of the NLC - e.g. that the chiefly title would alternate between two lineages - would endorse the decisions of their fathers. Thus the original legal settlement could itself become a source of dispute in later years.

The inability of colonial law to sustain the whole range of subsidiary rights still recognized at custom (e.g. those acquired by new periods of long co-residence) meant

some loss in the ability of the community to meet future
needs, especially those created by new arrivals. The
migratory habits of Fijians hardly ceased at Cession. When
the legal penalty for absenteeism was abolished in 1912, it
was again easy for a Fijian to exploit a political and
social relationship and move to another district or
province. Wherever the NLC had held its hearings, there
was no longer any way the outsider could acquire
proprietary rights except to lease from the true owners or
live on sufferance as a second-class vulagi, newcomer. (By
independence one-third to one-half of Fijians lived away
from their own lands.) Another loss of flexibility was that
the official lists of descent groups overlooked the
household as a real unit of society and did not allow for
the ongoing process of de facto segmentation and
amalgamation as kinship groups increased or decreased.
Inequalities of distribution were bound to increase with
time, for official lists of mataqali could not accommodate
the inherent fluidity of Fijian kinship structure. Not
that these kinds of academic observations are of much point
unless a practical way can be suggested for achieving a
periodic redistribution of land resources while maintaining
the finality and clear procedures that would seem
indispensable for preserving peace.

In later years the security of inalienable and
meticulously recorded Fijian land rights, the envy of other
Pacific peoples, was to become a tremendous problem for
land-seeking Indians. It has often been said in Indian
circles that Fijians seemed determined to deny an economic
future on the land for Indians and others even when the
owners themselves were unwilling or unable to bring their
lands into full production. The same complaint was
standard earlier in the century in local European political
comment, but it was poorly based. After the land sales of
1905-08, Europeans already had freehold title to 393,000
acres and in 1911 some of the best of these lands -
including prime river flats on the Dreketi and Sigatoka
Rivers - were lying idle. Add to this 320,000 acres of
Fijian land held by the government for leasing and it is
hard to credit the propaganda of the Planters Association
that the Fijian land monopoly was the main reason the
colony was slow to progress. [23] Yet the elected members of
the Legislative Council were constantly urging, in the
words of one, that 'the native owners should not be allowed
to defeat the best interests of the community and
themselves owing to mental inability . . . tradition,
superstition or sentiment'. [24]

Many government officers were in quiet agreement. After five years in Lau a magistrate wrote in 1914 that it was 'a most retarding influence on its development that most of the coconut land is tied up in the hands of idle natives, who will not lease it and will not use it themselves'. He estimated that where the Fijians were earning about £40,000 a year from their nuts, Europeans on the same lands would make £400,000, 'and one of the biggest assets of the Colony would not be lost'.[25] The notion that Fijian land was an asset of the colony, of the whole multiracial community, an asset wasted in the hands of the idle natives, underlay most of the non-Fijian political rhetoric or administrative comment on Fijian lands in the colonial period. The implicit invocation of the higher law that the earth belongs to all was not without effect, it will be seen, on the Fijians themselves.

Im Thurn's successor, Sir F. Henry May, was allowed to resume efforts to persuade the people that they should surrender voluntarily the control of surplus lands on equitable terms. 'No wise landlord', May lectured the Council of Chiefs in 1911, 'lets good agricultural land lie idle and unproductive', especially if there were tenants offering 'good hard gold' as rent. Six provinces (Tailevu, Cakaudrove, Ra, Rewa, Colo North and Colo East) admitted to having more lands they could lease. The chiefs resolved to hand over to the government the control of unused lands and lands under lease when such leases expired - the government to fix the terms of the leases as it saw fit. 'It is our wish that all future applications . . . be made direct to the Government. We fully trust the Government will safeguard our interests in dealing with our lands.' It was also agreed that the government deduct 5 per cent of rents by way of agency fees - increased to 10 per cent in 1912.[26]

It was soon revealed that the Fijian interpretation of 'waste and unused' and that of the government were widely divergent. Land was used in Fijian eyes if it yielded the occasional wild yam for the pot or timber for a house. Practically no good land was handed over in the desirable areas. The government decreed that from 1 January 1916 no further leasing of Fijian land would be allowed unless it had first been handed over to government control. Fijians were thus asked to forgo valuable rights without compensation, and not surprisingly there was some opposition from those who saw what was happening. Apolosi's friend Ro Tuisawau of Rewa and others protested that the disposal of their lands was their 'prerogative and

that of our descendants until the end of the world'.[27] Then
in 1916 the government legislated a new deal for the Indian
and other tenants of Fijian lands. If the owners refused
to hand over their leases to the government, the lessee
desiring an extension could demand compensation to the
value of his permanent and unexhausted improvements to the
land. The government hoped to prevent Fijians ejecting a
lessee unfairly - often at the instance of another Indian
coveting the lease and offering a bigger bribe. All
transactions in Fijian land were declared invalid unless
approved in writing by the Governor-in-Council.[28]

Opposition to government control was strongest in Ba
where many villages were short of land for their own needs.
A letter signed by 242 men of the Bulu and Nailaga
districts put their objection none too politely: 'If we
were to approve, what would happen to us in the future?
Where would we live? Or are our wives and children to live
in caves with the goats?'[29] Lease applications had
previously been regarded by Fijians as heaven-sent
opportunities for easy spoil. Unfortunately, in the
absence of complete surveys it was often still necessary
under the new system for an applicant to describe the
boundaries with the help of the owners; there was no way
government could prevent Indians from offering
'inducements' to Fijian owners to surrender their land in
the first place. The owners could adjust the amount to
compensate for the anticipated rent (decided by the
government). This 'undoubted burlesque' of the regulations
was not calculated to appeal to the Indian applicants the
government was trying to help.[30]

On the other hand it would be difficult to prove that
the surrender of control to the government or the
availability of land on easy terms led to the energetic
development of the colony. There was some consternation at
the Council of Chiefs in 1920 as to what the government
really desired in regard to unused lands. Ratu Pope
Seniloli even had a motion passed that the government
should 'bring from England men to occupy our lands and to
develop them and so to assist in the prosperity of the
natives'.[31] If Fiji offered such potential, why had the
settlers not come? And the government had disappointed
Fijians in its agency role. In the early 1920s rents were
tremendously in arrears. In 1923 outstanding rents in Nadi
were £3691 of the total rent roll of £5442. In Suva
arrears were about 65 per cent. Rents in Tailevu were in
some cases unpaid for seven or eight years. Landowners

were kept waiting for days at the offices of the Provincial Commissioners only to come away with nothing. [32]

If Fijians had reason to be disillusioned, the European colonists were still far from satisfied. In a memorandum to the Secretary of State in 1924, Sir Maynard Hedstrom acknowledged the difficulty of securing markets for crops - Australia had closed its door to Fijian bananas, for instance - but there were encouraging prospects for dairying, cotton and pineapple, he argued, which made it desirable that the Colonial Office reconsider its policy and allow native lands to be made more easily available for settlement. The Fijians were 'a primitive and underdeveloped people' who should not be allowed 'through caprice or through lack of knowledge, to hinder and obstruct the natural development of the Colony'. [33]

In the absence of Sir Cecil Rodwell, who agreed with Hedstrom, the Acting Governor, T.E. Fell, refuted the charge of Fijian obstructionism, citing the example of the Ra people who had surrendered 76,000 acres during the previous six years - the Tova Estate - while the Provincial Councils of Macuata, Cakaudrove and Bua in 1923 had reiterated their willingness to hand over surplus lands. Finally Fell predicted that a time would come when Fijians themselves would be able to develop their lands commercially: 'future generations may have surprises in store'. [34]

About 1930, when a large number of Indian sugar leases were up for renewal, some Fijians in those provinces expressed interest in working the land themselves. Landowners began to query the wisdom of surrendering, say, 10 acres of mataqali land for £5 a year and watching a single tenant make £150 from his lease. Although few Fijians were in a position to redeem their lands and compensate the tenants, the Indians were made uneasy by extremist propaganda and the atmosphere of resentment. Representatives of Indian planters were able to cite instances where some of their fellows had been made homeless by eviction. They pressed for longer leases of up to ninety-nine years arguing that they had severed their connection from India in every way and had made Fiji their permanent home. [35]

In 1930 the Council of Chiefs approved the principle of longer leases to Indians if Fijian needs were safeguarded, and in 1933 new leasing regulations increased the usual lease period from twenty-one to thirty years with provision for ninety-nine years in special cases - a loophole for Europeans with the right connections. The Provincial Commissioners had already been instructed to ensure that adequate planting lands were available to a village by demarcating non-leasable reserves. In memoranda to the government, CSR (sole sugar miller after 1926) said it was deeply concerned by the reluctance of Fijians to renew leases and the insecurity of its 4000 Indian sub-tenants on some 50,000 acres of Fijian land. The success of the Company's small-farm scheme, which had transformed the sugar industry since the end of indenture in 1920 and provided thousands of Indian families with a modest income, could be jeopardized by any suspension of Fijian goodwill. Half the industry was at stake. Although the Council of Chiefs was prevailed upon to approve legislation compelling Fijians reoccupying land to keep it under efficient cultivation or have it leased again, CSR argued that the measure was not sufficient: continuity of cultivation was still broken. In their opinion no successful Indian cane farmer should be refused renewal. The company despaired of ever being able to rely on Fijians for a regular cane supply as it had in Thurston's day. [36]

Fijian refusals to renew leases were most frequent in the Nausori area where 90 per cent of the mill's requirements were supplied by some 2000 small growers. Of thirty-four renewal applications in 1932, sixteen were refused, the Fijians usually stating that they wanted to plant the land themselves. In most cases the Fijians re-employed Indians to do all their work, and signed promissory notes to be honoured by the sale of the crops.[37]

On the western side there was much less trouble with the renewal of leases - 'no trouble at all' in Lautoka during 1935, reported the District Commissioner: 'Only one renewal was refused . . . and the Indian lessee had two other leases.'[38] In 1936 only four renewals were refused and again in 1938 the Fijians were adjudged most reasonable. The situation varied from year to year, from province to province, and prior to 1937 accurate statistics of Fijian refusals to lease were not kept. The problem was certainly not acute. [39]

Nevertheless CSR continued to press for absolute security for the tenants of Fijian lands against the threat of the owners resuming control and reducing or abandoning cane production. Reading the signs of the times, Ratu

Sukuna took it on himself to persuade the 1936 Council of Chiefs to make further concessions. In a speech lasting over an hour the emergent statesman reviewed the history of Fijian lands since Cession and paid tribute to the disinterestedness of the British government. Fijians were now faced with a new situation, he said, where they had to accept that they owed a moral obligation to the state to use their land. They all knew the parable of the talents. Did they also know that in other countries governments used death duties and taxes to redistribute the land more equitably? Better for the chiefs to propose their own scheme for the productive use of land than have forced on them something less congenial. The current system of leasing was wasteful - only the eyes of the land were taken - and corrupt:

> We can, surely, come to no other decision but to abolish a system that is capable of producing so much evil . . . gradually destroying our sense of purity and honesty of dealing and respect for others, qualities that are cherished ornaments of our civilization. I maintain that native lands can only be leased fairly if the Government has control . . . [40]

Only two men spoke against the motion, the Tui Cakau and his fellow member from Cakaudrove.

The real test of the resolution came with its referral to the nineteen provincial councils. Ratu Sukuna's speech was printed and distributed widely, and broadcast over the new weekly Fijian session on the radio. The chief addressed one or two councils personally. The final results were an extraordinary achievement for a viewpoint that had never before been put by a Fijian to his own people: twelve councils agreed unanimously and four by a large majority that after the determination of the amount of reserve land needed for their 'proper development', the surplus, including existing leases, should be handed over to the government for leasing to others. Only Cakaudrove was still opposed, in deference to their chief, and two councils were undecided. [41]

On the eve of his departure from Fiji in July 1938, Governor Sir Arthur Richards proposed a Native Lands Trust Ordinance to give effect to Ratu Sukuna's motion and empower the government to deal with all the Fijian lands in the colony without reference to the owners - the reserve

lands having been first set aside for exclusive Fijian use.
The Council of Chiefs approved Richards' proposals in 1938
and the final bill for the establishment of the Native
Lands Trust Board was approved by the Legislative Council
on 22 February 1940. The Indian members acknowledged that
Fijian owners had 'undoubtedly adopted a broad and generous
attitude to their lessees', but pressed for leases to be as
long as possible and even perpetual. Ratu Sukuna hailed
the legislation as a 'monument of trust in British rule, of
confidence in its honesty, and of hopes . . . that
Europeans, Indians and Fijians will settle down to labour,
sacrificing if need be community interests for the benefit
of the whole'.[42]

Fijian compromises for a multiracial society did not
extend so magnanimously to the political arena. The census
of 1936 found the 98,000 Fijians to be just under half the
total population, with the 85,000 Indians comprising 43 per
cent. Their crude death rate (10.27 per thousand for the
years 1928-37) was under half that of the Fijians (22.97),
so that the latter faced the demographic certainty that
within a decade they would no longer be the largest group.
The success of the Indians in gaining three elected members
in the Legislative Council after 1929, the comparative
prosperity of CSR tenant farmers, the growth of education
for Indian children, and the entry of over a thousand
Indians into commerce left no doubt that they would in time
become prosperous and influential.

The Fijian chiefs closed ranks finally with local
Europeans in the constitutional debates of the 1930s to
head off Indian demands for common electoral rolls. The
Indian case was powerfully argued on 'the recognition of
the principle of common and equal rights' and with an
idealistic vision of a future democracy in which Fijians
and Indians would come into their own. The prominent
lawyer S.B. Patel and other Indian leaders were at pains
to acknowledge that historic Fijian interests were still
paramount, but claimed that common franchise would diminish
racial friction and encourage all to pull together 'for the
good and welfare of Fiji as a whole'.[43] In defence of this
principle, the Indian members had boycotted the Legislative
Council from 1929 to 1932.

Fijian reaction was distinctly hostile. The Council
of Chiefs in 1933 recorded its 'strong and unanimous
opinion' that the 'Indian immigrant population should
neither directly nor indirectly have any part in the

control or direction of matters affecting the interests of the Fijian race'.[44] In 1935 the three Fijian members of the Legislative Council led by Ratu Sukuna published a long explanation that was hailed by church and business leaders as a persuasive case why Fiji should not only reject a common franchise but the franchise itself. 'A system that rests on the counting of heads', wrote the chiefs, or the 'notion that the people are the best judges of matters of vital importance to the welfare of a state' would be 'utterly incomprehensible' to a people who understood government as 'commands issued in the general interest by a hierarchy composed of chiefs, priests and elders'. In 1935 that was a remarkably archaic assessment of Fijian capabilities, but it was music to government ears when coupled with an evocative appeal to the Deed of Cession and the

> thoughts running in the minds of the chiefs, the feeling that they were handing over their country as a whole and their domains, each and severally, as a fief of the Crown; that they would in future be ruled autocratically but withal sympathetically; that from henceforth they were the vassals of the Great White Queen . . .

> After years of Crown colony government, there is nothing natives desire better than to be governed by the King's Representative with the help and advice of his senior officers and such European members of the Legislative Council as are, as far as possible, above the influences of local interests and prejudice.

The Chiefs noted that the European electorate would soon be 'white only in name, enlightened only in memory' due to the increase and low educational level of part-Europeans, and that Europeans would have no case at all on democratic grounds for denying Indians a similar opportunity to ensure 'the predominance of ignorance and prejudice'. Democracy itself, they concluded, should therefore give way to a racially balanced system of nominating enlightened representatives for each community.[45]

These arguments agreeably played to the fears of the European elite that they would lose their own position to part-Europeans, and that the Indians would triumph over all by sheer weight of numbers. Government response was rapid. In 1936 the municipal franchise was abolished in Suva and

Levuka to eliminate any possiblity of Indian control. Governor Sir Murchison Fletcher favoured a return to a Legislative Council comprising a majority of official members with nominated representatives of each community. The Colonial Office decreed finally that the Legislative Council would comprise sixteen official members, five Fijian members nominated from a panel of ten chosen by the Council of Chiefs, and an equal number of European and Indian members. Three of the five European and three of the five Indian members were still to be elected on communal rolls - an arrangement that lasted to 1963.

The false symmetry of these measures signalled that racial division was hardening into an accepted part of national life. Careful balancing of communal interests encouraged each community to cling to its own identity, to think instinctively in racial terms, to worry incessantly about political solidarity, and perhaps to miss the main point that Fiji's divided people would never to be able to loosen the grip of the Australian or New Zealand corporations and a few local Europeans over exports, imports and the internal market system.

Politically these changes made no compromise, then, over the paramountcy of Fijian interests to match the concessions made over land. The Fijians, it seemed, still had the separate space they needed to concentrate on their own development while the local Europeans and British officials held the fort. Nevertheless the new-found solidarity of the Europeans and Fijians in national politics and the frank admission of Fijian dependence on the trusteeship of the Crown obscured the deeper problem that neither the government nor the Fijians had really come to terms with the dilemmas of modernization and economic development.

Chapter 9

The dilemmas of development

Six decades after Cession the rationale for Britain's trusteeship was still that Fijians needed a lot of time to 'catch up'; the colonial timetable was leisurely and vague. As one Governor had put it: 'No one who has the interest of these islands at heart would unduly hasten the change in a people of whom it is literally true that less than 50 years ago they were only emerging from the Stone Age.'[1] Still, there was no dispute that ultimately Fijians would evolve, and would want to evolve, towards the liberal western ideal of individualistic, democratic man in an essentially capitalist society. Village Fijians probably had a poor grasp of that goal, but as Apolosi's Viti Company showed, they were generally receptive to innovation and programs of improvement.

Enthusiasm for education was another part of that search for the key to a vaguely conceived new level of welfare. As Ro Tuisawau once remarked, 'Education is the most useful thing of all for the present age and for the future'.[2] The Roman Catholic mission had responded generously to the demand for European teachers with the introduction of several teaching orders of nuns and brothers - by 1910 there were over fifty of these single-minded men and women committed to giving Fijians an education far superior to that the old Wesleyan village system had provided. Catholic policy was to educate boys and girls separately at centralized schools attached to the twenty-one mission stations. 'Our great effort', wrote Bishop Nicholas in 1929, 'is to have ALL our Catholic children in our BOARDING schools, and therefore can do what we like outside of school hours.'[3]

Members of the religious orders lived in community on mission stations. Physically and socially they were insulated from village life. They seem to have given little professional thought, in those unquestioning decades, to the wider societal impact of the academic curricula and teaching materials they imported from New Zealand, Australia and the United Kingdom. Their first concern was the personal and religious formation of individuals whose goodness of life would leaven the communities to which they returned. Their life-long dedication to the task and transparent integrity had a profound impact on many Fijians. What they may have lacked

130

in cultural sensitivity they often supplied in personal warmth and enthusiasm. Catholic schools received tremendous Fijian and Indian support, with the Marist Brothers schools in Suva generally acknowledged as Fiji's best. (In the latter, Indians were admitted alongside Fijians in the first decade of the century; in 1910 there was a single Indian convert, Xavieris, who confessed his sins regularly - in Fijian.) Catholic schools were also the first to introduce English (at Cawaci in 1892). The Wesleyan Annual Synod of 1899 reluctantly recognized that they would have to introduce some English in their own central school (at Navuloa until 1908) or lose their best pupils to the 'perverts of Rome'.[4] At the Queen Victoria School (founded by the government in 1906) the chiefs insisted that their sons were to be taught as the sons of Europeans were taught, and that they ought not to waste their time in manual labour - an argument that had found favour with Sir Everard im Thurn: 'After all it is education in the English language that the Fijian mostly needs if he is ever to play the part of an ordinary English subject.'[5]

The thrust for academic education came also from the chiefs in the provincial councils. On their own initiative in 1907 the Lauan chiefs voted £300 from provincial funds to obtain the appointment of an English master, the anthropologist A.M. Hocart, for their school at Lakeba. This school became the model for six government-assisted provincial schools which by the 1930s provided upper primary education for some 500 pupils chosen by the tikina for their rank and ability. The best pupils of the provincial schools went on to the Queen Victoria School.

Having lost the initiative in education, the Wesleyan mission gradually withdrew from the 600 or so village schools nominally under its control and, like the Catholic mission, concentrated its efforts on centralized district schools (34 in 1933). The Wesleyan educational centre at Davuilevu expanded to offer more technical training and teacher training as well as its large theological programs, and nearby the mission purchased the fine property 'Navuso' for £6000 in 1926 for an ambitious agricultural school.

On the whole the Wesleyan missionaries felt that the academic pace-setting of the Catholic schools, signalled by the introduction of Cambridge external exams in 1920, was doing an ultimate disservice to Fiji's youth. They resented how little effort went into supporting traditional

leadership and preparing Fijians for the village life eight
out of ten of them would have to lead. Not that Wesleyan
schools, any more than their competitors, tried to realize
the educational potential of centuries of accumulated
wisdom in the skills or arts of graceful and prosperous
living in island environments. Implicit in all the schools
was a 'hidden curriculum' that taught Fijian children to
expect nothing of value from 'the age of darkness' that
might be brought to bear on the problems of 'the modern
world'. At best, dances and songs might be encouraged for
their aesthetic and recreational value, exotic relief from
the 'real' business of the schoolroom as prescribed in
Cambridge or New South Wales.

The education of Fijian girls, fitfully attempted by
the occasional missionary wife, had not received serious
Wesleyan attention until the arrival in 1900 of Mary
Ballantine, an ex-prison wardress from Auckland who led a
famous little school at Matavelo in Ba. A smaller school
at Richmond, Kadavu, and ad hoc efforts elsewhere by the
handful of Methodist mission sisters hardly matched the
much greater effort of over forty Roman Catholic nuns in
thirteen girls schools by 1913. Yet as Catholic schools
reached less than one in six of the whole school
population, most Fijians girls were left with less
education than the little the boys received. In 1920 the
Reverend Wesley Amos blamed the '60 years criminal neglect'
by the government and his own mission for producing 'a
degenerated race of women lacking the capacity almost for
virtue'. There were, he claimed, 'thousands of
illegitimate marriages and thousands of paltry divorces and
thousands of separated homes'. [6]

If this was so, others wondered whether school
education was really the answer - to take girls, as the
nuns did, and supervise them carefully in their dormitories
during term then send them home with a smattering of
knowledge and a brace of medals to protect their virtue.
In the late 1920s there was a return to Sir George
O'Brien's thinking, that a new effort had to be made to
reach young mothers in their homes and to help them to rear
their children. Child mortality rates were still
distressingly high with children under 5 accounting for
more than a third of all Fijian deaths.

In 1927 a New Zealand nurse, Mrs Suckling, was
appointed as the first full-time child welfare nurse with
two Fijian assistants. They began in Tailevu by training a

small women's committee in each village. The committee's
task was to assemble the children daily to see that all of
them were properly bathed and dressed and fed, and to treat
minor ailments with a small stock of medicines. Dr Regina
Flood-Keyes Roberts, the wife of the American consul,
volunteered in December 1927 to supervise the dozen
villages in the Suva-Nausori district, and developed the
women's committee system a stage further. She had learned
from a similar experiment in Samoa in 1926 and 1927 that
unless the entire village became interested in the work and
the scheme had the active support of the chiefs, it was
doomed to failure.

When Dr Roberts descended on a village she did so in
style, having made sure that the Buli came with her and
that all would be present for a public weighing of the
infants after a general lesson on sanitation and health.
She made committee leaders stand to attention to give their
reports - the meetings were deliberately formal so that
when individual mothers were praised or blamed for the
state of their infants they could feel the full weight of
community feeling for or against them: 'A practice is made
to clap the hands for every child that has gained weight.'[7]

The effects were dramatic. Mothers vied with each
other to push those scales ever higher; the condition of
the children improved beyond belief. Dr Roberts was
probably instrumental in obtaining £2000 from the
government for child welfare work in 1928 and another £2000
from CSR. She also made it a fashionable cause amongst the
ladies of Suva. Mrs Seymour, wife of the Colonial
Secretary, started a baby show. It was to become a regular
feature in many provinces. In June 1928 the Methodist
mission provided a child welfare worker for Ba, and another
Methodist sister, Mrs Ruby Brewer, resigned the same year
to be able to work full time in the villages: 'That is my
only hope of getting out to these people. In this "I
surrender all" . . . as each child dies I know that I am
partly responsible for not going out earlier with
medicines, etc. I know this is my work.'[8] The dedication
of these overworked women is legendary. One of the
sisters, Miss Hettie Hames, is said to have delivered over
a thousand babies in Nadroga circuit.

Bishop Nicholas agreed to let nuns do child welfare
work in Namosi, the most backward province, but held out
little hope of success, recalling the failure of O'Brien's
hygiene mission. Père Guinard, who had lived in Namosi for

over thirty years, claimed that nurses were not needed:
the problem was nutrition. 'The children are starved', he
said; when he came to a village, often bringing food, they
swarmed around like a pack of hungry dogs. Parents left
their children at home with a few pieces of cold dalo, and
returned from their gardens in the evening when the
children were too tired to eat. [9]

These problems were overcome in most of the provinces
by the kind of social engineering that the child welfare
movement consciously or unconsciously employed. By 1937
there were six European nurses and sixteen Fijian nurses on
child welfare work, and scores of volunteers often led by
the wives of Rokos or DCs. Although child mortality rates
did not fall significantly until after World War II, the
general cleanliness of children, the incidence of yaws and
ringworm and other loathsome conditions was much improved.
When Mrs Brewer began her work in Ba in 1929, 440 of 450
children needed treatment. In 1933 she classified only 13
of the 473 children as 'poor' or 'frail' and enclosed
photographs to prove it.[10]

The child welfare movement was successful because it
was the kind of development that the people could 'make
their own'.[11] Women's committees and guilds expanded their
function to become an enjoyable and permanent part of the
life of village women, undoubtedly boosting their
self-esteem and disseminating much useful knowledge of
public health, nutrition, child care and crafts. The
movement was also an extension of a long colonial tradition
of initiating a small corps of villagers - Native Medical
Practitioners, obstetric nurses, provincial scribes,
constables and others - into useful skills of immediate
relevance, and either employing them locally or posting
them to various parts of the group as servants of the
Fijian Administration.

There was no incentive to force through more drastic
institutional reforms of village life against certain
opposition from Ratu Sukuna and others; the most
government felt it should do for rural development was to
encourage specific initiatives that seemed to promote a
more healthy society, one where Fijians would take 'a
serious part in the battle of life'. [12]

To salve the progressive conscience, some Fijians were
encouraged to take advantage of a provision written into
the Communal Services Regulation (1912 edition) by which

134

the Governor could grant exemption from communal services
to an individual wanting to take up commercial agriculture
or some business activity. The applicant had to apply
through his district council for the galala exemption, as
it was called, and pay in advance a fee of £2 10s. He had
to be able to show evidence of his enterprise. There was
no provision for credit of any kind, loans or technical
advice, nor any guarantee that after a year's exemption the
privilege would not be revoked. When it was easy to leave
a village for wage employment there was not much to
encourage a man to undertake the effort and risks of
commercial agriculture. Until 1929 perhaps a hundred
applications were granted each year, just sufficient for
the government to be able to reassure itself and the
Colonial Office that it was making efforts 'through a
process of education and training, to create in the native
an incentive to energy, and to grant him more individual
liberty'.[13]

Unimpressed with galala exemptions, the 1920 Council
of Chiefs had requested that provinces should be allowed,
if they wished, to revert to the payment of taxes in kind,
the only scheme that had ever succeeded in ensuring that
Fijians would be substantial producers while retaining the
full value of their produce and the benefits of a cash
income, yet without having to be dependent on European
employers. The Colonial Secretary opposed the resolution
'on general grounds' as a 'retrospective step involving
difficulty' - presumably to current employers of Fijian
labour, though the argument he advanced was pitched to the
vaguer certainties of the liberal ethos: 'The basis of the
inertness of the Fijian is, to my mind, due to . . . an
overburden of communalism, and the difficulty of individual
Fijians to assert and maintain individualism.' The Acting
Receiver General picked up the tune, protesting that the
resolution was 'a negation of the recognition of the Fijian
as an individual - it insists in an unmistakable manner
upon the perpetuation of the communal system. This is
retrogression . . . he should develop sufficiently to be
able to live and support himself and his dependents as
units of the community European civilisation has
evolved . . . '[14]

Such thinking was hopelessly out of tune with village
realities. Fijian authorities were not hostile, though, to
individual farmers who wanted some temporary relief from
their obligations to raise money for some reason. Taniela
J. Batiudolu of Lomaiviti, for example, successfully

applied in 1918 to manage full time a plantation where he
employed nineteen indentured Fijian labourers and seven
Indians to care for 8000 yams, 6000 yaqona, 4000 bananas,
1000 coconut trees and other food crops. He had run his
own store since 1915 and owned a 5 ton boat. Later his
exemption was cancelled by his own request because he had
accepted the post of turaga ni koro in his village and
wished 'to devote one year to improving his people'. The
request was not necessarily as altruistic as it sounds.
Undoubtedly he had built his success with the cooperation
and help of kinsmen as well as employees, and had a debt of
gratitude to repay.[15] In rural Fiji no man could literally
'go it alone', unless he wished to be a social outcast.

Fiji's commercial economy was not kind to small
producers. Opportunity had actually diminished since
Thurston's time. Without a government marketing
organization, farmers depended on local traders. In copra
provinces Chinese and other storekeepers encouraged Fijians
to morketi (mortgage) articles for up to a third of their
value with only one to three weeks to redeem their
property. Payments might be made with nuts (three to a
penny was the rate in 1927) and the balance made up by
working for the storekeeper at low wages. Traders also
took liens on growing nuts - a pernicious credit system
that took advantage of easy-going villagers.[16]

When Ratu Sukuna became District Commissioner of Lau
he tried strenuously to break the hand-to-mouth habits of
people cutting small lots of copra and selling locally at
deflated prices for grossly inflated trade goods. In 1934
yaqona bought in Suva for 2d sold in Lakeba for 6d; canvas
shoes, 3s 6d in Suva, were 6s 6d; black sulus rose from 2s
each to 6s:

> The native told all this will politely agree that
> the remedy is to sell and buy in Suva. If the
> initiative is left to him, nothing further will
> happen, for the average native prefers the
> certainty of the bird in the hand, bony and tough
> though it may obviously be, to better nourished
> ones so far away.

A direct consequence of the low produce prices obtained
locally was that to meet the payment of provincial rates,
the native tax, and the educational expenses of their
children, the men had to leave their wives and children in
the care of others to go and labour on plantations or, in

the 1930s, the gold mines of Vatukoula and Yanawai - 'and
for this Fijians will be counted virtuous; their industry
will be on men's lips as a sign of Fijian progress'.[17]

Ratu Sukuna's response was to reorganize the communal
cutting of copra as had been done in his father's day. In
1934 he made the village the unit of tax assessment in Lau
and Lomaiviti, investing the true chief of the village with
the obligation to meet the quota, and relieving the Buli of
the duty of hounding individuals:

> The payment of the tax is now a family
> affair . . . it is the Tribal chief that should
> conscript resources, make the biggest
> contribution, and organise the necessary labour.
> And the wise Buli works through his Tribal
> chiefs. Communal copra cutting . . . raises no
> conflict of interests in the native mind and so
> calls for no coercion unless official supervision
> by the Buli be so regarded.[18]

Those who were landless cut copra on the lands of
others. The copra was collected and transported to Suva
for sale by auction where, as in the old days, the larger
lots realized higher prices. The tabu on selling nuts
prior to tax-making halved the business of local traders,
who in most cases were customers of Burns Philp at Levuka.
The manager there, A.J.Acton, protested to the government
that the tabu had 'paralysed' trade: storekeepers would go
out of business. Ratu Sukuna replied that storekeepers who
bought from Burns Philp at a profit to the firm and then
sold to the people at an inflated profit to themselves were
providing a service of dubious value. Thurston's arguments
had been the same.[19]

Communal copra cutting was tried also in Macuata,
Cakaudrove and Kadavu with little success, suggesting that
the vital ingredient in Lau and Lomaiviti was the personal
inspiration of Ratu Sukuna himself and, in Lomaiviti, his
younger brother, Ratu Tiale W.T. Vuiyasawa (Native
Assistant to the Provincial Commissioner). Despite record
low copra prices, the scheme reduced Lau's arrears in rates
from £2913 in 1935 to £800 in 1936; the otherwise
universal problem of tax defaulters was no longer found in
Lau. For all this H.W. Jack, the Director of Agriculture,
regarded the scheme as 'iniquitous' and 'unfair to the
individual who is anxious to better himself'.[20]

Nothing Ratu Sukuna could say, or demonstrate empirically, would convince men like Jack that in every Fijian there was not an ego enslaved. In vain Ratu Sukuna showed the particular land problems of individuals his scheme had overcome and appealed to the capacity of existing village communities to surmount their own problems. The colonial officials judged on a priori grounds. If Burns Philp profits were down, there had been an unnatural manipulation of the marketplace; if the chiefs were encouraging the pooling of slender resources that all might jointly prosper, then individuality had been choked.

Nevertheless Jack did take the point that a government marketing organization would eliminate profits made by middlemen - £10,000 in 1936 from Fijian bananas, he estimated, where £2000 would have provided the department with a fleet of punts and boats to do the same job. His small, enthusiastic staff was successfully experimenting with export consignments of Fijian crops and saw no reason for not expanding its marketing activities. Jack used the example of a Tailevu man who had rejected a trader's offer of 3s per bag of sweet potatoes in 1936. He then persuaded the department to ship them to New Zealand on his behalf, and realized 10s 2d net per bag: 'The average Fijian has no idea of business, no organization to dispose of his produce co-operatively, and his experience of middlemen is such that he regards most offers made to him with suspicion. Hence he has no incentive to produce the crops for which markets are undoubtedly available within limits.' The bulk of the 15,000 tons of Fijian copra produced each year went through small traders, mainly Chinese, at a low price. It was depressing on Viti Levu to see many individuals spending days bringing down a few bags of maize or yaqona to hawk around a market centre when for a commission of 2 or 3 per cent the department could transport the market produce in larger lots at a much higher price. The Colonial Secretary, Juxon Barton, rejected even these proposals as 'a form of state socialism' that would do 'nothing but harm to the future of an already lethargic race'.[21]

Most of the Fijian farmers the Agriculture Department wanted to help were exempted men, galala, whose numbers began to increase after 1933 when the commutation fee was lowered to 10s and provision made for individuals to take out a licence to farm a piece of communal land. In the Waidina River in 1938 there were 39 of them who each supplied some 600 cases of bananas to the buyers, and elsewhere there were about another 650 who were experimenting with the new way of life.[22]

Many of the latter were protégés of the Reverend Arthur D. Lelean, the Wesleyan apostle of individualism. Lelean, nephew of the earlier missionary C.O. Lelean, was a powerful, energetic man with a reputation amongst Fijians (and later amongst Australians at Ballarat, Victoria) for peculiar psychic powers of divination. Constantly in trouble with mission superiors on account of his secretive ways and habit of recycling vakamisioneri collections back into his own development schemes, Lelean was the maverick of the Methodist mission, universally liked by the Fijians he helped, but regarded as eccentric and unbalanced by Europeans - not least because he had close ties with Apolosi's followers through a former mission teacher, Patemo Vai, one of Apolosi's lieutenants. Nevertheless Governor Fletcher asked Lelean to persuade Fijians to grow cane, and he took up the cause with true missionary zeal. For Lelean was passionately committed to making the Fijians an economic force in the colony.[23]

Fletcher had appealed to the CSR managers in Fiji to help Fijians make the 'changeover from the communal to the individualistic mode of life': 'I see no reason why, with sympathetic guidance, the Fijian should not make as good a peasant proprietor as the Indian.' The Ba manager, G.H. Allen, was sympathetic, for the Company was uneasy about its near total dependence on its 4000 Indian sub-tenants and 4500 small growers. In Bulu tikina, Ba, seven towns opened up 50 acres for cane and others followed suit, especially in Nadroga. By 1933 the Company had 411 Fijian growers supplying cane from their own mataqali lands.[24]

The Company also began experimenting in 1930 with Fijian tenants on its own estates. At Toko estate, Tavua, and Varoka, Ba, 500 acres were made available on exactly the same basis as to Indians - that is, 10 acre individual plots, with CSR field officers giving close supervision and training in the use of implements and horses: 'The scheme aims at making the Fijian self-supporting and developing the individual.'[25] A third project was begun at Navakai, Nadi, with 235 acres set aside for twenty-two Fijian tenants, twelve of whom had come from Nadroga. By 1933 one had been replaced but all were doing well; then in 1934 the whole of Nadi went football mad - there were

twenty-four teams using the one ground - and some of the
farmers became unsettled with their solitary workdays while
the carnival spirit prevailed. They wondered whether in
the search for freedom they had not found another bondage.
In 1935 the scheme collapsed - only two men worked well,
the majority not at all. Ten of the Nadroga men walked out
on a standing crop. Elsewhere the Company's efforts had
also failed except at Varoka where eight Fijian tenants
worked well under the more sympathetic leadership of one
Victor Clarke. Fijians seemed to do better as free
labourers on the Company estates where they were provided
with housing, land for planting root crops, and 1s 9d a day
on an easy-come easy-go basis.

In the Rewa delta there were on the average about a
hundred Fijian cane growers in the 1930s, a great number of
whom paid Indians to do the work and assigned them up to
half the crops: 'An amazing amount of jugglery goes
on . . .' Even though the Methodist agriculture school at
Navuso produced a few genuine cane farmers, the Nausori
mill manager was inclined to dismiss the Fijian effort on
the Rewa as negligible. They were too easily discouraged
by the bad weather that finally led to the abandonment of
cane growing in that area.[26]

In Ra province Fijians had little unleased land close
to the tramlines and there were only twenty-one cane
farmers on 67 acres in 1939. In Macuata (Labasa) the
Fijian contribution was minimal, but in Nadroga poor
resources made cane an attractive proposition. Every
village that had suitable land was growing cane by 1931 -
some 1000 acres in all, but generally in small patches and
of poor quality. Nadroga cane farmers were generally
villagers using their own land and still living within the
constraints of the provincial program of work.

However a large proportion of Fijian cane farmers in
the 1930s - there were 686 of them by 1938, 134 on CSR
estates - undoubtedly were seeking something of a new
life-style and were probably influenced by the constant
exhortations of government officials, company officers and
Lelean to become 'individualists' and embrace the dignity
of labour. Generally CSR was discouraged by the results of
its efforts. Depressing stories could be told of the
history of pieces of land as they changed hands. The
Lautoka Manager sent the extreme example to Sydney of 30
acres of land called 'Naikorokoro' which under direct
Company management produced 1135 tons in 1929. In the

hands of three Indians the yield fell to 324 tons by 1932.
The following year the property reverted to its 112 Fijian
owners including 40 able-bodied men. They produced 178
tons in their first year and about 70 in the second, with
most of the land reverting to bush. CSR officials argued
that virtues such as punctuality, essential to the milling
operations, were notoriously lacking in Fijians though in
other respects, such as the handling of machinery, they had
shown great natural aptitude. In other words, certain
cultural problems seemed insuperable. The Provincial
Commissioner of Nadi expressed the Company's frustration
when he wrote of the ailing Navakai scheme: 'It is
degrading and ignominious that we should all have to wait
on the Fijian's pleasure while he works spasmodically and
irregularly. Every time we are promised that the estate
"will be clean next time".' The Company estimated that it
lost £800 a year by allowing Fijians rather than Indians to
run the estate.[27]

In July 1936, G.H. Allen urged the Company to strike
at the roots of the Fijian problem by taking in boys and
training them in a disciplined environment for the skills
and habits of regularity and discipline they would need as
cane farmers. The General Manager, Sir Philip Goldfinch,
disapproved of the details of Allen's militaristic approach
(uniforms, bands, platoons, NCOs and a chiefly 'Adjutant')
but sanctioned a training farm on Drasa estate near
Lautoka. 'The keynote', he demanded, 'should be
simplicity, work, cleanliness, religious advantages, clean
living - and a certain amount of sport'. He rejected the
suggestion of the Education Department that cultural and
theoretical training should be included. Drasa was to be
strictly relevant and practical.[28]

And so it was for the community of eighty lads under a
Fijian Supervisor and European Field Officer who took over
Drasa in 1938 and worked from 6 a.m. to 3 p.m. learning
every aspect of cane farming by running the estate. The
Company kept them in food, clothing and pocket money and
gave them on graduation a lump sum of 5s for every working
week in the hope they would be able to establish
themselves. Unfortunately the boys went home at an age
when they were too young to have a say in anything. Their
families invariably commandeered the capital for the
welcome-home ceremonies, so the Company had to try and
place the graduates on its own estates. Only a minority of
Drasa graduates remained on the land, though many of them
applied their work habits to white-collar jobs. CSR, the

cynics said, trained the best waiters in Fiji.[29]

By World War II then, Fijians had been given many chances to become cane farmers and several hundred individuals had successfully laid the basis for a renewed Fijian presence in the sugar industry. Many more hundreds of Fijians preferred easier ways of earning money. A man could earn 3s 6d a day on the wharves at Lautoka and Suva. Discovery of gold near Vatukoula led to the opening of the Emperor and Loloma gold mines in the mid 1930s, and they employed nearly 2000 Fijians by the end of the decade. At the third annual general meeting of Emperor Mines Limited in Melbourne, in 1938, E.G. Theodore noted that while Fijians had no strong necessity to earn wages and could return to their village at any time, they were happy in the larger community of the mining settlement provided they had adequate housing and food. As workers they were easy to teach and supervise, and showed common sense. They were completely unorganized industrially: 'We are very happily situated', he told the shareholders, though occasionally provincial rivalries caused fights between the men. On 9-10 February 1936 a few hundred men from Ra and Tailevu were involved in several fights and the Tailevu men and their families fled the field. Theodore was advised to watch that Rewa and Verata were balanced against Bau. Parochialism, it seems, was exportable anywhere Fijians lived in groups.[30]

A smaller gold mine on Vanua Levu at Mt Kasi, Yanawai, provided employment for a constantly changing workforce of about two hundred men. To a much greater extent than on Viti Levu, the men of the outer provinces preferred to work for short periods, to pay their taxes and often to raise money for a community project such as a church or school. The turnover at Mt Kasi was full 30 per cent each month.

Other new developments came from within the Fijian Administration itself. Most of them were instigated by the local born Provincial Commissioner of Colo North and Colo East, Stuart Reay. Remembered by Fijians as an intimidating, resourceful man, Reay toured his provinces with immense amounts of luggage, including his personal food supply, fodder for his horses, and a sanitary 'thunderbox'. He delighted in outraging local custom by draping his horse with whatever plant was sacred to the women. In Nadrau it was the baka vine. As villagers related it forty years later, he once rode up trailing baka with an insolent grin, so as soon as he was seated for the welcoming ceremonies the women gathered in an adjoining house to set up a continuous howl of outrage and grief. 'When will they ever stop?' Reay asked his provincial constable, with feigned ignorance. 'Sir, they won't stop; you have done a fearful thing (ka rerevaki).' Finally a delegate came from the women to demand that Reay attend their 'court' before he opened his own. Reay went along for the sake of his ears and found himself arraigned before a lady 'magistrate' and her sister-in-arms as the 'interpreter'. 'O sa kila li ni tabu na baka? You [using the singular form with calculated disrespect] know, do you not, of the baka tabu?' Reay maintained the silence of consent - or bemused contempt - and was sentenced to furnish the village with twelve cows within a week. They were duly delivered at a cost of £2 each, drawn on the provincial funds.

Reay's otherwise undocumented sense of the farcical in his duties, and a liberal reading of his official powers, prompted him to exempt the village of Saumakia in Waima tikina of Colo East 'from the threat of the law and of official control' altogether. He was fed up with endless prosecutions for tax evasion and their complete indifference to his moral exhortations and overused threats, he said, and challenged them to manage their own affairs from the beginning of January 1933. Leadership reverted to the natural leaders of the villages. The experiment was a success. The people planted bananas and made a lot of money, and in 1934 their village was one of the best kept in Colo East. [31]

Could the model be transferred? Reay chose the Tavua people, as they were chronically short of food, sodden with yaqona, and resentful of authority. In March 1934 he took them to task: 'Why should it be necessary for the Government to force you to maintain dry roofs over your heads and to cultivate your gardens? If we washed our hands of you and left you to your own devices would you let your houses fall about your ears and abandon your gardens so you starved?' The Tui Tavua was so provoked that he challenged Reay to let them alone for a while and see the results. Reay accepted. Immediately in a fine speech the Tui announced that the lali drum would be sounded at dawn the following day and every day thereafter for the various mataqali to begin work. Waste land was to be cleared for cane, yaqona was tabu for the young men, and jaunts with taxi drivers tabu for the young women. Reay left the village feeling he had done his best day's work in years.

Within three weeks Tavualevu was a village transformed. A
new teacher's house had been built in two days whereas his
predecessor's had taken three weeks and fifteen
prosecutions. The tabu was effective, and the Tui
completely in control. Even after the first burst of
enthusiasm the experiment went well for several months in
the eight villages of the Tavua tikina. [32]

In January 1935 the experiment was extended to the
five villages of Nadrau, one of the districts in Colo North
that Lelean had stripped of most of its able-bodied men.
The results were disappointing. The Buli and the Tui had
to seek restoration of legal controls when they found that
their moral authority was insufficient to persuade men to
work. By contrast when Nakorovatu, Colo East, was exempted
in February of the same year, within three months the
village had repaired all its houses, dug a new latrine
system and planted 12 acres of bananas. In May the other
villages of Waima tikina were given the chance to emulate
Saumakia and also the three villages of Lutu tikina.
Soloira tikina was included at the beginning of 1936, and
Reay wondered whether the solution to half of the problems
of administration was not simply to leave the people to
themselves wherever traditional leadership was
self-sustaining. [33]

The need to restore regularly constituted legal
authority first became apparent in Tavua where the Buli had
only retained his bureaucratic powers to convene the
district council or sign lease applications and other
documents. The Tui Tavua as hereditary chief wanted to
displace the Buli entirely and virtually secede from the
Fijian Administration. Then in March 1935 the Tui died and
there was trouble over the succession.

The quarrel was a classically Fijian one absorbing
tremendous emotional energies while the mundane work of the
community was virtually abandoned. A mataqali in the
Buli's town of Korovou had the right at custom to offer the
yaqona to the Tui Tavua at his consecration. This custom
was ignored at the installation of the new chief and the
Korovou party declared the rites invalid. In July the
hundred days of mourning feast (burua) was attended by Ratu
Pope Seniloli and Deve Toganivalu. They intervened
unsuccessfully to achieve a settlement. Reay resumed
official control of the villages in August and asked Ratu
Sukuna to adjudicate. The Tavua people were asked to atone
(bulubulu) to Korovou for the breach of ritual. They

refused, so Reay declared the March ceremony invalid and
ordered another to replace it on 28 November. The people
sullenly refused to make the necessary preparations.

In desperation Reay called in Ratu Sukuna again, and
in this chief's presence on 12 December the two sides
agreed to reinstall the Tui immediately. The ceremony took
place in a grudging spirit, and Reay pondered the dilemma
of the administrator forced either to use a strong hand to
attain limited objects connected with hygiene - matters on
which the Fijian conscience was silent - or to respect the
autonomy of the people and allow traditional-type feuds
such as this to consume what seemed a grossly
disproportionate amount of their time and energy.[34]

On reflection Reay decided that village exemption
actually tended to reinforce the very 'communal system' the
government was pledged to modernize, even though
traditional leadership was less oppressive for individuals.
In the several villages where it was tried in 1935-37 the
final results were mixed. Some villages, especially in
Soloira, went into immediate decline because the chiefs no
longer had influence over the people. Others like Saumakia
thrived. Obviously much depended on the personal quality
of the traditional chiefs if autonomy was to work.

Elsewhere in Fiji there were similar experiments only
in Tailevu where Naila village was exempted in late 1931
and for several years grew fair quantities of rice and cane
vakoro (the village working together). Daku was exempted
in 1937 and did very well under its visionary chief, Ratu
Emosi, although its main source of income was firewood. It
was hard to generalize from these examples:

> In some communities of Fijians we get as much and
> sometimes more from voluntary effort than can be
> extracted by compulsion; in others the little
> more we get by compulsion is offset by the
> discontent engendered; we have reached a stage
> in Fijian development when the individual will no
> longer submit without protest to the curtailment
> of his liberty and the planning of his time and
> work by others, and the Communal Services
> Regulation may be said no longer to have the
> sanction of the community, except possibly in the
> more out-of-the-way islands. [35]

Although hardly qualified to speak for all Fiji (and
in trouble as soon as he tried), by 1937 Reay had done a
complete volte-face and was now convinced that a better
solution to the problems of Fijian villages was their
abolition. Communal and cooperative efforts, agricultural
'clubs' and the like had been tried, he argued, and found
wanting. Even at Naila, often held up as a showplace of
Fijian enterprise, nine men who were exempt individually as
galala to work and live on their own land were much in
advance of those working communally. [36]

Reay's new-found enthusiasm for lone galala seems to
have been based on a small sample of some thirty families
on Colo East and even fewer in Colo North who were already
living apart from villages. He frequently praised them in
his reports because all tended commercial crops, had
well-kept houses and compounds, children who helped the
family rather than ran loose in the villages; they paid
their taxes, were seldom in want, kept free of village
intrigues, reduced their involvement in ceremonial
observances, and appeared to Reay to be a lot happier. In
1938 Reay visited the Mogodro tikina of Colo West and was
similarly impressed with twenty-five settlers near Bukuya,
all in 'excellent' houses. They were typical of about a
third of the district who had begun to move out onto their
lands after 1935 on the suggestion of a former Buli. They
grew large quantities of yaqona for the Ba market:

> I feel justified in claiming from the Mogodro
> example, and from the example of the many
> settlers I have studied in three other provinces,
> that in Viti Levu outside the cane areas - and no
> doubt in Vanua Levu also - where men can be
> induced to break away from the village in this
> way there is an overwhelming chance of success. [37]

The Director of Agriculture naturally gave Reay strong
support. Jack had come to Fiji in 1934 after fourteen
years in Malaya where he had witnessed, he claimed, a
highly successful and sudden change-over from an
inefficient communal farming system to one of individual
smallholders intensively cultivating up to 3 acres and
living on their own land

> in pretty solid comfort, while producing 40% of
> the world's rubber and 80% of Malaya's copra:
> the Malay is now a man of independence and enjoys
> much more luxury than the Fijian and is far

happier in appearance, manner, and mode of living
on his little piece of land with his wife and
usually 3-4 children or more.

There was no hope for Fijians, Jack and his supporters
argued, until they became individual peasant proprietors
with 'some security from the lazy and improvident'. [38]

The arguments failed to convince some of the DCs who
valued the village as a centre of a polity that from its
slender resources could provide all its members with a
church, a school, a football ground or cricket pitch, a
bathing pool, piped water, mutual help in times of stress,
the opportunity to participate in councils or church
assemblies, and access to the advice of child welfare
workers, nurses and medical practitioners. Did the
proponents of village destruction, it was very fairly
asked, see beyond the shortlived benefits of commercial
production by galala to ask who would care for them in
their old age or what would replace the civilizing and
broadening influences of village life?

The views of the 'individualists' were put to the test
in Colo North about July 1937 in a decisive experiment with
policy repercussions for the next twenty years. Reay
called in the Qaliyalatina and Savatu people to Nadarivatu
and persuaded them that they should abandon their villages
and go out and live on their planting lands. Four villages
in Waima tikina, Colo East, were given the same choice.
According to oral accounts Reay used a great deal of
rhetoric and even fear - that there would be a great
shortage of food - to obtain his way. He indicated
ominously that anyone left in the villages would bear the
whole burden of the provincial program of work. The Waima
people were reluctant to move, hoping that the older
experiment of village exemption would continue. Some had
no suitable land away from the village. The men of
Qaliyalatina, who had had no taste of village exemption,
began building houses on their lands with more enthusiasm,
some in remote glens up to 16 miles from the village. Reay
assured Suva that the people were happy and that the women
who might have been expected to miss village life the most
were enjoying their freedom from the burdens of feeding
visitors, and their greater degree of privacy and comfort.
Or so they told the Commissioner.

Reay addressed the District Commissioners' Conference of 1938 - in the memory of a chief who was there, 'like a professor to so many students'. Old men in Mogodro had told him that scattered hamlets were the usual mode of settlement in ancient times, with occasional resort to fortified settlements in time of war. The centralized village was an aberration in the interior introduced in Gordon's time as a control device. The price paid by the people for settled government was a loss of individuality and independence. His latest experiment, then, should be understood as a harking back to a healthier state of society.[39]

The DCs were not convinced by Reay's arguments, fearing with the Colonial Secretary 'a hurricane flood of detribalization at any moment'. They wanted social changes to 'evolve', to come 'from within'. Finally they arrived at a compromise formula stating that the 'rural system', an extension of village society to embrace some Fijians living in groups on their own land and farming it systematically, was the 'next natural step in Fijian development'.[40] And so there, on the eve of war, the trustees of Fijian progress let the issues blur into abstractions.

Unquestionably the 1930s provided Fijians with greater opportunity and mobility than they had experienced before, and it was possible for a man to remove himself from obligations to his community and kindred for years at a time. Whether the net result was beneficial to Fijian societies depends on the value attached to such signs of 'progress'. Many individual Fijians had made particular choices that collectively threatened the viability of their villages and local government institutions. These alone ensured that there were wide areas of human life where Fijians were still masters of their destinies in a manner that could not prevail in the quarters, however congenial, provided by a foreign-owned mining company or a sugar mill or a copra plantation.

Chapter 10

Epilogue: rendezvous with the modern world

'It may be that to deny the omnipotence of the great
octopus of the modern world bespeaks an old-world outlook',
wrote Ratu Sukuna in 1934, 'but it is after all, of a
semi-feudal, semi-self-sufficing, society that we are, in
the main, treating.'[1] Six years later the war effort, the
tentacles of the great octopus, drew thousands of Fijian
men out of their narrow village world in response to Ratu
Sukuna's own appeals. Gladly accepting a commission as
Recruiting Officer with the rank of major in the minuscule
Fiji Defence Force, Ratu Sukuna welcomed the opportunity to
show the world and more especially the local Europeans and
British authorities his people's physical prowess,
intelligence, loyalty and capacity for sustained devotion
to a communal cause. He seems to have calculated that a
tremendous war effort by the Fijians would achieve several
of the goals he had espoused for twenty years: an expanded
role for traditional leadership, a renewed appreciation of
the Fijian capacity for community and cooperation, and a
secure compact with local Europeans to safeguard at the
national level vital Fijian interests such as land. In
none of these was he to be disappointed.

More immediately the future of the British Empire
itself seemed less certain as the German armies crushed
Holland and Belgium in May 1940 and France's defences began
to crumble. In July almost every eligible local European
was called up for training in the 1st Territorial
Battalion, and a second was raised at Ba. Ratu Sukuna
easily obtained fine Fijian recruits for a Regular Rifle
Company: 'young men could not bear the shame of not
participating in such a community effort . . . It was a
source of honour and pride to the Buli and his people if
they were well represented and none of their soldiers were
rejected . . . '[2]

New Zealand, assuming the defence burden of the South
Pacific colonies, built up its Second Expeditionary Force
in Fiji to 4000 men by the Pearl Harbour attack of 7
December 1941. The local forces were integrated into the
New Zealand command for operations and training. Following
the invasion of Rabaul and decimation of the Australian
defenders in January 1942, then the fateful surrender of
Singapore the following month, 'it was all too easy to

imagine a Japanese tide sweeping irresistibly over the
whole Pacific Ocean'.[3] Japanese troops landed on the New
Guinea mainland in March and occupied Tulagi in the south
Solomons in May, signalling a determined thrust south
towards Australia, but not impossibly a side sweep through
New Caledonia, Fiji and Samoa as well.

To meet this danger New Zealand increased its Fiji
garrison to 10,000 men, and Ratu Sukuna raised a second
battalion of Fijians at Lautoka. New Zealand officers
seconded to Fijian units developed a high regard for the
enthusiasm and soldierly qualities of the Fijian recruits.
In May they formed three commando units to develop further
the skills for which Fijians were to become celebrated.
Ambush, silent movement, acute observation and instant
response to attack at close quarters became the forte of
the Fijian jungle fighter. Field training developed close
personal bonds between New Zealanders and Fijians,
transforming the old colonialist code of automatic
deference to one of mutual respect and affection. For the
first time in decades ordinary Fijians could see and judge
a white man by the true measure of his integrity,
individual personality and professional competence. Both
were training for the field of fire where European lives
would depend as much on Fijian skill and intelligence as
the converse. Knowing there could be no racists (any more
than atheists) in foxholes, the New Zealanders seem to have
divested themselves of petty obsessions with white prestige
and shared their expertise willingly with Fijian officers
and NCOs. There were no invidious distinctions to hinder
the training of a totally professional fighting force.[4]

Unfortunately such distinctions could still be made at
the expense of the Indians when most accepted their
leaders' advice not to enlist at less than European scales
of pay and thus further institutionalize economic
inequality. Their 'indifference' - so it was construed -
to Britain's plight, the service of fewer than three
hundred in the military, the politically untimely
continuation of their pre-war struggle against CSR for
better cane prices, culminating in the refusal of CSR
tenants to harvest the 1943 crop, threw into sharper relief
the quality of the Fijian-European effort. Worst of all it
left the whole Indian community vulnerable to insinuations
of disloyalty and even 'subversion', serious charges that
could be delivered with those unpleasant aspersions on
manhood other wartime societies reserved for
pacifists.[5] (Not least in the legacy of these events was a

tacit understanding that the army would be virtually a
Fijian preserve.)

The 7500 men of the Fiji Defence Force came under
American operational control when the 37th Division of the
U.S. Army relieved the New Zealanders in June 1942. The
following month a new Governor, Major-General Sir Philip
Mitchell, arrived to mobilize the entire colony. Having
come 'to wage war', he stirred the Council of Chiefs in
September with a Churchillian appeal for another thousand
men:

> The business of brave men in time of danger is to
> fight, to suffer, to die if need be: but above
> all else to seek out the enemy and fight
> him . . . and if the enemy should come to our
> land we are going to fight him on our beaches and
> in the roads and fields and in the woods and
> hills, until we utterly destroy him and drive him
> into the sea. [6]

Perhaps, he concluded, Fiji's destiny was to be enrolled in
the stars with the other glorious islands of Malta and
Britain: Fiji had to be ready. The chiefs unanimously
urged that Fijian soldiers be sent overseas into action
without delay.

At the end of 1942 reluctant American consent was
given for thirty Fijian commandos to serve as scouts in the
Solomons. They so distinguished themselves that General
Patch, the area commander, successfully appealed for as
many as he could get. The 1st Commandos and the whole 1st
Battalion were emotionally farewelled in a march through
Suva on 13 April 1943. [7]

The commandos saw action on New Georgia and Vella
Lavella, and did much to enhance the growing reputation of
Fijian troops. After useful work on Florida and
Kolomgangara, the 1st Battalion was moved in November to
the front on Bougainville's east coast. Their aggressive
patrols brought on a determined Japanese attempt to seek
out and destroy them. In February 1944 they were saved
from encirclement only by the local knowledge of a resident
Fijian missionary, Usaia Sotutu, who led the battalion in
epic retreat over the Emperor mountain range to a west
coast beachhead. The battalion saw seven months of
continuous action on Bougainville for the loss of only
eighteen men and sixty-four wounded before they were

retired in July 1944.

Meanwhile the 3rd Battalion was in action from March to August 1944 bringing the total number of Fijians to fight with the Allies to 2071 and the death toll to forty-two. Sadness for these losses was quite eclipsed by popular exultation over the award of a posthumous Victoria Cross to Corporal Sefanaia Sukainaivalu. Twenty-nine other British decorations marked official recognition of Fijian valour and skill.

The war was such a disruption of village life that many feared the dislocation would be permanent. Neglected womenfolk were unwilling or unable to repair their houses, and some tikina had less than a score of men available for the program of work. In April 1944, a year past the peak of the war effort, there were still 9503 Fijians working for wages, or 36.5 per cent of able bodied males between 16 and eighty. Nearly 7000 men were in uniform or directly employed by the military.[8] Clearly, firm plans had to be made for post-war reconstruction, and especially in relation to the place of the village and the old problem of those who wanted to strike out on their own.

Ratu Sukuna was particularly sensitive about the encouragement the Department of Agriculture had given to its protegés to supply food for the forces as individual contractors. They had been very successful, and H.W. Jack, still Director of Agriculture, was unrepentantly drawing some future policy implications of his own: 'I maintain very strongly', he wrote in 1943, 'that those who wish to farm individually should be encouraged to do so and to exercise this freedom of choice without compulsion as British subjects.' Ratu Sukuna countered that agricultural officers and their Fijian assistants were operating lucrative closed markets for the exclusive benefit of a few. Government should look to the long-term results of undermining the villages, for which the earlier experiments (see Chapter 9) had provided some dramatic evidence.

Mogodro and Qaliyalatina had become bywords for desolation and depression. Reay's glowing accounts of the benefits of the individualistic peasant existence had no counterpart in the actual experience of the people for whom there was more to life than digging on their own land or carrying produce to Ba. The young men found the isolation unbearable and fled to the coast to join the army or get a job; the women stayed for long periods in the nearest

villages, while the old and sick often fended largely for
themselves. Ministers could get no one to church; the
schools were empty of children living too far away;
village meetings and customary observances all suffered.
As the chiefs had predicted at their first Council in 1875,
life outside a strong communal organization became a
struggle for subsistence devoid of stimulation; the deep
valleys no longer echoed to laughter or song. (In the
words of one informant the people 'just went to sleep'
until at the end of the war most of them were regrouped at
Navala on the Ba River. Old men interviewed in Colo North
had nothing good to remember about Reay's scheme, although
forty years later there were survivors still scattered in
the bush.)

Governor Mitchell himself rode through this district
(from Ba to Nadarivatu) and confirmed that it was indeed a
'melancholy wilderness'. He wrote to the Colonial
Secretary:

> I hope we have heard the last of this lunacy and
> that it is generally recognized that the Fijian
> community is the basis of Fijian society and that
> for Government to intervene to destroy it is
> stupid, if not indeed wicked . . . Even if the
> exempted man succeeded in the sense that his
> sponsors understand success, that is to say even
> if he earned more money for himself and less
> obligation to his fellows, nothing would be
> proved which has not already been proved by the
> melancholy condition to which the same philosophy
> [of individualism] has brought Europe. [9]

Ratu Sukuna had made a powerful convert. Having
himself visited the much-vaunted individualists in Colo
North in 1941, the chief had condemned the experiment as
'foreign in conception, novel in thought, and socially
disruptive in form':

> The reality of the position is that some natives
> do well as individual growers where a market is
> assured; others succeed for a time and then,
> finding regular work irksome, either return to
> their villages or become rolling stones; some
> again stay on to escape social obligations,
> producing barely enough for their own
> requirements while living in hovels. In sickness
> and in old age all return for aid to the village

community. [10]

Though since regarded by scholars as the arch-conservative spokesman for outmoded orthodoxy in Fijian affairs, Ratu Sukuna developed a telling critique of the vague liberal ideology underpinning the colonialist preference for individualism. He insisted that his British colleagues were unconsciously affected by the discredited Enlightenment hypothesis of a blissful state of nature, implicit in their enthusiasm for the virtues of an isolated life in the bush. The historical reality in Fiji, as he saw it, was that moderately autocratic personal authority, religious and kinship ties had been the principles of a sophisticated social order redeeming the people from utter chaos and primitive subsistence. The premise that civilization could now flourish in the bush in isolation and that the best settlers were individualists was a utopian product of the myopic liberal mind and ignored the practical wisdom of centuries. Nor could he countenance the forced dependence of individual growers on the cruel, externally determined cycle of local and international gluts and shortages. For market fluctuations always rebounded hardest on primary producers, a world-wide phenomenon beyond dispute. It was much worse when they were, as in the interior, totally without organizations of their own.

Ratu Sukuna was also keenly aware that centuries of western civilization and modern industrialization had produced the characteristic individualism and capitalist milieu of European culture:

> Without this background and an assured market the villager cannot by ukase be changed overnight into an individualist, nor can he in isolation find new vigour and moral purification . . . Freedom the new individualist does not understand. His word for it is tu galala, which means freedom not in the sense of laissez-faire, but in the sense of freedom without an object. [11]

He defended the village as still 'the most natural, the most convenient, and the cheapest unit of administration and for bestowing most effectively those inestimable gifts civilization can bring to a native race - medical attention, education in the broadest sense of the word, and religious teaching'. [12]

Even before inspecting the effects of village
dissolution, Governor Mitchell had determined to move
quickly to reorganize the Fijian Administration in
accordance with Ratu Sukuna's views. He appointed the
chief himself as the new Talai, now restyled Secretary for
Fijian Affairs with an ex officio seat on the Executive
Council. The Fijian Affairs Ordinance of 1944
reconstituted the old Native Regulations Board as a much
more powerful Fijian Affairs Board, chaired by the Talai,
and comprising only the Fijian members of the Legislative
Council and a Legal Adviser. The objective was to tie more
closely together the Executive Council, the Great Council
of Chiefs and the members nominated by the latter for the
Legislative Council. In other words a small interlocking
directorate of Fijians close to the government was to have
unambiguous control over the whole Fijian Administration.
The Fijian Affairs Board assumed control over the local
government finances and all administrative positions of
consequence, as well as any other, undefined, special
Fijian interests. Mitchell noted that the significance of
these changes was that Fijians would be ruled by 'Officers
and organizations truly native in composition and outlook
and able . . . to carry the confidence of the native
people . . . '13 At provincial level Rokos and magistrates
were freed of direct European supervision, despite parallel
appointments of District Officers, often European, to
attend to the business of other government departments and
the affairs of the whole population. For those with
memories such as Ratu Sukuna had of his boyhood years in
the 1890s, Fijian colonial history had come full circle.

In the rapidly approaching era of decolonization it
was a quite novel defiance of liberal concepts of progress
and individualism to reissue the Native Regulations with
the privileges of chiefs nominally intact and stringent
conditions governing the release of individuals from
communal programs of work. For post-war Fijian policy, as
guided until 1958 by Ratu Sukuna, did not construe progress
as the right to live a life free from obligations, nor as
the sabotage, in the name of democracy, of the capacity of
village leaders to maintain the social security of all. 14

On the other hand Fijian leaders shared the
aspirations of their people for better houses, education
and medical services. They shared too a general anxiety
about the faster population increase of the Indians and the
outcome of their efforts to win an equal place in the
colony's affairs. Fear of Indian domination was

deliberately stirred by European elected members of the legislature seeking to exploit the lack of Indian support for the war effort or to carry over the euphoria of wartime European-Fijian solidarity into a permanent post-war political alliance. Local born Europeans now unctuously identified themselves with the British authorities as 'trustees' of the Deed of Cession and took up the cry 'Fiji for the Fijians': 'those of us who have the interests of the Fijians as heart know the writing is on the wall, and it spells disaster for them', warned A.A. Ragg in 1946.[15]

European propaganda about 'the Indian menace' strengthened Ratu Sukuna's appeals for a greater Fijian effort to bring their lands into full production. He pinned his faith on the capacity of the renovated Fijian Administration to inspire communal efforts at village level. A major innovation, which illustrates his approach, was to bring all Fijian copra production under centralized control, eliminating most of the European and Chinese middlemen. A compulsory saving scheme in the form of a cess of £10 sterling on every ton of copra funded a Fijian Development Fund which was used mainly to finance more permanent housing. The goal, as always, was to achieve a state of collective financial and social security without breaking up the villages. He was perhaps unreasonably confident that Fijians would work as enthusiastically for their collective well-being as they would for themselves. In parliament he defended the element of compulsion as

> the normal kind of compulsion which is exercised daily in native society and which is its lifeblood. Without it, Sir, village life at this stage would come to a stand- still . . . From time immemorial, communal work of a compulsory nature has been regarded as normal; so also the levy for a common purpose. It naturally follows that these services are enforceable in the Native Regulations . . . [16]

Ratu Sukuna's generally progressive goals were thoroughly in tune with village aspirations and needs, but the renovated machinery of administration was not. The corporate strength of the old tikina based on the local chiefly domain, the vanua, still the most effective unit of cooperation, was often sacrificed in the amalgamation of two or three tikina into one (reducing the total number from 184 to 76). For Ratu Sukuna was as impatient as any English official with the parochialism of district politics

156

and inveighed against it often. Similarly, in an effort
that was a complete failure, he urged smaller villages to
combine into more viable and attractive communities capable
of burning a few 'bright lights' of their own.[17] Fijians
clung tenaciously to smaller groupings and their own
chiefs. It was a singular Buli indeed who could get people
not his own to work gladly under him in the old way as if
he were their own chief. And it was a rare village which
felt properly represented by an outsider-Buli speaking for
its needs on the provincial council. Ratu Sukuna had
over-estimated the dynamics of traditional organization in
trying to stretch it in new directions and control it
bureaucratically. The result, in the opinion of many keen
observers, was a fundamentally flawed administrative
machinery marked by rigid authoritarianism and village
apathy, leading in some areas to a near paralysis of
effective local leadership.[18]

There were new problems, too, at provincial level with
a siphoning of power from the Rokos and District Officers
to powerful District Commissioners responsible for four or
five provinces, so that, for instance, there was little the
Roko Tui of Nadroga and Navosa could do without reference
to the District Commissioner Western at Lautoka.[19] He in
turn answered closely to Suva, and supervised an
ever-growing corps of economic development and agricultural
officers whose influence reached down to village level, not
always in coordination with the provincial office. The
Roko's leadership was thus compromised or bypassed, while
the annual provincial councils, usually dominated by the
new officials, were inclined to rubber-stamp their wishes
without real debate.

A critical weakness of official reliance on communal
labour was that local authorities could, and often did,
withdraw their labour force from agriculture to domestic or
social tasks, principally house repairs. The Fijian
Development Fund was never able to make housing
improvements on a scale that would diminish the burden of
communal work. Secondly, the government was not willing or
able to control personal movement, so that by 1956 a
quarter of the Fijian population had chosen wage employment
or life outside the village. The 'burden of obligations'
fell ever harder on those that remained. Finally, inherent
in any form of communal development was the need for
inspired personal leadership close to the people. Ratu
Sukuna's bureaucratic, top-heavy and highly ceremonious
administrative machine was simply inadequate to engage with

the risks of commercial agriculture. A hurricane, a new pest or disease, or a sudden fall in prices could undo years of patient work when growers were ultimately dependent on a single export commodity, usually copra, a laissez-faire economy, unskilled leadership and minimal technical or financial assistance. 'To sum up', wrote Belshaw in his scathing review of the post-war years, 'the effects of Fijian Administration on the economic growth of the Fijian people have been little short of disastrous, and the source of much difficulty lies within the structure and philosophy of the Administration as a political unit.'[20]

Two major official inquiries published in 1959 and 1960 warned the Fijians that Ratu Sukuna's design for slow evolution from within was utterly bankrupt. Professor Spate declared: 'The main point is clear: a people cannot contract out of the century it lives in, nor can it be sole judge of the terms on which it enters, for modern economic life has also its own logic.'[21] The road forward, the right philosophy, the right way to modernize was firmly to espouse democracy and individualism, to become a nation of independent farmers and so-called free agents within the capitalist economy.

The critiques were telling, much as many Fijians were angered by the Eurocentrism of their faith in capitalist models and naive if well-intended recommendations such as an assurance in the Burns Report that Fijian cultural life could be adequately sustained by the equivalent of Highland Games and eisteddfods - pleasant ornaments on the structures of a better, that is, Anglo-western, way of life.[22] On another front the government was already under strong pressure from London and the International Labour Organization to abolish the last vestiges of 'forced labour'. The dismantling of the communal system began in earnest in 1961 with a series of amending regulations, removing all communal obligations and the program of work and finally abolishing the body of Fijian regulations in favour of increased regulatory power for provincial councils.[23] The Fijian courts and their relatively harsh and speedy sanctions were no longer available to local leaders: a man could now evade his taxes with relative ease, and only moral disapproval could be brought to bear on the lazy or improvident.

It was only logical to take the next step and abolish the Bulis and the tikina councils, and to give provincial councils directly elected majorities (in 1967).

Councillors (<u>mata</u>) represented large constituencies with
the same problems of unity experienced by the amalgamated
<u>tikina</u>, leaving many villages without a sense of
participation and commitment to the province.[24] Not
surprisingly there were spontaneous movements in many
provinces in the 1970s to reconstitute the 'old <u>tikina</u>'
(pre-1944) with which people still identified for church,
sporting and cultural events; for the old <u>tikina</u> was
still, after all these years, the locus of their best
corporate energies. (At the time of writing these
extra-legal entities under traditional leadership were
being given some encouragement and recognition by
authorities rather disillusioned by the fruits of
provincial democracy, and further changes were in the air.)

Fijians first exercised the franchise at national
level in 1963 when constitutional amendments provided for
two nominated Fijian members and four elected from a
communal roll. Similar and equal provision was made for
Indian and European members, reducing the official
government majority to one. Britain then began pushing
towards self-government and independence at a faster pace
than most Fijians would have wished. A Constitutional
Conference in London in 1965 agreed on the continuation of
three communal electoral rolls, with the Chinese and other
non-islander minorities being counted in with the Europeans
on the 'General' roll, and Pacific Islanders with the
Fijians. A new system of cross-voting allowed voters of
all races to vote together for a member from each race for
'national' seats, in addition to voting for a communal
seat, so that each elector voted for four candidates.
Ministerial government followed in 1967. Finally a
Constitutional Conference in 1970, attended in London by
the entire Legislative Council, incorporated similar
principles into the constitution for independence, but
reducing the relative weight of the 'General'
representatives to eight of the fifty-two members (twelve
Fijians, twelve Indians and three 'General' elected on
communal rolls, ten Fijians, ten Indians, and five
'General' elected on national rolls through cross-voting).

In most other respects the Constitutional Instruments,
handed to Ratu Sir Kamisese K.T. Mara by Prince Charles at
a simple ceremony on 10 October 1970, provided for a
Westminister-style government with the British Sovereign as
Head of State represented by a Governor-General. (Fijians
had remained attached to the throne - was any village home
without a picture gallery of the Royals? - and would not

countenance the republican sympathies of most Indians, whose leaders, in the prevailing spirit of compromise, did not press the matter.) A crucial feature of the legislature was that eight of the twenty-two members of the new upper house of review, the Senate, were to be appointed by the Great Council of Chiefs (with seven nominated by the Prime Minister, six by the Leader of the Opposition and one on the advice of the Council of Rotuma, a local government body for that island, established in 1927 and comprising a District Officer, traditional chiefs and district representatives). The consent of six of the eight chiefly nominees had to be obtained to enact any legislation affecting certain entrenched measures - previous colonial laws - or new legislation regarding Fijian lands, customs and administration. In short the constitution gave iron-clad security, short of revolution, to the paramountcy of Fijian interests articulated at Cession, defended against Europeans by Gordon and Thurston, weakly maintained by their successors, never threatened by the Indians, and reaffirmed effectively in 1944 by Governor Mitchell and Ratu Sukuna in alliance with the local European elite.

The triumph of Fijian political and European economic interests at national level, matched by the unambiguous commitment of Indian leaders to national peace, allowed the ascendant Fijian leaders to foster multiracial participation in selected areas of national life such as higher education and the civil service, while accepting as historically determined the sharp racial boundaries in community life. Fiji under Alliance Party multiracial governments moved very comfortably into the international arena, enjoying an unexpected and enviable reputation for stability, despite the continuing problems of Indian farmers in negotiating with the Native Lands Trust Board for adequate leases. The rapid demarcation of Fijian reserves in the 1960s by the Native Lands Commission had removed nearly a million and a half acres from future non-Fijian use, while existing Indian tenants on these lands had the bitterness of seeing their leases expire and the land, in many cases, revert to bush, even where the Fijian owners themselves would have been glad not to lose their rents. The government did legislate, however, in 1976 to extend existing ten-year leases for twenty years and ensure that new leases would be for a minimum of thirty years - the payoff to landlords being a five-yearly review of the rents.[25] It still meant there were few Indians who could look forward to passing on to their sons the land they worked for decades. This condition made for high mobility and openness to any avenue to success, including emigration to a few countries such as Canada willing to take skilled people Fiji could ill afford to lose.

Independent Fiji sustained an elaborate architecture of compromise, a balance of imbalances which prompted an anthropologist writing in 1977 to suggest that Fiji 'offered an unusual lesson for students of race relations: it may be the development of a culture that admits racial contention, allowing it to be acted out in regularized ways rather than repressing or denying it, which facilitates control of conflict and the achievement of integration'. [26] G.B. Milner has paid tribute to the Fijian demonstration of a 'modest, unassuming, though unmistakable self-confidence, this silent, amiable though eloquent protest against the monotony and the impersonal universalism of the Western world . . . a cultural achievement of the first order'. [27] Such claims are beyond empirical demonstration, but will ring true to those who have lived any length of time in the homes of ordinary Fijians, not least the shanty-dwellers on the fringes of Suva.

When the history of these decades can be written in detail, however, the facts of economic power may well diminish the triumph of Fijian political leadership and that enormous sense of unity, vitality and cultural pride for which Fijian leaders have gladly acknowledged their general debt to the British colonial arrangements analysed in this book. Two Australian multinational groups - Carpenters and Burns Philp - effortlessly maintained their domination, not to say stranglehold, over the importing, wholesaling and retailing sectors, while Fijians continued to be under-represented in the upper status levels of the workforce, especially in commerce. Though the government was forced to acquire CSR's sugar interests in 1973, and set up a most successful Fiji Sugar Corporation, there was little inclination to apply the model elsewhere. For the economy remained heavily dependent on foreign investment, most visibly in the tourist industry, with minimal restraints on the expatriation of profits. On the other hand new ventures such as pine-growing and cattle schemes were designed for a much greater local and Fijian participation. A country as small as Fiji with unemployment figures as large as New Zealand's could not afford to close the door on any kind of investment that would create jobs and compensate for the tragic loss of self-sufficiency in the villages.

The dilemmas of rural development throw into sharper relief some of the basic achievements of earlier colonial organization. For the simple basic needs that filter up from the villages through the modern administration in the required language of 'development priorities' are often requests for new housing, repairs to old housing, the clearing of drains and wells, the cutting of grass and undergrowth - the very tasks that were once attended to by the Bulis with communal labour.[28] Brookfield and his colleagues have admirably delineated for eastern Fiji the growing dependency of 'marginalized' peripheral areas on external subsidies and direction, accompanied by a paradoxical mix of 'disgust at the breakdown of traditional co-operation' and 'an equally general wish for greater individual opportunity'.[29] While generally predisposed, of course, to encourage the latter still further, they document the (irretrievable?) collapse of the ability of outer-island villages to exploit ancient horizontal linkages with other villages to redistribute resources in normal times and to survive major disasters such as hurricanes or droughts. Suva sends American food and relief workers where once Moala may have sent seed-yams and kinsmen.

And so after sixty years of sporadic rhetoric and twenty of effective policy, one dimension of individualism, self-reliance, may have finally taken hold of village life wherever leaders are absent, lacking or ignored. It means that young men or poor men cannot call on mutual aid in the construction of houses without a prohibitive outlay of food and cash for the builders; and there are old men and women who have none to care for them. If such individualism is accompanied by legalism, inequalities in land distribution (as owning units increase and decrease) cause corresponding inequalities in the distribution of wealth. Families are much less inclined to share wealth, if only to protect their aspirations for children whose future remittances may be the only way their parents and elderly relatives will survive in the villages at all. Already one finds, as Nankivell reports of Taveuni, 'truly desperate cases' of poverty and neglect, and this on the famed 'garden isle' of the group.[30] And it can be safely said the housing standards of Fijians are the worst they have been in centuries, with thin reed walls and stone-weighted sloping iron roofs 'almost universal' in most new settlements and extremely common in villages.[31] Fijians have never had less to abandon when opportunity beckons elsewhere.

Yet others insist that wherever Fijians live, not least in Suva, groups still dominate their lives politically, culturally and socially. 'Urban Fijians', writes Nation, 'are no more individualistic than their village cousins.'[32] Personal expenditure flows freely to the support of weddings, funerals, festivals, church collections and other social projects, as it always did through the whole colonial period. Named social groups remain at the very heart of Fijian life. Perhaps the emasculation of the communal system and the triumph of liberal concepts of democracy has not, after all, produced a new race of individualists; it has left many villagers, though, in a perilous state of marginalization and dependency. In the 1980s they have the unenviable task of regaining basic self-sufficiency and security while satisfying the desire of their remaining young people to achieve higher productivity, higher incomes, and greater self-realization from the interplay of their human and natural resources.

The Spate report offered Fijians in 1959 only two choices: individualism or 'a rigid authoritarian collectivism'.[33] The witness of this history is that at least until World War II Fijians had a special talent for a modest, low-energy but quite admirable and prosperous design for living and working together that avoided both extremes - a design which maintained enriching continuity with the past despite colonialist disparagement of everything they encapsuled in the words, na itovo vakaviti, the Fijian way. Perhaps the best hope for an uncertain future is that Ratu Sukuna's memorable defence of Fijian communal values in the colonial period will inspire strategies for more fully human modes of community development. The simplistic prescriptions of individualism, so clearly pernicious had they guided colonial policy in the 1870s, seem to have been equally bankrupt in the 1970s. Other than doubting that communal development can be led by teams of bureaucrats answering to the centre, it is surely premature to preclude the rise of innovative leaders closer to the groups with which Fijians still largely identify.

By and large Fijians commanded the banks if not always the main-stream of their colonial history. At independence their leaders resumed command of the sweep of the stream itself, with all its conflicting eddies and currents. Their challenge, in the face of urbanization without industrialization, unemployment, marketing problems for sugar and copra, and continuing institutional weaknesses in local administration, is to ensure that neither Fijians nor Indians in sufficient number ever begin to feel that the stream has ceased to carry them, or has marooned them in stagnant pools on the fringe. In a world that is running out of easy answers, no one will be surprised if the entire nation looks to its own Fijian heritage for some of the arts of living well on islands, and to select aspects of its colonial experience for containing the continents.

Notes to text

Introduction

1. See Deryck Scarr's life of Thurston: _I, the Very Bayonet_ and _Viceroy of the Pacific_; R.A. Derrick, _A History of Fiji_; J.D. Legge, _Britain in Fiji 1858-1880_ and for the best short account of the nineteenth century period leading into this book, Deryck Scarr, 'John Bates Thurston: Grand Panjandrum of the Pacific'.

2. Ratu Peni Tanoa to the NC, 5 March 1908, CSO 08/1174.

3. See David Wilkinson's open letter to Sir Everard im Thurn, _Western Pacific Herald_, 3 July 1908, for another account of Cession from the Fijian viewpoint.

4. See Deryck Scarr, 'John Bates Thurston, Commodore J.G. Goodenough, and Rampant Anglo-Saxons in Fiji'.

5. Much of the Indian story in Fiji has been told by K.L. Gillion in _Fiji's Indian Migrants_ and _The Fiji Indians_.

6. Peter France, _The Charter of the Land_, has the best impressionistic survey of pre-Cession Fiji.

7. Sir Arthur Hamilton Gordon, _Paper on the System of Taxation in Force in Fiji,_ p. 178. See France, _Charter of the Land_, p.108.

8. See Ian Heath, 'Towards a Reassessment of Gordon in Fiji'.

9. After 1904 the Council of Chiefs submitted a panel of six to the Governor, and two were given seats on the Legislative Council, three after 1929. Since independence the Council chooses eight of the twenty-two senators comprising the upper house.

10. Legge, _Britain in Fiji_, has an exhaustive discussion of the system summarized here and further elaborated as needed in the chapters below.

11. Figures supplied by Deryck Scarr. His _Viceroy of the Pacific_ has a full discussion of the taxation system.

12. Legge, Britain in Fiji, pp. 193-4.

13. France, Charter of the Land, p. 123.

14. ibid., p. 139.

Chapter 1. New white men without knowledge

1. Sir Everard im Thurn's address, 14 October 1907,
   Legislative Council Debates, 1907.

2. Sir George T.M. O'Brien to Sir Ian Anderson, 30
   November 1901, CO 83/73.

3. Fiji Times, 9 September 1899.

4. Norma McArthur, Island Populations of the Pacific, pp.
   26-32.

5. Basil Thomson, The Indiscretions of Lady Asenath,
   p.186.

6. G.R. Burt to the Governor, 12 February 1892, CSO
   92/620.

7. Frank Spence to the CS, 11 February 1892, CSO 92/252.

8. W. Slade to the CS, 18 February 1892, CSO 92/645.

9. Report of a Commission of Enquiry Appointed to Enquire
   into the Decrease of the Native Population (1896),
   p. 38.

10. The turaga ni koro of Cautata, William Sutherland's
    minute, 13 December 1910, CSO 11/784.

11. S. Smith's minute, 10 June 1898, Kadavu Provincial
    Council Book.

12. W. Scott's minute, 12 April 1911, Serua Provincial
    Council Book.

13. Ratu Tevita Suraki's report, 29 November 1898, CSO
    98/5154.

14. Basil Thomson, The Fijians, pp. 228-32.

15. W.L. Allardyce's minute, 6 December 1902, CSO 02/5451.

16. Thomson, The Fijians, pp. 229-30.

17. O'Brien's minute, 8 January 1898, CSO 89/42; address to the Legislative Council, 7 October 1898, CP 33/99.

18. O'Brien to CO, 31 December 1897.

19. Walter Carew's minute, 11 July 1896, and Sir John B. Thurston's, 14 December 1896, CSO 96/2425.

20. See letters of appointment, 14 October 1898, CSO 98/3498.

21. O'Brien's marginals, CSO 00/2693 and minute, 19 September 1900, CSO 99/3534.

22. Spence diaries at CSO 99/38, 00/3534.

23. Excerpts from Sydney Smith's 1900 diaries, CSO 02/5838.

24. Nailatikau to O'Brien, 7 May 1900 and O'Brien's minute, 18 May 1900, CSO 00/1628.

25. Proceedings of the Council of Chiefs, 1902.

26. Na Mata, May 1899, pp. 74-5.

27. ibid., March 1899, p. 47.

28. For the hygiene mission see CSO 99/1777, 99/3149, 99/4930.

29. O'Brien's address to the Legislative Council, 27 September 1899, CP 29/00.

30. See O'Brien to Bishop Vidal, 10 November 1898, PMB microfilm 455.

31. W.L. Allardyce to the Commissioner of Colo North, 31 January 1899, CSO 99/567.

32. CP 29/00

33. _Na Mata_, July 1905.

34. ibid., August 1905.

35. Proceedings of the Council of Chiefs, 1875.

36. O'Brien's minutes, 9 December 1898, CSO 98/4850.

37. See CSO 99/1483, 5426.

38. O'Brien to CO, 31 December 1897.

39. _Fiji : Report for 1900_, HMSO London, 1901.

40. W.L. Allardyce's memorandum, 6 December 1902, CSO 02/5457.

41. Islay McOwan to the Receiver General, 3 June 1901, CSO 01/2522.

42. CSO 02/5457.

43. Nathaniel Chalmers to the Receiver General, 1 June 1898, CSO 98/525.

44. O'Brien's minute, 13 May 1898, CSO 98/525.

45. William Sutherland's minute, 19 June 1901, CSO 01/2740.

46. Ratu Isikeli Tubailagi to the NC, 15 November 1901, CSO 00/3795.

47. R. Booth to the assistant CS, 20 October 1900, CSO 00/3795.

48. W.L. Allardyce's minute, 9 December 1898, CSO 98/4850.

49. W.A. Scott to the NC, 21 August 1904, CSO 04/4229.

50. Ratu A. Finau to the NC, 10 February 1903, CSO 00/2215.

51. O'Brien's minute, 23 June 1900, CSO 00/2215.

52. William Sutherland to the CS, 1 July 1909, enc. Sir Charles Major to CO, 6 July 1909, CO 83/92.

53. Sutherland's minute, 20 January 1913, CSO 13/5856.

54. H.B. Cox's minute on im Thurn to CO, 26 October 1906, CO 83/83.

Chapter 2. The assault on land rights

1. Sir Everard im Thurn's diary, 11 October 1904, im Thurn Papers.

2. Address to the Council of Chiefs, April 1905, im Thurn Papers.

3. Fiji Times, 20 March 1909.

4. See Gordon to CO, 25 March 1881, in Sir Arthur Hamilton Gordon, Fiji, vol. 4, pp. 516-17.

5. See Introduction.

6. F. Spence to im Thurn, 31 January 1909,enclosed in CSO F37/93.

7. Lord Stanmore (Gordon) to CO, 29 August 1908, CO 83/86.

8. Im Thurn's minute, 6 December 1907, CSO 06/3236.

9. Im Thurn to CO, 2 November 1907, CO 83/86 and 18 March 1908, CO 83/87.

10. Im Thurn's minute, 11 January 1906, CSO 05/4118. See also CSO 05/4029, 05/4556.

11. Proceedings of the Council of Chiefs, 1903, Resolution VI: 'it is our unanimous wish that the Government have the entire control of leasing such land, fixing the terms and the rents for it'.

12. Sir Charles Major's minute, 24 January 1905, and Francis Baxendale's minute, 15 March 1905, CSO 05/1206.

13. Im Thurn to CO, 22 March 1907, CO 83/85.

14. Im Thurn to CO, 26 October 1906, CO 83/84.

15. ibid. The ordinance was approved with the proviso that the Colonial Office's approval be obtained prior to actual resumption.

16. Madraiwiwi to the NC, August 1906, CSO 06/2854.

17. David Wilkinson to the NC, 13 August 1906, MM L/14; copy enclosed in CSO F37/93.

18. See im Thurn to CO, 12 June 1907, CO 83/85.

19. CO to im Thurn, 26 October 1907, CO 83/86.

20. Im Thurn to CO, 18 March 1908, CO 83/87.

21. See CSO 06/3236, 06/3651, 06/3602, 07/4816.

22. W.A. Scott to the NC, 30 July 1909, CSO 09/6393.

23. Komai Sawakasa and others to the NC, 1 November 1909, CSO 09/9295.

24. Letter read to the Tailevu Provincial Council, November 1909, CSO 09/9295.

25. Petition of the Planters Association to the Right Hon. the Secretary of State for the Colonies, 30 January 1908, article 117.

26. Im Thurn to CO, 26 October 1906 and 22 March 1907.

27. Rev. A.J. Small to im Thurn, 14 March 1908, CSO 08/1174.

28. Im Thurn's minute, 16 March 1908, on Tanoa and others to the NC, 5 March 1908, CSO 08/1174.

29. See Peter France, The Charter of the Land, pp. 159-61.

30. Stanmore to CO, 29 August 1908, CO 83/86; im Thurn to CO, 15 April 1908, CO 83/87; CO to im Thurn, 15 July 1908, CO 83/88.

31. France, Charter of the Land, p. 165.

Chapter 3. The erosion of hereditary privilege

1. Ai Tukutuku Vakalotu [The Church Times] March 1932, pp. 10-11.

2. Proceedings of the Council of Chiefs, 1892, Resolution III.

3. David Wilkinson's memorandum ('Lala or Fijian Service Tenures'), 18 December 1875, CSO 00/3434.

4. Wilkinson to the CS, 6 January 1898, CSO 98/215. His singular spelling is no reflection on the quality of his observations.

5. Francis Baxendale's minute, 21 October 1904, CSO 04/4229.

6. W.A. Scott to the NC, 21 September 1904, ibid.

7. Im Thurn's note, 16 November 1904, im Thurn Papers, ms2, item 10.

8. Im Thurn's opening address, 10 April 1905, Proceedings of the Council of Chiefs, 1905; J. Baleiricau and others to im Thurn, 7 April 1905, CSO 05/1971.

9. Im Thurn's minute, 29 June 1905, CSO 05/2720.

10. Letter to the editor, Na Mata, September 1906, pp. 138-9.

11. Letter to the editor, Na Mata, September 1908, pp. 136-7.

12. Ratu Joni Madraiwiwi to the Governor, 26 October 1913, CSO 14/1745.

13. But see the conflict between Bau and Verata on this very point in Chapter 5.

14. See G.V. Maxwell to the CS, 11 July 1917, CSO 17/5947.

15. Rusiate R. Nayacakalou, Fijian Leadership in a Situation of Change, p. 316.

16. CSO 01/1058; Ratu A. Finau to the CS, 21 October 1905, CSO 05/4533.

17. W.A. Scott's minute, November 1909, Kadavu Provincial Council Book.

18. Similarly the chiefs protested in 1932 when the government removed from the Communal Services Regulation three items that seemed to offend the Geneva Convention on forced labour effective 3 June 1932: the transport of mail and government officials, the conveyance of the sick and the assistance of NLC surveyors. The chiefs said that by the abolition of free transport 'a chiefly custom of our land would be done away with' - see Sir Murchison Fletcher to CO, 9 November 1932. The government was glad to allow the provincial councils separately to re-enact these 'forced labour' provisions.

19. Proceedings of the Council of Chiefs, 1911, Resolution XVIII. The Rokos of Tailevu and Rewa held out unsuccessfully for compensation.

20. Proceedings of the Council of Chiefs, 1912.

21. D.R. Stewart's minute, 22 April 1919, SNA 19/1095.

22. Sir John B. Thurston to Ratu Epeli Nailatikau, 30 July 1894, CSO 94/2049. The following year relief supplies of rice were sent to the island - CSO 95/2579.

23. Similarly, disputes over land near the Nausori mill broke out whenever CSR required further leases. In 1885 there was an unpleasant confrontation at Nausori between the Chief of Namata with his men and the Bauans under Ratu Epeli. The Namata chief feared that some of the Bauans were bent on armed violence and on depriving him of all his lands - Ratu Marika Toroca to Lt Governor, 6 December 1886, CSO 93/3676. A further dispute over 'Nokonoko', some 70 acres on the Bau-Namata boundary, was resolved in favour of Namata by W.L. Allardyce in 1894 - ibid.

24. As spoken by Ratu Busa, 26 October 1907, CSO 05/3764. Im Thurn minuted: 'The Bau chiefs seem always to have played at young blackbirds in their nest doing nothing but opening their mouths.'

25. See Sir F. Henry May to CO, 25 October 1911, for a longer summary and the chiefs of Bau to CO, 14 May 1909, CO 83/99.

26. Ratu Marika Toroca's conflict with the Bauans is analysed in Deryck Scarr, 'A Roko Tui for Lomaiviti'.

27. J. Green's minute, 1 January 1916, CO 83/127.

28. William Sutherland's minute, 2 March 1911, CSO 10/7259.

29. A. Erdhardt's minute, 16 October 1912, CSO 12/6371.

30. See CP 17/06. Prior to 1906 the turaga i taukei received 8s in the £, but was expected to distribute it according to custom to the lesser chiefs - few did. In 1906 therefore, ignoring the actual social organization of the people, a new division was made: 1s for the turaga i taukei, 2s for the head of the yavusa (a descent group of third-order inclusiveness) and 3s for the chief of the legal land-owning unit, the mataqali. The Roko and the Buli were given 1s each whether or not they were landowners. After 1912 the government deducted 2s, leaving 10s to the mataqali members.

31. See evidence of Wilisoni Tuisawau and Sorita Batei, CSO 12/6371. Inoke Nawa, ex-Buli Bureta (Ovalau) stated that the reason they had not sent first fruits to the Vunivalu for some years was due to orders from the European magistrate in charge of Lomaiviti.

32. Report of the NLC proceedings in Lomaiviti, 16 November 1916, CP 14/17.

33. CSO 16/7067.

34. Wainiu's evidence, ibid.

35. Sir Cecil Rodwell to CO, 31 August 1922.

36. J.S. Neill's minute, 20 November 1925, CSO 23/2888.

37. A.L. Armstrong's report, 19 June 1923, CSO 22/4936.

38. Wainiu to Sir Arthur Richards, 20 August 1937, CSO F50/68. In 1940 and in 1942 the Council of Chiefs unsuccessfully asked that the Vunivalu receive a salary.

Chapter 4. The new politics of chiefly power

1. Journal of Rev. Thomas Baker, 6 Ausust 1859, Mitchell Library, Sydney, reference courtesy of Deryck Scarr.

2. Madraiwiwi to the Governor, 26 October 1913, CSO 14/1745.

3. ibid.

4. Madraiwiwi to the NC, 19 April 1907, CSO 07/1452.

5. See CSO 07/5549 for Adi Vasemaca. For many details I am indebted to Ratu Tiale Vuiyasawa.

6. See CSO 07/5286. There were 300 acres already under nuts.

7. William Sutherland's minute, 31 March 1908, CSO 07/5624.

8. The Vunivalu of Bau was installed first as Tui Kaba and his wife as Ranadi Kaba. Some time later the original inhabitants of Bau now living at Namaciu on Koro (the kai Butoni) installed him as Vunivalu, and several months after that the kai Levuka of Lakeba installed him and his wife as Tui and Ranadi Levuka. See Niko Rabuku to the NC, 9 April 1907, CSO 07/1452, explaining the irregularity of the previous month's proceedings, and accompanying papers.

9. Wainiu had long been trying to discredit Kadavulevu; for instance in August 1911 he charged Kadavulevu with supplying liquor to Pita Raori and with beating one Loga twenty times with a stick until the man bled - Wainiu to the Governor, 9 August 1911, CSO 11/6509.

10. Wainiu to the Governor, 18 August 1913, CSO 14/1686.

11. William Sutherland's minute, 14 October 1913, CSO 13/8213.

12. Fiji Times, 7 October 1913.

13. Rabici to the NC, 30 May 1914, CSO 14/5063.

14. CSO 16/8918.

15. See, for example, G.V. Maxwell to the CS, 4 December 1917, CSO 17/201 and memorandum, 10 November 1919, CSO 19/31.

16. Toganivalu to the NC, 26 June 1908, CSO 07/4137; Na Mata, March 1909, pp. 44-6.

17. Cyril Francis's minute, 19 October 1912, CSO 12/5197.

18. See Islay McOwan's minute, 3 July 1908, CSO 08/3045.

19. See CSO 08/6325 and Vuama Vakabati and others to the Governor, 11 October 1911, CSO 11/8814.

20. Sutherland's minute, 26 November 1908, CSO 08/6325.

21. Qasevakatini to Cyril Francis, 25 November 1908, CSO 08/6325.

22. The presiding officer of the 1909 Provincial Council, W.A. Scott, gave as the reason for the move that 'The Roko wishes Councils to be held at different places each year so as to lend impetus to planting' - n.d. [November 1909], Kadavu Provincial Council Book. But the Council did not move from Yale in 1911. Few Tavuki chiefs came to these meetings. Ratu Asesala was conspicuously absent in 1910.

23. Chiefs of Tavuki to the Governor, 11 October 1911, CSO 11/8814.

24. Qasevakatini to Buli Tavuki, 24 August 1911, CSO 11/404.

25. Vuama Vakabati and others to the Governor, 11 October 1911, and Sutherland's minute, 15 November 1911, CSO 11/8814.

26. Qasevakatini to Sutherland, 8 December 1912, CSO 12/7932.

27. David Wilkinson's report on Serua, CSO 99/1575.

28. A comparison of the kinship units listed in the NLC final report on Serua, 1932, with those made by David Wilkinson in 1899 is the main documentary basis for the

inferences made here and amply confirmed in many
conversations in villages of the province. Fijian
readers will appreciate that out of consideration for
prominent living personalities I have not broached the
related question of the publicly disputed right of Ratu
Aseri's mataqali to exclusive possession of the chiefly
titles Na Ka Levu and Vunivalu.

29. Sir F. Henry May to CO, 3 May 1911, CO 83/101.

30. Rev. A.J. Small to Rev. W. Bennett, 5 June 1909, MM
F/1/1909.

31. See CSO 04/4656, 13/3500, 19/1859.

32. G.V. Maxwell's minute, my emphases, 21 May 1919, CSO
19/1859; Komave's petition to secede at CSO 13/3800.

33. Ratu Aseri to DC Navua, 17 October 1917, CSO 17/10162.

34. H. Disbrowe's minute, 28 October 1921, SNA 21/1137.

35. Evidence at CSO F50/27/19; Sukuna's memorandum 3
January 1934, SNA 32/552.

36. Words of a Galoa informant, 26 August 1973.

37. ibid: 'Sa turaga levu duadua ga vei keda o Ratu Aseri.'

38. At the time of writing, Ratu Sukuna's official
biography by Deryck Scarr was going to press. I was
able to check some details from the early chapters in
draft, by kind permission of the author.

39. Sukuna's memorandum in Sir Cecil Rodwell to CO, 23 July
1923, CO 83/165.

Chapter 5. The continuities of village life and politics.

1. Walter Carew to the CS, 24 April 1896, CSO 96/1431.

2. See CSO 08/1240. For a detailed analysis of 114
appointments of Bulis see T.J. Macnaught, 'Chiefly
Civil Servants?...'

3. Sukuna to the CS, 21 April 1933, CSO F15/1.

4. Regulation III of 1912, Part III.

5. Sukuna to the CS, 16 April 1940, CSO F15/1.

6. Colo East Provincial Council Report, 1929.

7. Rev. Wesley Amos to Rev. A.J. Small, 13 June 1918, MM
    F/1/1918. The other party to the exchange would have
    been the Bauans.

8. I am indebted in part for this description to the
    eye-witness account of Rev. Robert Green in his
    unpublished memoirs.

9. Rusiate R. Nayacakalou, Tradition, Choice and Change in
    the Fijian Economy, p. 69.

10. H.C. Monckton's minute, 17 September 1939, CSO F50/6.

11. Ratu J.L.V. Sukuna, Policy with Regard to Fijian
    Communal Obligations.

12. CSO F15/1.

13. CSO 13/1463.

14. Parochialism is a major theme of John Nation, Customs
    of Respect.

15. Nailatikau to Sir John B. Thurston, 1 September 1890,
    CSO 90/1734; CSO 90/3091.

16. Ravoka to the SNA, 21 January 1921 and other papers at
    SNA 21/230.

17. CSO 22/5611, 22/1127, 22/1728, 23/1622.

18. Ratu J.A. Rabici et al. to the Governor, 13 November
    1923, CSO 23/1725.

19. CSO 23/4338.

20. A.J. Armstrong's minute, 16 February 1925, CSO 25/2441.

21. Buli Verata to DC Rewa, 28 August 1930, CSO 30/3068.

22. Sukuna's diary, 12 September 1933, CSO F15/5.

23. ibid., 5-12 September 1933.

24. CSO F23/7. The following year he was exiled to Batiki.

Chapter 6. Apolosi R. Nawai and the Viti Company

1. For Tuka, see Deryck Scarr, Viceroy of the Pacific, passim, and Thurston's masterly despatches to CO, 15 January, 16 February, and 5 July 1886, 1 June and 4 July 1887, 12 August 1891.

2. Stories such as these, which are legion, are equally as often ascribed to Apolosi as to Navosavakadua, one clue to a linkage impossible to document firmly in the records.

3. Sukuna's memorandum, 12 March 1917, CSO 17/2286. See also Chapter 2.

4. Sydney Smith to the CS, 29 October 1912, CSO 12/7021.

5. The ordinance (XXVII of 1913) was based largely on G.V. Maxwell's recommendations at CSO 13/3087.

6. K.J. Allardyce to the CS, 5 February 1915, CSO 15/1166.

7. Oral accounts on which this paragraph is mostly based were gathered informally at Lutu village in 1973, and are not necessarily reliable.

8. Sukuna's memorandum, 12 March 1917, CSO 17/2286.

9. Na Mata, January 1914.

10. Kuruduadua to the Provincial Commissioner of Colo East, 28 January 1914, CSO 14/1975.

11. Recast from an awkward paraphrase of Ilaisa Seru's evidence, restricted file.

12. Escott's minute, 3 June 1914 and other papers at CSO 14/4758.

13. Ratu A. Finau to the CS, 18 February 1914, CSO 14/2413.

14. Proceedings of the Council of Chiefs, 1914.

15. ibid., 1917 and CSO 14/4712.

16. CSO 14/4385, 14/19313, 14/10287.

17. Registrar of Companies to the CS, 25 November 1916, CSO 16/9253.

18. Apolosi's circular to the Bulis of Nadroga, 17 March 1915, CSO 15/2851. See also Gaunavou R. Nawai and David L. Toma's, Ai Tukutuku Bibi . . .

19. Fiji Times, 30 March 1915.

20. Fijian text, ibid; Gilchrist Alexander, From the Middle Temple to the South Seas, p. 72.

21. Restricted files and George Barrow to the Governor, 5 April 1915, CSO 15/3130.

22. Escott to CO, 7 December 1917, CO 83/139.

23. Na Mata, January 1916; Escott's text of verbal warning read to Apolosi in Korovou gaol, September 1916, CSO 16/6390.

24. H.E. Snell to the CS, 28 March 1917, CSO 17/3093.

25. Rev. C.O. Lelean to Rev. A.J. Small, 16 November 1916, MM F/1/1916.

26. From a conversation with miners at Vatukoula in 1973, and A. Thompson's personal communication, 17 November 1975.

27. Lutu files are restricted.

28. Co to Escott, 11 July 1917, CSO 17/7208.

29. Unless a source is cited hereafter the files are restricted.

30. Escott to CO, 7 December 1917, with enclosures, CO 83/141.

31. Sukuna's memorandum, 12 March 1917, CSO 17/2286.

32. Escott to CO, 7 December 1917, CO 83/141.

33. H. Long's minute, 28 February 1918, CO 83/141.

34. I could not locate the Fijian original of this remarkable document.

35. For the narrative of these years see my earlier account in Deryck Scarr (ed.), More Pacific Island Portraits, pp. 186-92.

Chapter 7. The vein of discontent.

1. See Legislative Council Debates, 1969, pp. 780-842 for European, Fijian and Indian testimony on the prevalence of black magic in Fiji and Ratu Penaia L. Latianara's article in Pacific Islands Monthly, September 1973, pp. 21-5.

2. A.J. Armstrong to the CS, 20 January 1937, CSO F50/46.

3. Ratu A. Finau to the NC, 8 March 1906, translation enclosed in CSO F50/47.

4. Rev. Colin Bleazard to Rev. A.J. Small, 22 April 1906, and Small to Rev. B. Danks, 31 July 1906, MM F/1/1906. The teachers were suspended and began a Free Church of their own.

5. H.C. Monckton to the CS, 29 July 1914, CSO 14/6993.

6. Nathaniel Chalmers to the CS, 11 January 1905, CSO 05/303.

7. David Wilkinson's minute, 27 January 1905, CSO 05/303.

8. A.B. Joske to the NC, 17 February 1908, CSO 08/974.

9. See Joske to the Commissioner of Colo East, 1 August 1891, CSO 91/2344.

10. This account is based on a mass of sworn Fijian testimony at CSO 14/6189, 14/7090 and attached papers.

11. Sitiveni's evidence, 11 July 1914, CSO 14/7090.

12. Sailosi's evidence, 11 July 1914, CSO 14/7090.

13. CSO 14/7297.

14. W.E. Russell to the CS, 14 December 1914, CSO 14/19450; Picherit to the CS, 15 February 1915, CSO 15/1621.

15. See CSO 17/7444, 18/3529, 18/9707.

16. Rev. Harold Chambers to Small, 22 May 1918, MM F/1/1918; SNA C19/18; CSO 18/6336; Escott to CO, 4 June 1918 and 13 June 1918, CO 83/142.

17. See Stuart Reay's diary, 1934, passim, CSO F13/21; Reay to the CS, 25 May 1935 and 25 August 1936, CSO F13/1. I visited the area in September 1974 but found the subject too sensitive to broach. Dr Karl Erik Larsson did extensive fieldwork in the area but has not yet published an account of these events.

18. W.A. Scott's memorandum, 4 January 1910, CSO 10/1242.

19. See CSO 23/2576, 27/1115.

20. Isley McOwan's minute, 21 March 1927, CSO 27/1115.

21. CO to Sir Henry Jackson, 8 May 1903, CO 83/76.

22. E.R. Leach, 'Ourselves and Others', Times Literary Supplement, 6 July 1973, pp. 771-2.

23. Proceedings of the Council of Chiefs, 1917, 1923 and passim; J.S. Neill's minute, 27 January 1925, CSO 23/2576.

24. Sukuna's minute, 22 March 1926, CSO 26/797.

25. Native Regulation IV of 1927; SNA 23/242, 26/942; Proceedings of the Council of Chiefs, 1933, Resolution XXV and reply; and 1940 Resolution XXIX; CSO F50/74.

26. Rev. Wesley Amos to Small, 9 February 1915, MM
    F/1/1915; Rev. W. Brown to Small, 22 February 1913, MM
    F/1/1913; Rev. A.G. Adamson to Rev. R.L. McDonald, 22
    August 1917, MM F/1/1927.

27. Small to Rev. W. Deane, 26 January 1911, MM F/1/1911,
    and to Brown, 17 May 1905, MM F/1/1905.

28. Chambers to McDonald, 19 June 1933, MM F/1/1933.

29. See Ratu Sukuna's annual reports at CSO F15/1.

30. Sukuna to the CS, 21 April 1937, CSO F15/1.

31. Rev. C.O. Lelean to Small, 14 July 1909 and 9 December
    1909, MM F/1/1909.

32. Small to Brown, 21 September 1904, MM F/1/1904. For the
    related issue of lay representation see A. H. Wood,
    Overseas Missions of the Australian Methodist Church,
    vol. 2, chapter XXXVIII.

33. McDonald to Rev. J.W. Burton, 26 January 1923, MM
    F/1/1923.

34. Chambers to McDonald, 26 February 1933, MM F/1/1933.

35. See charter documents requesting canonical approval
    from Rome, Records of the Roman Catholic Mission, PMB
    microfilm 454.

36. Mosese Buadromo (President) to the Acting Under SNA, 14
    September 1925, SNA 25/1194.

37. A.W. Seymour to CO, 2 August 1933.

38. Drekitirua to McOwan, 5 November 1928, CSO 29/771.

39. Ravai to SNA, 22 August 1933, SNA 33/1537.

40. CSO 30/2704. Ahmed Ali, Fiji and the Franchise, pp.
    158-93, has a full discussion.

Chapter 8. Compromise for a multiracial society

1. W.L. Allardyce's minute, 21 May 1889, CSO 89/415.

2. CSO 09/7249.

3. The CS to the European Stipendiary Magistrates, 13 August 1910, CSO 10/6561.

4. See also K.L. Gillion, The Fiji Indians, pp. 13-16.

5. Ratu J. Madraiwiwi, Ratu J.A. Rabici and Deve Toganivalu to the Governor, 2 February 1915, CSO 15/1034. In the preceding year the Council of Chiefs had been told it was necessary to bring native administration 'more closely into touch' with European administration.

6. This account follows Gillion, The Fiji Indians, pp. 18-46.

7. Y.M. Helliet to the Bishop, 23 April 1922, Records of the Roman Catholic Mission, PMB microfilm 466.

8. Rev. Stanley Jarvis to Rev. A.J. Small, 31 August 1921, MM F/1/1921. See Gillion, The Fiji Indians, Chapters 2 and 3 for an account of the strike from government records.

9. Ratu Pope Seniloli, Ratu S. Seniloli and Ratu J.A. Rabici to the Under SNA, 16 November 1921, CSO 21/6741.

10. Minutes of the meeting, January 1922, CSO 21/6741.

11. Copy of D.R. Stewart's speech, 12 December 1923, at CSO 23/4265.

12. F. Raiwalui and others to the Acting Governor, 10 October 1924, CSO 24/7028.

13. Ratu Pope Seniloli and others to the Governor, 25 April 1925, CSO 25/1524; Sir Eyre Hutson to CO, 6 May 1925; CO to Hutson, 16 June 1925.

14. As told by S.M. Lambert, A Doctor in Paradise, p. 166.

15. T.E. Fell to CO, 7 and 15 February 1924, CSO 24/4078; SNA 27/602.

16. See Peter France, The Charter of the Land, pp. 165-75.

17. David Wilkinson to the NC, 6 October 1905, CSO 05/4556. Marshall D. Sahlins, Moala, pp. 271-87 has a local study of actual land tenurial practices for the 1960s.

18. Sukuna's memorandum, 21 May 1932, CSO F50/27/3.

19. In 1903 Ratu Josefa Lala, then Tui Cakau, subdivided the holdings of the mataqali Valelevu into individual holdings retaining five blocks and five dowry portions for his own use. On his death a commission settled these lands to his immediate heirs and they passed to his son Ratu G.W. Lala who was eventually, after a long dispute with a rival claimant, installed as Tui Cakau (1936). See CSO F50/27/1.

20. Sukuna to the CS, 8 August 1930, SNA 29/1564.

21. As reported by A.A. Wright's minute, 29 March 1934, CSO F50/27/9.

22. Sir Murchison Fletcher's minute, 21 March 1934, CSO F50/27/9.

23. Native lands actually under lease, 30 April 1911, comprised 140,974 acres (rental £23,500), with approximately 1800 Indians holding a very small proportion. The government paid small rents (total £643) for only half the Fijian land held for leasing. See CP 14/11.

24. McCrae, 14 October, Legislative Council Debates, 1907.

25. R. St Johnstone to the CS, 9 January 1914, CSO 14/1349.

26. See CO to Sir F. Henry May, 31 May 1911, CO 83/100; May's address, 27 June 1911 and Resolution XIV, Proceedings of the Council of Chiefs.

27. Ro Tuisawau and others to the Governor, 6 December 1915, Na Mata, January 1916.

184

28. Native Land (Leases) Ordinance, XXIII of 1916, CSO 16/9016.

29. Ruveni Naisua and 241 others to the NC, 8 October 1915, CSO 15/9101. See also Buli Nausori to the NC, 22 December 1915, CSO 15/10912 for similar dissatisfaction in the Rewa districts.

30. H.E. Snell to the CS, 25 March 1917, CSO 17/3093.

31. Proceedings of the Council of Chiefs, 1920; D.R. Stewart's report, 15 December 1920, CSO 20/8025.

32. CSO 23/4018.

33. Sir Maynard Hedstrom's memorandum, 4 August 1924, in CO to the Acting Governor, 5 November 1924.

34. T.E. Fell to CO, 20 February 1925. See also CSO 23/4117, 25/53.

35. Datwari and other leaseholders to the General Secretary of the Moslem League, 21 April 1933, CSO F37/42.

36. See correspondence and resolutions of the Council of Chiefs at CSO F37/42/2.

37. H.C. Monckton to the CS, 10 March 1933, CSO F23/7. The notes were signed successively for amounts less than £20 to render inapplicable the Native Dealings Ordinance of 1904.

38. R.N. Caldwell to the CS, 31 March 1936, and A.E. Howard to the CS, 6 August 1939, CSO F16/2.

39. This conclusion is based on the annual reports of the Provincial Commissioners and figures for applications refused 1937-39 in Lautoka, Macuata and Nadi.

40. Ratu J.L.V. Sukuna, A Vosa nei [the speech of] Ratu J.L.V. Sukuna, Bosevakaturaga 1936. Translation in Juxon Barton to CO, 17 November 1936.

41. For Cakaudrove, see the Cakaudrove Provincial Council Book 1935-1938, pp. 14-15.

42. Farewell address of Sir Arthur Richards, 21 July 1938,
CP 53/38; Proceedings of the Council of Chiefs, 1938,
Resolution XL (carried 38-3); <u>Legislative Council
Debates</u>, 1940, pp. 105-8.

43. S.B. Patel to H.S.L. Polak, 31 October 1929, cited by
Gillion, <u>The Fiji Indians</u>, p. 136.

44. Proceedings of the Council of Chiefs, 1933, Resolution
XVIII, CP 8/34.

45. Ratu Deve Toganivalu, Ratu Pope Seniloli Cakobau and
Ratu J.L.V. Sukuna 'for and on behalf of the senior
Chiefs of Fiji' to the Acting CS, 5 November 1935.
Edited text published CP 47/35.

Chapter 9. The dilemmas of development

1. Sir F. Henry May to CO, 3 May 1911, CO 83/101.

2. Tuisawau's report on Resolution IV of the Rewa
Provincial Council, 11 April 1899, copy at PMB
microfilm 455.

3. Nicholas to F.J. Corder, 25 March 1929, PMB microfilm
454.

4. Minutes of the Synod, October 1899, MM F/4/B.

5. Im Thurn's message, 10 October, in <u>Legislative Council
Debates</u>, 1907.

6. Rev. Wesley Amos to Rev. A.J. Small, 30 March 1920, MM
F/1/1920.

7. Dr R.F.K. Roberts, 'Routine of Child Welfare Work',
n.d., CSO 28/5904.

8. Mrs Ruby Brewer to Rev. R.L. McDonald, 1 October 1928,
MM F/1/1929.

9. As reported by DC Navua to the CS, 31 March 1927, and
Nicholas to the CS, 19 January 1928, CSO 27/2033.

10. CSO 30/1179; SNA 33/1347, 33/1348.

11. See SNA 28/1659 for a spontaneous request from the daughter of Buli Cicia and five of her friends to begin a program in their village.

12. A favourite phrase of Governor May - 19 December 1911, Lomaiviti Provincial Council Book.

13. See CSO 17/2206, Na Mata, September 1917; Fiji: Report for 1920, HMSO, London, 1921, pp. 9-10.

14. T.E. Fell's minute, 10 November 1920, and H.W. Harcourt's 15 February 1921, CSO 20/7813.

15. CSO 18/8754, 18/10217. Other examples at CSO 12/1017, 13/2997.

16. Frequent observations such as these are in the Lau Provincial Council Book. See also SNA 29/2101, CSO F15/1.

17. Sukuna to the CS, 23 March 1935 and 17 March 1939, CSO F15/1.

18. Sukuna to the CS, 14 August 1936, CSO F15/1.

19. A.J. Acton to the CS, 22 April 1936, and Sukuna's memorandum, 'The Tabu in Lomaiviti 1934-1936', CSO F2/175.

20. H.W. Jack to the CS, 5 August 1939, CSO F2/175, and minute, 15 September 1939, CSO F15/1.

21. Jack to the CS, 16 November 1936, and Juxon Barton's minute, 17 February 1937, CSO F2/132.

22. See CSO F50/32, 30/783, 30/1288, F2/17.

23. Rev. A.D. Lelean to McDonald, 5 March 1931, MM F/1/1931. I am indebted to Mrs A.D. Lelean for her reminiscences. Lelean destroyed all his papers.

24. Sir Murchison Fletcher to H.K. Irving, 23 February 1931, CSO F2/121; Irving to the SNA, 30 May 1934, CSO 30/590.

25. C.E. de F. Pennyfather's minute, ? May 1930, CSO 30/590 and papers at CSO F2/121.

26. A.J. Armstrong's diary, 23 July 1935 and passim, CSO F23/4.

27. J.W. Gittins' diary, 19 August 1935 and passim, CSO F19/5.

28. Sir Philip Goldfinch's note, ? August 1936, CSR records, Sydney, R1-0, 1.

29. In 1966 of 2417 Fijian cane farmers, 195 were ex-Drasa. By then 677 boys had graduated. The school had problems of student unrest in the 1950s and 1960s. Ex-Drasa farmers I interviewed at Penang in August 1974 deplored the school's closure in 1967 and insisted it had been a happy place.

30. Report of the third annual general meeting of Emperor Mines, 11 November 1938, CSO 13/39/1; J.E. Windrum to the CS, 18 February 1936, CSO F50/53.

31. Stuart Reay's diary, 7 May 1934 and passim, CSO F13/2.

32. ibid., 8 March 1934 and passim.

33. Reay's diary, and reports at CSO F13/1.

34. ibid.

35. Reay to the CS, 11 April 1938, CSO F13/1.

36. See A.J. Armstrong to the CS, 13 March 1939, CSO F23/7.

37. Reay's memorandum, n.d. [1938], CSO F50/16.

38. Jack's minute, 7 January 1936, CSO F20/2.

39. Reay's suggestion needs research - see diary, 21 March 1938, CSO F13/2 and memorandum at CSO F50/16.

40. Barton's minute, 9 October 1936, CSO F13/2; Proceedings of the District Commissioners' Conference, CSO F50/16.

Chapter 10 : Rendezvous with the modern world

1. Sukuna to the CS, 29 September 1934, CSO F15/1.

2. Asesela Ravuvu, Fijians at War, p. 15.

3. Glen Barclay, A History of the Pacific, p. 191.

4. See Ravuvu, Fijians at War for an evocative Fijian account and R.A. Howlett, The History of the Fiji Military Forces, 1939-1945.

5. See K.L. Gillion, The Fiji Indians, Chapter 9.

6. Fiji Times, 17 September 1942.

7. This summary follows Ravuvu and Howlett.

8. Unless cited, references hereafter are to restricted files.

9. Part of this report is cited in the Acting Governor's address to the Great Council of Chiefs, 1944, CP 10/45.

10. Ratu Sukuna's Memorandum, Policy with Regard to Fijian Communal Obligations.

11. ibid. See also Ratu Sukuna's speech and the debate in Legislative Council Debates, 1944, Fijian Affairs Bill, especially pp. 5-6.

12. Native Lands Trust Report on Ba, 1941, National Archives of Fiji.

13. Sir Philip Mitchell to CO, 16 July 1943, CP 24/1943.

14. Ratu Sukuna's annual reports were published in the Legislative Council Journal. See especially CP 2/51, 5/53 and 29/55.

15. Legislative Council Debates, 16 July 1946.

16. ibid., debate on the Fijian Development Fund Bill, 20 April 1951.

17. The classic but in some respects antiquarian or at least ahistorical account of the post-war Fijian social and political system is G.K. Roth, Fijian Way of Life.

18. The most influential publications of 'the development writers' are: Cyril S. Belshaw, 'The Effect of Limited Anthropological Theory on Problems of Fijian Administration' and Under the Ivi Tree; Sir Alan Burns, T.Y. Watson, and A.T. Peacock, Report of the Commission of Enquiry into the Natural Resources and Population Trends of the Colony of Fiji, 1959; O.H.K. Spate, The Fijian People; R.F. Watters, Koro.

19. The three Colo provinces lost their identity on reorganization, as did Nadi and Lautoka (merged into Ba, as they were prior to 1920), thus reducing the number of provinces from nineteen to fourteen.

20. Belshaw, Under the Ivi Tree, p. 236.

21. Spate, The Fijian People, p. 21.

22. Fiji Times, March-April 1960 has several reports of the Fijian opposition to the Burns Report.

23. Amending regulations dismantling aspects of the communal system can be found in Fiji Royal Gazette, 1961-62, prior to the final Fijian Affairs (Amendment) Regulation, 14 December 1962, which had been approved by the Great Council of Chiefs.

24. See John Nation, Customs of Respect, for a detailed study of provincial politics.

25. See Michael Moynagh, 'Land Tenure in Fiji's Sugar Cane Districts since the 1920s'.

26. Robert Norton, Race and Politics in Fiji, p. 160.

27. Milner's introduction to Roth, Fijian Way of Life, 2nd edn, p. xxvii.

28. Nation, Customs of Respect, p. 58.

29. UNESCO/UNFPA, Population, Resources and Development in the Eastern Islands of Fiji, p. 236.

30. P.S. Nankivell, 'Income Inequality in Taveuni District', in Brookfield et al _Taveuni_, p. 295 and _passim_.

31. UNESCO/UNFPA, _Population, Resources and Development in the Eastern Islands of Fiji_, pp. 173, 211.

32. Nation, _Customs of Respect_, p. 38.

33. Spate, _The Fijian People_, p. 9.

Bibliography

1. Documents held in the National Archives of Fiji, Suva

The most important collections for this study are:

    (i)   Records of the Colonial Secretary's Office 1897-1940.
    (ii) Records of the Secretariat for Native Affairs 1918-35.

Note: For the CSO series prior to 1930, regrettably, it is not possible to direct the reader to files collected under subject headings — they once were so organized for administrative use but later the bundles were broken up. And so, for example, to write the story of the beginning of the Apolosi movement in 1913 there is no collection of Apolosi files to consult: it is necessary to sort through 10,535 files for 1913 that have been reshelved in their original numerical order in twenty-one large bundles — perhaps 30 feet high if stacked, and similarly through the years to 1929. Letter registers and subject indexes describing individual files have to be used by anyone whose time is limited, but they are never fully reliable or consistent. From 1930 to 1940 the CSO files (but not the SNA files) are collected much more conveniently under broad subject divisions prefixed by the letter F and a number, e.g. F50 is the prefix for all files on Fijian Affairs; F50/6: the Council of Chiefs papers 1931-39; F50/13: correspondence relating to sorcery; and so on.

Other important collections are:

    (iii)   Provincial Council Records Books (incomplete).
    (iv)   Proceedings of the Council of Chiefs.
    (v)   Despatches to and from the Secretary of State for the Colonies.
    (vi)   Methodist Mission Collection.

2. Official publications

    (i)   Government of Fiji

        Fiji Blue Book
        Fiji Royal Gazette
        Journal of Legislative Council
        [Colony of Fiji.] Legislative Council Debates
        Native Regulations 1912, 1928, 1948
        Report of the Commission Appointed to Inquire into the
           Decrease of the Native Population, 1896.

    (ii)   Colonial Office, Great Britain

        Colonial Reports — Annual. Fiji, 1897-1939

3. Im Thurn Papers, Royal Anthropological Institute of Great Britain and Ireland, Microfilm, Research School of Pacific Studies, Canberra.

4. Records of the Roman Catholic Mission, Suva

  Pacific Manuscripts Bureau, Canberra: microfilm, PMB 435, 452-5, 459-9, 466.

5. Records of the Colonial Sugar Refining Company, Sydney

  Access was given to files on Drasa Training Farm

6. Newspapers and periodicals

  Ai Tukutuku Vakalotu, Suva
  Fiji Times, Suva
  Na Mata, Suva
  Native Medical Practitioner, Suva
  Na Viti 1924-30, Suva
  Pacific Islands Monthly, Sydney

7. Unpublished

Ali, Ahmed, 1974. Fiji and the Franchise: a history of political respresentation, 1900-1937, Ph.D. thesis, Australian National University.

Cato, A.C., 1951. A survey of native education in Fiji, Tonga, and Western Samoa, with special attention to Fiji, Ph.D. thesis, University of Melbourne, 1951.

Fisk, E.K., 1974. The traditional economy as a basis for rural development. Based on a paper presented at the Third Regional Conference of Directors of Agriculture, Livestock Production and Fisheries arranged by the South Pacific Commission at Lae, Papua New Guinea, February. Typescript in my possession, courtesy of the author.

Geddes, W.R., 1948. An analysis of cultural change in Fiji, Ph.D. thesis, University of London.

Green, Rev. Robert. Memoirs. Typescript in possession of author, Melbourne.

Janssen, Rev. Herman, 1972. Religion and secularisation. Cultures, Christianity and development. The Catholic Church and the Development of Peoples in the South Pacific Conference. Typescript, Commission for Justice and Peace, New Zealand Episcopal Conference.

Nayacakalou, Rusiate R., 1955. Tradition, choice and change in the Fijian economy, M.A. thesis, University of New Zealand.

―――― 1963. Fijian leadership in a situation of change, Ph.D. thesis, University of London.

Peacock, Allan T., 1960. Economic problems of a multiracial society — the Fiji case, seminar paper, University of London. Typescript, National Archives of Fiji.

Rutz, Henry John, 1973. Local-level responses to induced economic change in the Waidina Valley, Fiji: a case study in anthropological economics, Ph.D. thesis, McGill University.

Sukuna, Ratu, J.L.V. (Sir Lala), 1940. Address to the Defence Club. Typescript courtesy of Mr L.G. Usher, Suva.

―――― n.d. Notes on Lau. Typescript, National Archives of Fiji.

―――― n.d. Notes on customs regarding lands. Typescript, National Archives of Fiji.

—— 1943. Memorandum for District Commissioners' Conference. Typescript, National Archives of Fiji.

—— 1944. Policy with regard to Fijian communal obligations (memorandum for Administrative Officers' Conference). Typescript, National Archives of Fiji.

Walter, Michael, A.H.B., 1971. Changing principles of social organisation in the Exploring Islands of Northern Lau, Fiji, Ph.D. thesis, Australian National University.

Young, John, M.R., 1969. Frontier society in Fiji, 1858-1873, Ph.D. thesis, University of Adelaide.

8. Published

Note: This list includes all secondary works cited in the text and a few secondary sources I found useful and which are not to be found readily in the standard bibliographies.

Alexander, Gilchrist, 1927. *From the Middle Temple to the South Seas.* John Murray, London.

Barclay, Glen, 1978. *A History of the Pacific from the Stone Age to the Present Day.* Sidgwick and Jackson, London.

Belshaw, Cyril, S., 1964. *Under the Ivi Tree: Society and Economic Growth in Rural Fiji.* Routledge and Kegan Paul, London.

—— 1965. 'The effect of limited anthropological theory on problems of Fijian administration', in Roland W. Force (ed.), *Induced Political Change in the Pacific*, Bishop Museum Press, Honolulu, pp.63-73.

Brewster, A.B., 1921. 'The history of Nadrau'. *Transactions of the Fijian Society for the Year 1920*, Suva, pp.16-19.

—— 1922. *The Hill Tribes of Fiji.* J.B. Lippincott, Philadelphia.

—— 1937. *King of the Cannibal Isles: a Tale of Early Life and Adventure in the Fiji Islands.* Robert Hale, London.

Brookfield, Harold, C. and Hart, Doreen, 1971. *Melanesia: a Geographical Interpretation of an Island World.* Methuen, London.

Brookfield, Harold (ed.), 1973. *The Pacific in Transition: Geographical Perspectives on Adaptation and Change.* Australian National University Press, Canberra.

—— et al., 1978. *Taveuni: Land, Population and Production*, UNESCO/UNFPA Fiji Island Report no. 3, Canberra, ANU Development Studies Centre for UNESCO.

Burnett, Frank, 1923. *Summer Isles of Eden.* Sifton Praed, London.

Burns, Sir Alan, Watson, T.Y. and Peacock, A.T., 1960. *Report of the Commission of Enquiry into the Natural Resources and Population Trends of the Colony of Fiji, 1959.* Fiji Legislative Council Paper 1 of 1960, Government Printer, Suva.

Burton, Rev. J.W., 1910. *The Fiji of Today.* Kelly, London.

Capell, A., 1953. 'The nature of Fiji totemism'. *Transactions and Proceedings of the Fiji Society of Science and Industry 1940-1944*, Suva, pp.59-67.

—— and Lester, R.H., 1941. 'Local divisions and movements in Fiji', Oceania, XI:313-41, XII, 1952:21-48.

Cavalevu, J.D., 1971. 'The Fijian community and its development'. Transactions and Proceedings of the Fiji Society 1966-1967, Suva, pp.131-42.

Chapple, W.A., 1921. Fiji, Its Problems and Resources. Whitcombe and Tombs, Auckland.

Coulter, John Wesley, 1942. Fiji, Little India of the Pacific. University of Chicago Press, Chicago.

Crocombe, R.G., 1971. Review article. Journal Polynesian Society 80(4): 505-20.

Daws, Gavan, 1974. 'Looking at Islanders: European ways of thinking about Polynesians in the eighteenth and nineteenth centuries'. Topics in Culture Learning, East-West Center, Honolulu, 2:51-6.

Deane, Rev. W., 1921. Fijian Society or the Sociology and Psychology of the Fijians. Macmillan, London.

Derrick, R.A., 1957. A History of Fiji, rev. edn., Government Printer, Suva.

Finucane, M.I., 1901. 'The islands and peoples of Fiji. Proceedings of the Royal Colonial Institute, XXXII:32-53.

Fisk, E.K., 1970. The Political Economy of Independent Fiji. Australian National University Press, Canberra.

—— and Honeybone, D., 1971. 'Belshaw's "Emergent Fijian Enterprise" after ten years'. Pacific Viewpoint, XII:2, pp.123-40, September.

Fison, Rev. Lorimer, 1903. Land Tenure in Fiji. Government Printer, Suva.

Foster, Harry, L., 1927. A Vagabond in Fiji. John Lane, London.

France, Peter, 1966. 'The Kaunitoni migration: notes on the genesis of a Fijian tradition'. Journal Pacific History, 1:107-13.

—— 1968. 'The founding of an orthodoxy: Sir Arthur Gordon and the doctrine of the Fijian way of life'. Journal Polynesian Society, 77(1):6-32.

—— 1969. The Charter of the Land: Custom and Colonization in Fiji. Oxford University Press, Melbourne.

—— 1971. 'Fijian administration during the past decade'. Journal Administration Overseas, X(3):192-200.

Fraser, John, A., 1954. Gold Dish and Kava Bowl. Dent, London.

Fraser, R.M., 1968. 'A social and economic history of Ra Province'. Transactions and Proceedings of the Fiji Society 1962-1963, Suva, pp.93-112.

Geddes, W.R., 1945. Deuba: a Study of a Fijian Village. The Polynesian Society Inc., Wellington.

—— 1959. 'Fijian social structure in a period of transition', in J.D. Freeman and W.R. Geddes (eds), Anthropology in the South Seas. Avery, New Plymouth, New Zealand.

Gillion, K.L., 1962. Fiji's Indian Migrants: a History to the End of Indenture in 1920. Oxford University Press, Melbourne.

—— 1977. The Fiji Indians: Challenge to European Dominance 1920-1946. Australian National University Press, Canberra.

Gordon, Sir Arthur Hamilton (First Baron Stanmore), 1879. Letters and Notes Written during the Disturbance in the Highlands (Known as the 'Devil Country') of Viti Levu, Fiji, privately printed, 2 vols, Edinburgh.

—— Paper on the System of Taxation in Force in Fiji, Read before the Royal Colonial Institute, 18 March 1879.

—— Fiji: Records of Private and of Public Life 1875-1880, 4 vols, Clark, Edinburgh: vol.1, 1897; vol. 2, 1901; vol. 3, 1904; vol. 4, 1912.

Gorrie, Sir J., 1883. 'Fiji as it is'. Proceedings of the Royal Colonial Institute, XIV:159-99.

Groves, M., 1963. 'The nature of Fijian society'. Journal Polynesian Society, 72(3):272-91.

Heath, Ian, 1974. 'Towards a reassessment of Gordon in Fiji'. Journal Pacific History, IX:81-92.

Hocart, A.M., 1929. The Lau Islands of Fiji. Bernice P. Bishop Bulletin no.62, Honolulu.

—— 1952. The Life Giving Myth and Other Essays, ed. Lord Raglan, Tavistock, London.

—— 1952. The Northern States of Fiji. Occasional Publication no.11, London, Royal Anthropological Institute of Great Britain and Ireland.

Howlett, R.A., 1948. The History of the Fiji Military Forces 1939-1945. Crown Agents, London.

Hubner, Baron Joseph A. von. Through the British Empire, 2 vols, John Murray, London.

Im Thurn, Sir Everard, 1913. 'Native land and labour in the South Seas', in F.J.C. Hearnshaw (ed.). King's College Lectures on Colonial Problems. Bell and Sons, London, pp.35-71.

Jarre, Rev. Raymond, 1955. 'Notes sur les changements survenus dans les coutumes Fidjiennes depuis l'occupation Européene'. Journal de la Société de Océanistes, XI:15-36.

Joyce, R.B., 1971. Sir William MacGregor. Oxford University Press, Melbourne.

King, Agnes Gardner, 1920. Islands Far Away. Sifton Praed, London.

Lambert, S.M., 1942. A Doctor in Paradise, 2nd Australian edn, Dent, Melbourne.

Larsson, Karl Erik, 1960. Fijian Studies. Ethnografiska Museet, Göteborg.

Legge, J.D., 1958. Britain in Fiji 1858-1880. Macmillan, London.

Lester, R.H., 1941. 'Kava-drinking in Viti Levu, Fiji'. Oceania, XI, 2 December, pp.97-121; XII, 3 March 1942, pp.226-54.

—— 1953. 'Magico-religious secret societies of Viti Levu, Fiji'. Transcripts and Proceedings of the Fiji Society of Science and Industry 1940-1944, Suva, pp.117-34.

Luke, Sir Harry, 1945. Britain and the South Seas. Longmans, London.

McArthur, Norma, 1967. Island Populations of the Pacific. Australian National University, Canberra.

Macnaught, T.J., 1974. 'Chiefly civil servants? Ambiguity in district administration and the preservation of a Fijian way of life'. Journal Pacific History, IX:3-20.

—— 1979. 'The man from Ra: Apolosi R. Nawai', in Deryck Scarr (ed.), More Pacific Island Portraits, Australian National University Press, Canberra, pp.173-92.

Mara, Ratu Sir Kamisese, K.T., 1975. 'Address to the Royal Commonwealth Society, London, 16 May, News from Fiji, XXIX:7, 16 May.

Mayer, Adrian, C., 1961. Peasants in the Pacific: a Study of Fiji Indian Rural Society. Routledge and Kegan Paul, London.

Meller, Norman and Anthony, James, 1968. Fiji Goes to the Polls: the Crucial Legislative Council Elections of 1963. East-West Center, Honolulu.

Memmi, Albert, 1965. The Colonizer and the Colonized. Orion, New York.

Moynagh, Michael, 1978. 'Land tenure in Fiji's sugar cane districts since the 1920s'. Journal Pacific History, XIII(1-2):53-73.

Nacola, J., 1970. 'Villagers in dilemma on the eve of Fiji's Independence', in Marion Ward (ed.), The Politics of Melanesia (Fourth Waigani Seminar), Research School of Pacific Studies, Canberra, pp.131-43.

Nankivell, P.S., 1978. 'Income inequality in Taveuni district: a statistical analysis of data from the Resource Base Survey', in H.C. Brookfield et al., Taveuni: Land, Population and Production, UNESCO/UNFPA Fiji Island Report no.3, Canberra, ANU Development Studies Centre for UNESCO.

Nation, John, 1978. Customs of Respect: the Traditional Basis of Fijian Communal Politics. Development Studies Centre Monograph no.14, Australian National University, Canberra.

Nawai, Gaunavou [Sereima] R. and Toma's [sic], David L. [?1966]. Ai Tukutuku Bibi E Baleti Ratu Avalosi R. Nawai. S.S.P. Press, Nadi.

Nayacakalou, Rusiate R., 1964. 'Traditional and modern types of leadership and economic development among the Fijians'. International Social Science Journal, XVI(2):261-72.

—— 1971. 'Manipulating the system', in R. Crocombe (ed.), Land Tenure in the Pacific. Oxford University Press, Melbourne, pp.206-26.

—— 1975. Leadership in Fiji. Oxford University Press, Melbourne.

Norton, Robert, 1977. Race and Politics in Fiji. St Martin's Press, New York and University of Queensland Press, St. Lucia.

Petition of the Planters Association to the Right Hon. the Secretary of State for the Colonies, Suva, 30 January 1908.

Quain, Buell, 1948. Fijian Village. University of Chicago Press, Chicago.

Ravuvu, Asesela, 1974. Fijians at War. South Pacific Social Sciences Association. Suva.

Ross, C. Stuart, 1909. Fiji and the Western Pacific. Thacker, Geelong.

Roth, G.I., 1951. Native Administration in Fiji During the Past 75 Years. Occasional Paper no.10, Royal Anthropological Institute, London.

—— 1973. Fijian Way of Life, 2nd edn, Oxford University Press, Melbourne.

Rutz, Henry J., 1973. 'Uncertainty and the outcome of a development situation'. Canadian Review of Sociology and Anthropology, X(3):231-52.

Sahlins, Marshall D., 1962. Moala: Culture and Nature on a Fijian Island. Michigan University Press, Ann Arbor, Michigan.

St Johnstone, T.R., 1918. The Lau Islands (Fiji) and Their Fairy Tales and Folk-Lore. The Times, London.

────── 1922. South Sea Reminiscences. Fisher Unwin, London.

Scarr, Deryck, 1965. 'John Bates Thurston, Commodore J.G. Goodenough, and Rampant Anglo Saxons in Fiji'. Historical Studies, Australia and New Zealand, XI(43):361-82, October.

────── 1970. 'A Roko Tui for Lomaiviti: the question of legitimacy in the Fijian administration 1874-1900'. Journal Pacific Hisotry, V:3-31.

────── 1973. 'Cakobau and Maafu: contenders for pre-eminence in Fiji', in J.W. Davidson and Deryck Scarr (eds), Pacific Islands Portraits, rev. edn, Australian National University Press, Canberra, pp.95-126.

────── 1973. I, the Very Bayonet. The Majesty of Colour vol. I, Australian National University Press, Canberra.

────── 1980. Viceroy of the Pacific. The Majesty of Colour vol.II, Pacific Research Monograph no.4, ANU, Canberra.

────── 1979. 'John Bates Thurston: Grand Panjandrum of the Pacific', in Deryck Scarr (ed.), More Pacific Island Portraits. Australian National University Press, Canberra, pp.95-114.

Smith, Norman, 1960. Maori Land Law. A.H. and A.W. Reed, Wellington.

Snow, P.A., 1969. A Bibliography of Fiji, Tonga and Rotuma. Australian National University Press, Canberra.

Spate, O.H.K., 1959. The Fijian People: Economic Problems and Prospects. Fiji Legislative Council Paper 13 of 1959, Government Printer, Suva.

────── 1965. Let Me Enjoy: Essays, Partly Geographical. Australian National University Press, Canberra.

Spencer, Dorothy, M., 1941. Disease, Religion and Society in the Fiji Islands. Monographs of the American Ethnological Society, II, Philadelphia.

Sukuna, Ratu, J.L.V., 1936. A Vosa nei Ratu J.L.V. Sukuna, Bosevakaturaga 1936 [Fijian text of his speech to the 1936 Council of Chiefs.] Government Printer, Suva.

Sutherland, W., 1926. 'The Tuka Religion'. Transactions of the Fijian Society 1908-1910, reprinted Suva, pp.51-7.

Thompson, Laura, 1940. Fijian Frontier (Studies of the Pacific no.4). Institute of Pacific Relations, New York.

────── 1940. Southern Lau: An Ethnography. Bernice P. Bishop Museum Bulletin no.2, Honolulu.

Thomson, Basil, 1898. The Indiscretions of Lady Asenath. Innes, London.

────── 1908. The Fijians: a Study of the Decay of Custom. Heinemann, London.

Toganivalu, Deve, 1912. 'The Customs of Bau before Christianity'. Transactions of the Fijian Society for the Year 1911, Suva.

────── 1924. 'Fiji and the Fijians during the 50 Years Now Ending 1874-1924'. Transactions of the Fijian Society for the Year 1924, Suva.

UNESCO/UNFPA, 1977. Population and Environment Project, 1977. Population Resources and Development in the Eastern Islands of Fiji: Information for Decision-Making, General Report no.1, Canberra, Development Studies Centre for UNESCO.

Vandercook, John, W., 1938. Dark Islands. Heinemann, London.

Wallis, Mary, D., 1851. Life in Feejee or Five Years among the Cannibals. Heath, Boston.

Ward, Alan, 1974. A Show of Justice: Racial 'Amalgamation' in Nineteenth Century New Zealand. Australian National University Press, Canberra.

Ward, R.G., 1961. 'Internal Migration in Fiji'. Journal Polynesian Society, 70(3):257-71.

———— 1965. Land Use and Population in Fiji: a Geographical Study. HMSO, London.

Waterhouse, Joseph, 1866. The King and People of Fiji. Wesleyan Conference Office, London.

Watters, R.F., 1965. 'The development of agricultural enterprise in Fiji'. Journal Polynesian Society, 74(4):490-502.

———— 1969. Koro: Economic Development and Social Change in Fiji. Clarendon, Oxford.

———— 1970. 'The economic response of South Pacific Societies'. Pacific Viewpoint, II(1):120-44.

West, F.J., 1960. 'Problems of political advancement in Fiji'. Pacific Affairs, XXXIII(1):23-37.

———— 1961. Political Advancement in the South Pacific: a Comparative Study of Colonial Practice in Fiji, Tahiti and American Samoa. Oxford University Press, Oxford.

———— 1966. 'The establishment of the Fijian administration: Part I. Sir Lala Sukuna'. Journal Overseas Administration, V(4):258-67, October; Part II: VI(1):43-9, January 1967.

Whitelaw, J.S., 1965. 'Constitutional change in Fiji', Journal Polynesian Studies, 74(4):503-11, December.

Williams, John A., 1969. Politics of the New Zealand Maori: Protest and Co-operation 1891-1909. University of Washington Press, Seattle and London.

Williams, T. and Calvert, J., 1859. Fiji and the Fijians, ed. George Stringer Rowe, Appleton, New York.

Wood, A.H., 1978. Overseas Missions of the Australian Methodist Church, vol. 2, Fiji. Uniting Church in Australia Publications Committee, Melbourne.

www.ingramcontent.com/pod-product-compliance
Lightning Source LLC
Chambersburg PA
CBHW040143270326
41928CB00023B/3324